# THE ULTIMATE GUITAR TONE
## HANDBOOK

A Definitive Guide to
## Creating and Recording Great Guitar Sounds

### Bobby Owsinski and Rich Tozzoli

Alfred Music Publishing Co., Inc.
P.O. Box 10003
Van Nuys, CA 91410-0003
alfred.com

Produced in association with Lawson Music Media, Inc.

ISBN-10: 0-7390-7535-7 (Book & DVD)
ISBN-13: 978-0-7390-7535-7 (Book & DVD)

Cover Photos
Background texture: © iStockphoto.com / mandala • Foreground soundwave: © dreamstime.com / Carlos Castilla
2nd row / sixth column, concert: © iStockphoto.com / dwphotos • 5th row / forth column, rock star with guitar: © iStockphoto.com / Nathan McClunie
7th row / second column, concert: © iStockphoto.com / dwphotos • All other photos: © Bobby Owsinski

# Contents

# Foreword

One of the reasons that this book came about is because, like my co-writer Rich Tozzoli, I've become a connoisseur of guitar tone over the years. To me, there's nothing better than a great-sounding acoustic guitar or electric guitar and amp rig. Over the years I've spent gigging, and especially in the studio, I think I've learned just what a "good" guitar tone is, especially in terms of how it fits in the mix.

It wasn't always that way though. Way back when I first started playing and gigging I was just like so many young players, searching for the elusive tone I heard on records and in my head, trying every amp and pedal I could find, and eventually resorting to some crazy combinations that led me further away from tonal nirvana instead of closer to it. But I had two revelations that led me to listen to electric guitar tones with new ears.

The first came when I was jamming in a garage one day with slide guitarist extraordinaire Gerry Groom, bass player and LA studio stalwart Paul III, and the amazing drummer Michael Wright. Gerry was a protégé of Duane Allman (of the famous Allman Brothers Band), and was so close to Duane that Duane willed Gerry his beloved Les Paul when he died. Gerry had amazing chops and a lot of experience, and was once dubbed by Jimi Hendrix' former manager "the next great American guitar player." I was no pup either. I had been playing about 15 years at the time, and had a couple of major-label record deals under my belt (back when they actually meant something).

Gerry plugged his 1960 Les Paul Black Beauty into his 1964 Fender black-faced Super Reverb and the sound was glorious with lots of sustain and some really great-sounding overdrive. I plugged my 1981 Strat into a small rack (which was popular at the time) full of distortion devices, chorus units, EQs and noise gates, which then went into a fabulous 1977 Marshall JMP 100-watt half-stack. While Gerry's guitar sang with richness and as much sustain as he wanted, mine sounded thin and buzzy, although just as loud. After about a half-hour of jamming, Gerry looked at my rack and sneered, "Why do you even use that crap? You'd sound a lot better without it."

I loved my pedals and rack gear and the way they made me sound while I played by myself, but I had to admit that his rig sounded better than mine by a mile. He had the sound that I kept trying to get by using all the pedals and rack gear, but he got it by using none of them!

I unplugged everything and went straight into the amp, turned it up, and…wow! It really did sound better once I tweaked the amp's controls a bit. I was a little bit shocked by how high I had to turn the amp up to get the sound, but there it was, the sound that I heard on countless records and that I'd been trying to achieve. It was that simple.

The next revelation came shortly afterward when I was producing and playing on a record. I was playing the same Strat with a '66 Fender silver-face transition-model Twin. I still wasn't totally confident about foregoing my rack so it was still plugged up, but after many, many takes of just not getting a sound that fit, I unplugged the rack, ran straight into the amp and turned it up. Once again, there was the perfect sound. At that point, the lesson had finally sunk in about where my tone was coming from.

After that, I began to rent the vintage gear that I couldn't afford, and I listened closely to the great players who I worked with who always had the best gear. Through this process, I've developed my own reference point for what works. My preferences aren't that far off from currently accepted wisdom on tone, but now I personally know it to be true.

I hope that this book helps guide you on your quest for the ultimate tone. It's a personal journey to be sure, and one that's both fun and frustrating, and almost never-ending. But we're guitar players, and we wouldn't have it any other way.

*Bobby Owsinski*

Recording guitars, both electric and acoustic, is a deep passion of mine. It's been a lifelong pursuit to always find the best tone and never settle for mediocrity. I've been lucky enough to work with amazing guitar players throughout my career, and after every session, I've walked away with another small nugget of information.

Coming up the "chain," I've also learned from some top-notch engineers how they record the instrument and amplifiers—different styles, techniques, placements, attitudes and approaches.

Through all of this knowledge, I've built a mental database that I rely upon every time I approach a guitar-recording session, be it my own or one I'm producing for another artist. No two sessions are ever the same—not just because of the differences in microphones, preamps, amps and guitars, but because of the player. Every single player is unique. And therein lies the timeless beauty of the instrument. I hope this book can help you capture the best guitar sounds possible, and that you share them with the world.

*Rich Tozzoli*

## SPECIAL THANKS

### From Rich Tozzoli:
Thank you first and foremost to my friends and family for all their support! Special thanks also to Vincent Miraglia for all the amp knowledge, Dick Boke for the words of wisdom, Paul Antonell, Pete Moshay, Chuck Ainlay, Hernan Romero, Al DiMeola, John Holbrook, Chipman, Weider, Ace, Ray Levier, Scott Moore, Rob DiStefano, Joe Capozio, Elaine Ashburn for the graphics, Dave Murphy, Hutch and Brian, Blunder, the gang at Creation Audio Labs, Lisa Kelly for the pics, Brian Mackewich, Howard Massey, Bruce MacPherson, Michael McConnell, Dave Crane, Mitch Thomas, Rich Maloof, Emile Menasche, Mike Levine, Andy Munitz, David Ondrick, Ray Maxwell, Annette Genovese, Rob Reich, Howard Sherman, Nathan Eames, Sarah Jones and especially to Bobby O for the drive and teamwork to get it done.

### From Bobby Owsinski:
Thanks to everyone who helped us along the way especially John Jennings, Dusty Wakeman, Paul III, Chris Pierce, and especially Rich T. for being a great partner in finding a way to express into words a never-ending pursuit.

# PART ONE:
## ELECTRIC GUITARS AND AMPLIFIERS

## Chapter 1:

## What is Tone

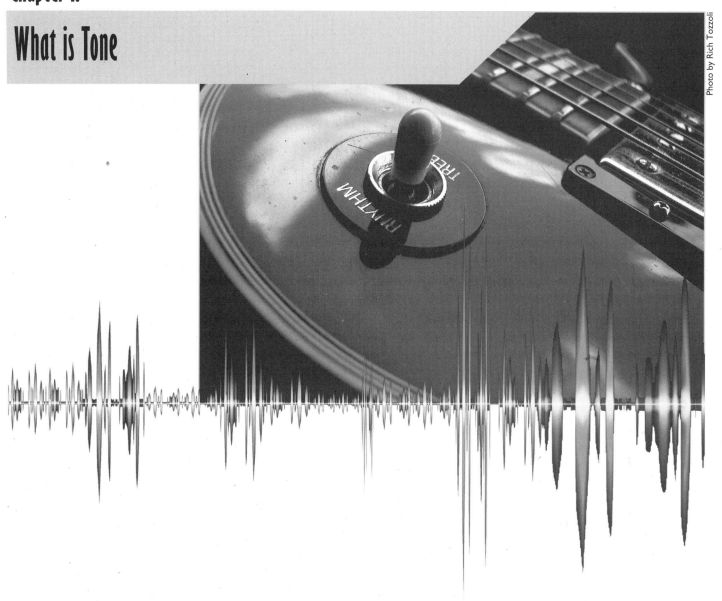

Photo by Rich Tozzoli

What exactly is this thing called tone? That's the great question, isn't it? The thing that makes the answer so interesting is, the perfect tone is different to the ears of different guitar players, engineers, producers, other musicians and listeners. To a kid playing thrash metal, it could be the buzziest, most processed, over-the-top distorted sonic assault that comes just short of burning the walls down in the rehearsal room; while to a jazz player, it could be the silkiest, mellowest Wes Montgomery-like sound that flows like milk over the listener's ears. Or the answer could be anywhere in between. For acoustic guitars, it could be the classic full-bodied tone of a pre-war Gibson J-45, the mid-heavy sonics of an inexpensive import or the pristine clarity of a modern luthier's mahogany dreadnought. Who's to say? If you love what you hear, then it's good to you.

To the average player, the perfect tone is as much a matter of feel as it is the sound coming from the instrument. In fact, feel and sound are completely intertwined because it won't sound good unless it feels good, and vice-versa. We're usually more forgiving of our sounds when we perform live because of the unpredictable environment, but in the studio, we have the perfect opportunity to perfect our tone.

## Studio Ears

We can truly evaluate guitar tone in a studio recording session because everything is under a sonic microscope. The more experienced the musician, engineer and producer, the better their tone reference point. That's why we'll refer to the insights of several top recording engineers, acclaimed musicians, and producers during the course of this book.

But there's another important factor that contributes to tone: the way the instrument sounds in the context of the song. Often, everyone involved deems an instrument or sound wonderful when played by itself, only to find that it overwhelms or underwhelms the song, which defeats the purpose of what we perceive as good tone. That's why so many types of guitars, amplifiers, pedals and effects exist, because there's always a perfect combination that compliments the song.

## It's All in the Fingers

It's amazing what happens when even an inexperienced player picks up and plays a fifty-year-old Martin D-45 or a '58 Les Paul, or plugs into a 1959 Fender Bassman or Marshall Plexi. The air comes alive, and even a neophyte immediately knows why these musical marvels are so revered. They're desirable not only because so few were made, but primarily because they sound so good. But a lot more goes into tone than the rig; the main ingredient is really the player. If Eric Clapton picks up your guitar, he'll still sound like Eric Clapton. But if you pick up his guitar, you won't sound like him!

I had an experience once playing with guitar great and ex-Rolling Stone Mick Taylor. Mick relied on rental gear or even guitars and amps supplied by fans for a series of dates. No matter how bad some of the gear was (and some of it was total crap), or how different it was (guitars and amp models varied every night), he always sounded like Mick Taylor; same tone, no matter what. It just goes to prove—it's all in the fingers first.

# Other Factors in the Search for Tone

So what else goes into getting a great tone? Many engineers and producers feel that the player and the gear contribute about 50 percent to the overall recorded sound. Of course, that proportion is somewhat arbitrary, but consider these other factors.

## THE ROOM

The environment is a huge factor in achieving the ultimate tone on a recording, especially when recording acoustic instruments (if I were to place an arbitrary percentage on its contribution, I'd say about 20 percent). Even on close-miked instruments and amplifiers, the room has far more responsibility for the ultimate sound than many players realize.

That's one of the reasons that finding the perfect placement in the room is so important. When tracking, you try to find the most comfortable position in the room that provides the best interaction among the players with the least leakage (in some cases, leakage is desirable). But during overdubs, the search for the best tone becomes paramount, which is why we need to find the best-sounding part of the room to record. We'll discuss this more in Chapter 7.

## THE MICROPHONE

The type of microphone used will contribute to tone, although not as much as you might think. The positioning of the microphone is actually more of a factor than the microphone itself, contributing about 20 percent to the overall sound. Consider mic placement as your "acoustic EQ," because it contributes heavily to the instrument's tone in the track.

Contrary to popular belief, the microphone choice only contributes about 10 percent to a recorded guitar's overall sound, although with acoustic guitars this may be a larger percentage due to the fact that there are no amplifiers involved and the guitar itself is projecting all the tone. The microphone selection is the final small element that takes a good sound and makes it great. We'll discuss mic selection and placement more in Chapter 6.

## CHANGE YOUR TONE

So what do you do if something doesn't sound right? There are a lot of things to try before you reach for the EQ. Try the following steps, in order:

1. Change the mic placement on the instrument or amp.

2. Change the mic itself.

3. Change the placement of the instrument or amp in the room.

4. Change the strings on your guitar.

5. Change the instrument or amp that you're miking.

6. Change the mic preamplifier.

7. Change the amount of compression and/or limiting (from none to a lot).

8. Change the room you are recording in.

9. Change the player (the producer's decision).

10. Come back and try it another day (also the producer's decision).

# Tone Killers

While many factors go into a good tone, a few can kill it just as easily if you're not careful. Let's look at a few of the most common problems.

## DISTORTION

Most guitar players love distortion, but a little goes a long way, especially in the studio. Nothing can kill the sound of a guitar track as fast as too much distortion. Many times, the tone that sounds perfectly great in the open air of the tracking room becomes an undefined din when blended into a recording. It's common for an engineer or producer to ask a guitar player to back off on the distortion or overdrive during recording, usually to the player's dismay. Listen to recordings of some of the greats such as Jimmy Page and Pete Townshend. It doesn't take as much distortion as you may think for these players to sound "heavy." Both had intense backing bands which helped create a sense of power without the need for a huge amount of saturation of the amps.

Playing with distortion and sustain can give you a false sense of your ability by covering up a lot of mistakes and technique problems. The way to get around this is to learn to play completely clean. You might not like what you hear at first, but with practice, you'll find that it'll make you a much better player, because you can hear all the nuances that you're either doing well or need work on that you just can't hear through the distortion. If you can sound great clean, you'll sound even better dirty!

## EFFECTS PEDALS

Today, almost every player has a huge stockpile of various types of effects pedals, and some players sport huge pedalboards. Pedals can be your greatest asset or your weakest link, depending upon how they're set up and used.

If they're set up incorrectly, pedals can generate a huge amount of noise and affect your signal level and tone even when they are bypassed, which is why high-end pedalboards and interface systems are desirable in professional applications, as we'll discuss in Chapter 8. Sometimes, an engineer will prefer to dial in an effect via a plug-in or a piece of outboard gear rather than having the guitar player add it at the source, especially when it comes to reverb. Sometimes the sound of the guitar player is so good that it must be captured as-is. Remember, you can't remove the effects once they're recorded in your signal path. If you add them later, they can be adjusted to fit the song.

Regardless of the situation, using too many effects in line at once usually adds up to about the same thing as too much distortion; a muddy wash of sound rather than a clearly-defined expression of ultimate tone. Of course, if your name is Tom Morello, The Edge or Steve Lukather, that statement may not apply thanks to your subtle effects touch.

In the studio, we're constantly looking for the right sound that fits the song and that requires the willingness to experiment. Guitars, amps, effects—even something as subtle as the strings or a pickup—all make a difference in the final product. But regardless of the means you use to come to your tonal end, the key word is discretion. A little goes a long way!

# Chapter 2:

## The Evolution of the Electric Guitar and Amplifier

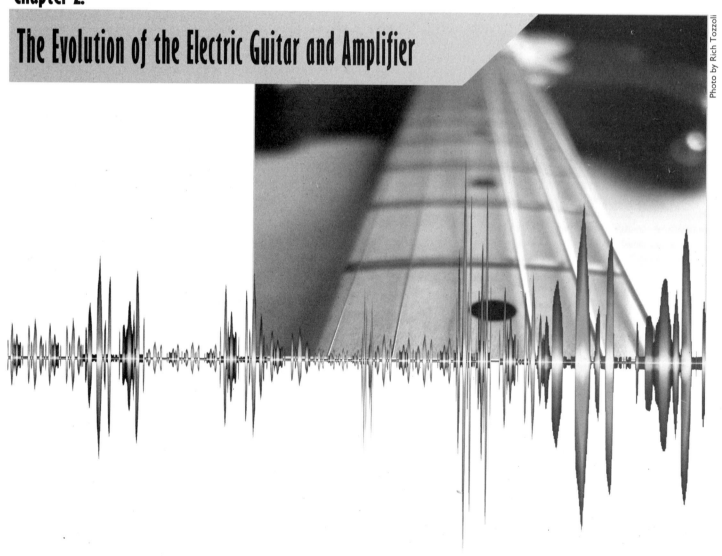

Photo by Rich Tozzoli

If you're a guitar player, you know that the guitar is more than the instrument itself; it's the embodiment of everything that goes into creating the sound, from the body to the strings to the pickups to the cable to the effects to the amplifier (which we can further break down into tubes, speakers, cabinets, etc.). Let's take a look at the development of the instrument as a whole over the decades.

## The 1890s: Development of Steel Strings

The electric guitar has roots in the acoustic version in many ways, but none more significant than the development of steel strings. The strong X-bracing pattern developed in the 1850s by Christian Frederick Martin, the founder of today's CF Martin company, and later improved in 1880 by Chicago guitar maker Joseph Bohmann, opened the door for the bridge and tailpiece combination patented by Charles Geiger in 1891. These innovations were put to use immediately by the John Church company, for what many believe to be the first steel-string guitar. By 1896, the giant instrument manufacturer Lyon and Healy was shipping its Jupiter, Columbus and Marquette guitars with factory-installed steel strings.

## The 1920s: Picks and Pickups

In 1921, the CF Martin Company was the first major guitar manufacturer to focus production on steel-string guitars, in an effort to overcome a big deficiency of the acoustic guitars of the time: not enough volume.

The first guitar pickup can be attributed to Lloyd Loar, a master luthier responsible for Gibson's revered L5 guitar and F5 mandolin (among others), who pioneered the F-hole and extended neck, and moved the bridge closer to the guitar's body. Loar was well-versed in acoustics, and used this knowledge to improve the design of the guitar body for maximum projection.

Loar was fascinated with the idea of amplifying acoustic instruments, and after leaving Gibson in 1924, he opened the Vivi-Tone company. It was there that he designed and patented the first guitar pickup, and created the first amplifier designed specifically for musical instruments.

The 1920s also saw another creation that impacts players to this day: the plastic pick. Until 1922, guitarists shaped pieces of bone, shell, wood, cuttlebone, metal, amber, stone or ivory into picks. Luigi D'Andrea and his son Tony purchased a sheet of tortoiseshell-colored celluloid and shaped pieces into the pick shape that we use today. Soon, D'Andrea Picks offered a number of pick shapes, and in the late '30s, began to imprint guitarist's names on custom picks (the first model was made for the then-popular Nick Lucas).

# The 1930s: Birth of the Electric

It's a popular misconception that Leo Fender was the originator of the first electric guitar. In fact, the first electric guitar was developed by Rickenbacker in 1931 and produced in 1932. The famous Frying Pan model (see Figure 2.1) was designed by George Beauchamp, with Rickenbacker holding the patent. These guitars were nicknamed Frying Pans because of their unusual shape and material; they were made from cast aluminum and were played on a person's lap, using a steel slide much like today's lap steel guitar. By 1935, Rickenbacker had built its reputation as a manufacturer of electric guitars, and became the first to build a solid body out of Bakelite plastic and wood.

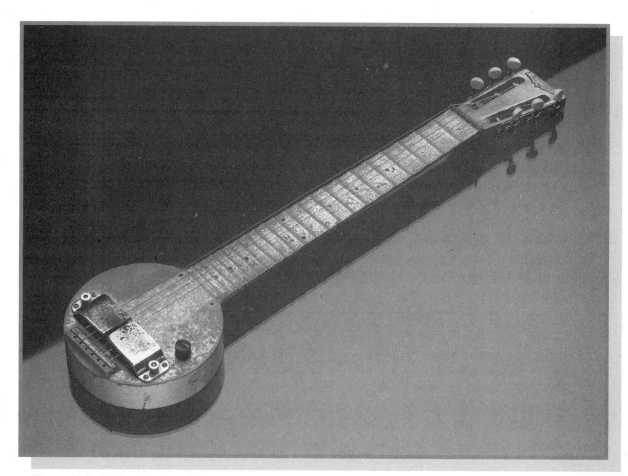

*Figure 2.1: Rickenbacker "Frying Pan": the first electric guitar*

Other companies noticed Rickenbacker's innovations and created their own electric models. Epiphone was a premier banjo maker at the time, but correctly predicted that soon there would be an increased interest in guitars. Its Emperor dual-pickup F-hole hollow-body was released in 1935.

Vega released an electric mandolin in 1936.

In 1935, Gibson commissioned the prominent slide guitarist Alvino Rey to assist the company in the development of a guitar pickup, which was eventually built by Gibson's Walter Fuller. Originally incorporated into a lap steel, the pickup was attached to a standard F-hole archtop guitar in 1936 and designated the ES-150 ("ES" for Electro-Spanish and "150" for the price in dollars). The ES-150 (see Figure 2.2) became the first commercially successful electric guitar, as it immediately found a home in the many jazz bands of the day. Sold in a set with a cable and the EH-150 amplifier, it gave guitarists enough volume to take a more prominent role in their ensemble.

At the same time, a name that would figure heavily in electric guitar development began to experiment with pickups attached to acoustic guitars: Les Paul. The guitarist and inventor was frustrated by the feedback problems that plagued amplified acoustic instruments, and after hearing about a solid-body violin developed by Thomas Edison, became intrigued by the idea of a solid-body guitar. As we all know, he was to play a major part in the development of the electric guitar, although that would come some years later.

Rickenbacker wasn't only the first company to commercially produce an electric guitar, it was also the first to produce an amplifier line. In 1932, three versions of its 12-watt, 3-input M-11 amplifier (see Figure 2.3) were introduced, at $62.50, $65 and $70. The 15-watt M-12, with a bass-reflex speaker cabinet, was released in 1933. In fact, during the 1930s, Rickenbacker was the premier amplifier company, although the actual sales numbers were relatively small.

By the end of the 1930s, most electric guitars had evolved to include the volume and tone controls that we know today, many of them even mounted to a metal cover plate.

*Figure 2.2: 1937 Gibson ES-150*

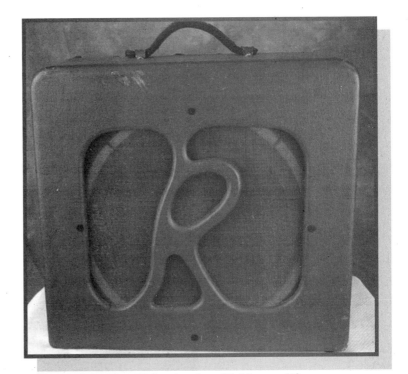

*Figure 2.3: The Rickenbacker M-11 amplifier*

# The 1940s: The Instrument Evolves

While the 1930s saw the creation of the electric guitar, the 1940s were all about refinement of the concept, as the newfound interest in amplified instruments grew.

In 1941, Les Paul used Epiphone's workshop on Sundays to build his now legendary "Log" guitar (see Figure 2.4). Convinced that this would be the solution to the feedback he'd been experiencing on stage, the Log was a simple 4x4 wood post with a neck attached to it, along with some homemade pickups and hardware. After being ridiculed for using the Log on a club gig, Paul attached two cutaway halves of an acoustic guitar to the wings to give the appearance of a real guitar. In 1946 Paul took his Log guitar to Gibson and was laughed out of the building, a move the company would almost come to regret.

*Figure 2.4: Les Paul's "Log" guitar*

In 1945, former Rickenbacker employee Doc Kaufman and electronics tinkerer Leo Fender opened the K&F Manufacturing company to make lap steel guitars and matching amplifiers. Fender believed that he could build a more compact pickup using smaller magnets than were the norm, and that the demand for amplifiers would ramp up as World War II ended. K&F's first steel guitar/amplifier combo was sold only as a set and was aimed more at students and beginners than seasoned pros.

In 1947, Fender bought out Kaufman and changed the name of the company to Fender Electric Instrument Company, with the new logo appearing on every product. The first Fender amp, the Model 26, was very simple, offering no controls (not even a volume control). The Model 26 was soon followed by the Champion 600, another beginner's amp, similar to today's Champ. Fender soon followed that model with its first serious amplifier, the 2-channel Dual Pro (its name was later changed to the Super), which featured two 6L6 tubes and a 15-watt output—a sample of things to come. (See Figure 2.5.)

*Figure 2.5: The Fender Dual Pro*

In the same year, Gibson introduced the ES-350, the first guitar to have a cutaway. While this feature seems like a no-brainer today because it's so common, the cutaway was a major innovation for its day, although it presented numerous manufacturing problems at the time.

In 1948, Paul Bigsby, who was making mostly steel guitars, built a solid-body guitar for guitarist Merle Travis (see Figure 2.6) that featured a vibrato tailpiece. This guitar would have a huge influence on Leo Fender's first guitar design, although there is some question as to who copied who, since Bigsby's operation was close to Fender's in Fullerton, California.

*Figure 2.6: Bigsby's Merle Travis guitar*

In 1949, Gibson introduced the first 3-pickup guitar, the ES-5 Switchmaster (see Figure 2.7), and Leo Fender prototyped his first electric guitar, which would soon start a revolution in the industry.

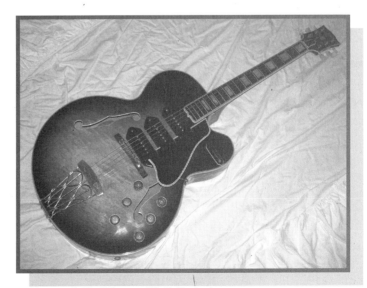

*Figure 2.7: Gibson ES-5 Switchmaster*

# The 1950s: Breakthrough Developments

In a decade of many innovations, perhaps the most profound were the 1950 releases of Fender's first electric guitar, the single-pickup Esquire, and the 2-pickup Broadcaster (which would soon change its name to Telecaster to avoid a trademark clash with a Gretsch drum set called "Broadkaster"; see Figure 2.8). Leo Fender wanted to make a solid-body guitar because it was easier to produce than an acoustic electric, so he stripped the guitar down to its essential elements and had it manufactured from easily assembled parts. The result was a guitar with a unique sound and an affordable price.

*Figure 2.8: An original Fender Broadcaster*

By 1951, electric guitars made up half of Gibson's total sales, so the company decided to get serious in the market, introducing the Super 400 and the L-5, both of which contained the revered P-90 pickups, cutaways and individual bridge saddles. Gibson went back to Les Paul, whom the company had laughed at five years earlier, and asked him to help design a solid-body guitar. The result was the Les Paul Gold Top (see Figure 2.9), introduced in 1952 (also with single-coil P-90s).

*Figure 2.9: 1952 Les Paul Gold Top*

1952 was also a significant year for Fender, which introduced the first version of its Bassman amplifier (see Figure 2.10). Although designed to be a companion to the Precision Bass introduced in 1951, the Bassman soon became a favorite of guitarists everywhere, and to this day is held as somewhat of a Holy Grail of guitar amps.

*Figure 2.10: 1958 Fender Bassman*

1952 saw Paul Bigsby build the first double-neck instrument, featuring a guitar and mandolin, for Nashville guitarist Grady Martin. Gibson followed in 1958 with its own double-neck, the EDS-1275 6- and 12-string later made famous by Jimmy Page (see Figure 2.11).

*Figure 2.11: Gibson EDS-1275 double-neck*

Leo Fender's master stroke in guitar design came in 1954 with the introduction of the Stratocaster, probably the most widely played and influential guitar ever made (see Figure 2.12). Slow selling until popularized by Jimi Hendrix in the late '60s, the Strat has gone on to become the biggest-selling guitar of all time. Designed by Fender, George Fullerton and Freddie Tavares, the Strat was unique in so many ways. First, it had a rather space-age (for the day) double-cutaway body that was contoured to better fit the player's body. It also had frets set directly into the maple neck (instead of a fingerboard), as well as unique semi-locking tuning machines that all pulled from the same side of the neck. Add to that a simple-yet-effective vibrato system, two-tone double-coat paint (on sunburst models) and sideways output jack, and you have a guitar that's been unmatched in innovation 50-plus years later. Of course, the one-piece pickguard that allowed all electronic components to be mounted on a single easily removable surface is a standard used on many electric instruments to this day.

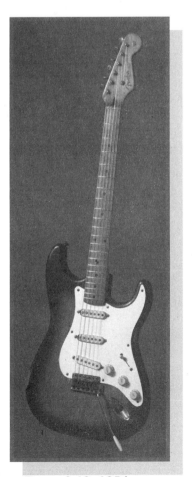

*Figure 2.12: 1954 Fender Strat*

1954 saw Gretsch's first entry into true electric-guitar building with the single-cutaway Country Club model. Two years later, Gretsch would be the first manufacturer to release a semi-solid guitar, with its seldom-seen-today White Penguin (see Figure 2.13).

*Figure 2.13: Gretsch White Penguin*

In 1954, the Les Paul was upgraded with the Tune-O-Matic bridge and the now-familiar stop tailpiece (see Figure 2.14). The Tune-O-Matic bridge was a real advancement in that the bridge was now fully adjustable, so intonation could be precisely set within minutes. At the same time, Gibson redesigned its P-90 pickups to use alnico magnets, which provided more output and a sweeter tone.

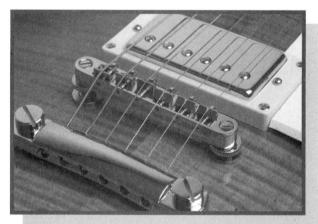

*Figure 2.14: Les Paul with Tune-O-Matic bridge and stop tailpiece*

In 1956, Rickenbacker introduced two instruments featuring the innovative "neck through body" construction that was to become standard for its later products. The same year, Fender introduced the Vibrolux, the first amplifier with "vibrato" (see Figure 2.15). Vibrato was actually an incorrect term, since it means a cyclic change in pitch while the Vibrolux produced a change in volume known as tremolo. To this day, Fender still uses the term vibrato instead of tremolo.

*Figure 2.15: 1960 Fender Vibrolux*

Also in 1956, Vox introduced the AC-15, which would go on to become one of the most beloved amps of British guitarists, and would lead to the development of the famous AC-30 (see Figure 2.16)

*Figure 2.16: Vox AC-30*

In 1957, Gibson engineer Seth Lover designed the first dual-coil humbucking pickup, which radically reduced external hum and noise from being captured by the guitar. Humbuckers were incorporated into most Gibson electric guitars from that point forward. The same year, Gibson acquired Epiphone. Also in 1957, Rickenbacker introduced its 4000 Series bass, a must-have for every serious rock bass player in later years.

1957 was also the year that guitar maker Kay Musical Instruments, which had up to that point manufactured beginner guitars for department store brands, came out with its own guitar, the Barney Kessel signature model. Kay was also the manufacturer of the Sears Silvertone brand, which has gone on to vintage fame. In 1968, the Kay name was sold and used for a line of poorly-made imported student guitars.

1958 was a big year for guitar innovation. First, Gretsch introduced its famed White Falcon stereo guitar (see Figure 2.17) in an effort to take advantage of the stereo audio craze that was just taking off.

*Figure 2.17: Gretsch White Falcon*

1958 also saw the introduction of the Fender Jazzmaster, which featured two independent circuits for rhythm and lead, although jazz players were always cool to it (see Figure 2.18). That year, Fender also introduced custom colors, which were essentially the same DuPont lacquers used on autos at the time.

*Figure 2.18: A vintage Fender Jazzmaster*

In 1958, Gibson introduced the radical Explorer (see Figure 2.19), Flying V, and Modern designs, in an effort to keep up with the success that Fender was having with solid-body guitars. While these models never sold well, the company's innovative semi-solid ES-335 "thinline" acoustic guitar design (see Figure 2.20), complete with double cutaways, proved a big success. With sales of the Les Paul declining, Gibson changed the guitar's finish to a cherry sunburst, which has become one of the most prized and sought-after guitars today, mostly because it was discontinued in 1960.

Also in 1958, Rickenbacker introduced its Capri Series double-cutaway semi-acoustic guitars, which would later become the famous 300 Series.

*Figure 2.19: Gibson Explorer*

*Figure 2.20: Gibson ES-335 "Dot Neck"*

Not a company known to lag behind, Gibson introduced the ES-345 stereo model to compete with Gretsch and take advantage of stereo recordings in 1959, as well as the ES-345 and ES-355 models, which featured a new "Varitone" switch that let players select tonal presets.

# The 1960s: Amps and Distortion

With the sudden popularity of the electric guitar thanks to The Beatles and the "British Invasion," market-leading Fender and Gibson guitars became a bit too expensive for the average beginner guitar player, which led to an influx of poor-quality imported instruments that were difficult to play. That didn't discourage many new guitarists, though, as bands and players flourished like never before.

Sales of pricier instruments continued to thrive, which led to the major companies fighting for market share. In 1960, Gibson experienced a decline in sales, due to strong competition from Fender. In 1961, impressed with the cutaway design of the Stratocaster, Gibson modified its Les Paul line with a model that was thinner and lighter than earlier models and featured double cutaways and a vibrato system (see Figure 2.21). These modifications were made without Les Paul's knowledge, and as a result, he asked that his name be removed from the instrument and parted ways with the company shortly thereafter. In 1963, the guitar's name was changed to "SG," which stood for Solid Guitar. Variations on this design evolved into products such as the less-expensive Les Paul Juniors, Specials and Melody Makers.

*Figure 2.21: 1961 Les Paul SG*

At the time, tubes were thought to be the weak link in the amplification chain, and many companies began to integrate the new technology of transistor amplification into their product lines, because of their lower heat and weight and longer life. Kay was the first company to implement the design in 1962, followed by Gibson in 1963, Vox in 1964 and Fender in 1966. Players were not impressed, to say the least, and these models have never been sought after in any vintage.

Musicians have always loved distorted guitar, but in the early days, most of the time distortion was achieved by accident. From Ike Turner's defective amp on 1951's "Rocket 88," to Link Wray's blown speakers on his 1958 instrumental hit "Rumble," to the legendary 1961 Marty Robbins "Don't Worry" recording session with a malfunctioning console preamp that generated a now-famous "fuzztone," guitar players had trusted that magic sound to be a product of fate. Glen Snotty, the recording engineer at that fateful Marty Robbins session, managed to duplicate that sound in 1962 in the first known instance of a distortion stompbox, which soon became a popular device on the Nashville scene. That same year, this became the basis of the first commercially released distortion pedal, the Maestro FZ-1 Fuzz-Tone (see Figure 2.22), although sales were slow until Keith Richards used one on the Stones' seminal "Satisfaction" in 1964. The sound of the guitar would never be the same again, as distortion and the stompbox became front and center of the rock guitarist's sound.

*Figure 2.22: Maestro FZ-1 Fuzz-Tone stompbox*

Maestro put another groundbreaking effect in the hands of guitarists with the Echoplex EP-1 (see Figure 2.23), a small tape-based delay unit with a movable head that allowed the guitar player to change the delay time.

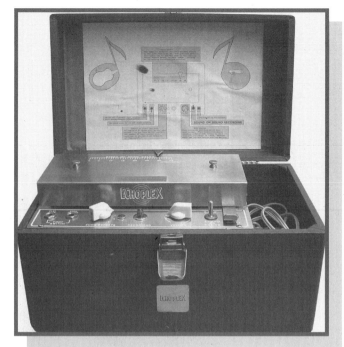

*Figure 2.23: Echoplex EP-1*

In 1962, the National Dobro Company changed its name to Valco and introduced a line of fiberglass guitars (see Figure 2.24). These didn't resonate with the public much at the time, but they are prized collector's items today.

*Figure 2.24: Valco Sahara*

One of the biggest events in guitar history came in 1962, when Jim Marshall built his first amplifier in the back of his music store. Soon came the familiar Marshall stack with the famous amp head and 4x12 cabinet, both of which are standards of rock music to this day. By 1964, Marshall's first factory had 16 full-time employees producing 20 amps a week. In 1965, Marshall introduced its first Bluesbreaker combo amp and the famous 100-watt head and stack.

In 1963, Rickenbacker developed an electric 12-string, the 360/12 (see Figure 2.25), which featured a headstock that enabled all twelve machine heads to be mounted on a standard headstock, instead of the elongated type used by Gibson and Fender. Its distinctive jangly sound soon became the centerpiece of Beatles and Byrds records, among many others.

1965 was a pivotal year for Fender as founder Leo Fender, burned out from nonstop work and in poor health, sold his company to media giant CBS. The move would have far-reaching implications for many years to come as CBS's cost-cutting led to a general reduction of quality. CBS believed that the future was in solid-state amplifiers and introduced new models to an almost hostile reception. As time went by, Fender guitars and amps produced before the sale to CBS ("pre-CBS") became sought after, and still are today.

1967 was another seminal year in the history of the electric guitar, marked by the release of the wah-wah pedal by Warwick Electronics/Thomas Organ Company, which has become a staple of almost every modern guitar player's sonic arsenal.

In 1968, after high-profile players like Jimmy Page, Mike Bloomfield, Keith Richards and Eric Clapton used the instrument to great acclaim, Gibson reintroduced the Les Paul. Also in 1968, Micro-frets, a little-known company from Frederick, Maryland, released the Orbiter, the first wireless guitar, which used an FM transmitter and receiver.

*Figure 2.25: Rickenbacker 360/12 Headstock*

## The 1970s: Big Amps and Boutiques

The '70s saw an evolution in both guitars and amplification, but more and more, pedals came into play. In 1970, Electro-Harmonix introduced the famous Big Muff Pi distortion and the LBP-1 (Linear Power Booster), the first overdrive device. In 1972, MXR, in Rochester, N.Y., came out with its Phase 90, Distortion+ and Dyna-Comp pedals, among many others. But the '70s are known mostly for the "watt wars," when each manufacturer tried to make a louder amp than its competition.

While other manufacturers built larger and larger amplifiers, Mesa-Boogie went in a different direction in 1972 by adding a master volume, then switchable channels. Also in 1972, Guitar Center began its quest to control the retail end of the business as it opened its second store in San Francisco (the first was in Hollywood, across the street from today's flagship store on Sunset Boulevard).

Gibson and Fender both went through major changes in the '70s. Gibson suffered through absentee corporate management and as a result, saw little in the way of guitar innovation. Fender, thanks to the penny-pinching of CBS, made cosmetic changes as it scrimped on quality. The four-bolt neck was changed to three, a new "improved" micro-tilt neck and truss-rod system and even a new Seth Lover-designed Humbucking pickup was incorporated in some models, none of which were hits with their customers. Perhaps the best thing that Fender did during this time period was adding a 5-way pickup selector to the Strat, which eliminated the need to delicately balance between selections on the previous 3-way switch.

While the major manufacturers remained saddled by their past, new boutique guitar makers sprang up. In 1972, B.C. Rich began producing unusually shaped guitars (see Figure 2.26), and guitars with aluminum necks (allegedly for improved sustain) debuted from Travis Bean in 1974, then Kramer Guitars in 1975 (see Figure 2.27). In 1976, Dean Guitars launched the guitars that would soon become the face of metal like the Razorback and Bolt, and Ibanez made a number of quality instruments, such as the Artist and the Iceman, that have since become collectibles.

*Figure 2.26: B.C. Rich Bich*

*Figure 2.27: Kramer with aluminum neck*

## The 1980s: Mass Production, Improved Effects

The '80s didn't see much in the way of guitar innovation, but the decade saw more manufacturers jump into the business, especially from overseas. Beginning in the early '80s, the Japanese began to manufacture instruments of roughly the same quality as the major American manufacturers, but at more affordable prices. Yamaha, Ibanez, Aria and Kawai all provided highly playable instruments at prices so competitive that Fender developed the Squire line of low-cost look-alike instruments, and produced them in Japan to take advantage of the low manufacturing costs. Soon, other guitar makers would follow suit.

In order to keep manufacturing costs down at home, the major manufacturers turned to CNC (Computer Numerically Controlled) woodcutting to improve cut precision and use wood more efficiently (see Figure 2.28). Guitar manufacturing would never be the same, as general instrument quality rose, but instruments with exceptional nuances disappeared as a result of mass production.

*Figure 2.28: CNC precision woodcutting machine*

The '80s saw the introduction of the Floyd Rose tremolo, a device that was invented in the '70s but didn't become widely available until 1982. The Floyd Rose allowed guitarists to radically lower and raise pitch over a much wider range than previously possible, and still magically remain in tune.

As guitarists began to use pedals more, they grew frustrated by the time it took to set them up, as well as the amount of floor space required onstage or in the studio. Enter the multi-effects device. The first units were primitive, but they soon evolved into the sophisticated devices that we know today. Always at the forefront of stompbox and guitar pedal technology, Ibanez led the way with the introduction of the UE-300 in 1982 (see Figure 2.29).

*Figure 2.29: An original Ibanez UE-300 multi-effects unit*

While weekend warriors opted for multi-effects pedals, pro guitarists had more complex needs. They wanted to get the same sound live that they were used to getting in the studio by using their rackmount studio devices, but the studio units weren't suited for stage use, in terms of fast switching and interface to non-studio hardware. Custom switching systems like Bob Bradshaw's RS-10 eliminated the challenges of using multiple amps, rack effects and pedals onstage by letting users program complex signal-routing setups that could be accessed instantly by stomping on a single switch (see Figure 2.30). As these systems grew progressively larger, it became clear that the most efficient way to incorporate everything was to use a separate preamp from the amplifier, and the first rack-mounted guitar preamps were born (see Figure 2.31).

*Figure 2.30: Bradshaw switching system*

Bigger wasn't always more beautiful though. In 1982, Tom Sholz, the founder and guitar player of the band Boston (and an engineer for Polaroid), built a multi-effects device that captured his distinctive sound in a box that was the size of the popular Sony Walkman. The first case of modeling (however primitive) and direct recording was born with his "Rockman" (see Figure 2.32).

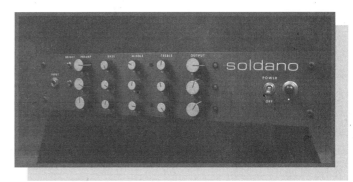

*Figure 2.31: Soldano X88 rack-mounted preamp*

One of the most significant events of the decade came in 1984, when CBS tired of the musical instrument industry and sold Fender back to a few of its senior executives. The new company started out with a major disadvantage since no factories were included in the deal, but soon restored product quality, and began its slow growth into the manufacturing powerhouse it is today.

*Figure 2.32: The Rockman*

As metal became a big part of the music scene in the '80s, guitarists lusted for more distortion, overdrive and sustain. Manufacturers responded by building amps with more gain stages to give guitarists more control over their amp sound. High-gain amps by Soldano (see Figure 2.33), Mesa/Boogie, VHT and others soon became the norm, although whether the tone actually improved is debatable.

During the '80s, custom pickups became the norm, with many guitarists swapping their stock factory units for hotter or quieter versions. Companies like Seymour Duncan and DiMarzio even supplied pickups to various guitar manufacturers, but these pickups mostly remained popular after-market products.

*Figure 2.33: Soldano SLO-100*

Finally, a huge advance that is often overlooked:
In the '80s, the inexpensive guitar tuner was born. During previous decades, the only options for tuning a guitar were a very expensive strobe tuner, a cheesy pitch pipe, a tuning fork or an extremely good ear. After companies like Boss and Korg started offering affordable digital chromatic tuners, guitarists no longer had an excuse for being out of tune.

## The 1990s: Wireless Goes Mainstream, Amp Modelers Debut

Guitar and amp innovation slowed in the '90s, yet a number of significant events occurred. In 1993, Ken Parker and Larry Fishman designed the first guitar built from composite materials. The Parker Fly was extremely lightweight, and was one of the first instruments to combine both magnetic and piezoelectric pickups, allowing the guitarist to access both electric and acoustic tones. (See Figure 2.34.)

Although modern wireless microphone technology debuted in 1976 with Nady's first compander system, it wasn't until the mid-'90s that systems of sufficient quality came within the financial reach of the average musician when Nady and Samson introduced affordable systems with price points of only a few hundred dollars.

In the '90s, new sources for vacuum tubes were discovered in Russia, China and Yugoslavia. The tubes were found in the nick of time, because existing stocks of western-made tubes began to dwindle. Tube amp lovers everywhere breathed a sigh of relief.

*Figure 2.34: The Parker Fly guitar*

In 1996, Line 6 debuted its AxSys 212, the first modeling amplifier somewhat capable of reproducing the sound of vintage amps and speaker cabinets (see Figure 2.35). Fender, Vox, Marshall and other companies would eventually follow as the technology improved, became more widespread and grew less expensive.

In 1998, Line 6 continued its path of innovation by introducing the Pod, the portable amp-modeling processor that could be used for direct recording or personal rehearsal.

*Figure 2.35: Line 6 AxSys 212—the first modeling amplifier*

# The 2000s: Modelers, Reissues Recreate the Classics

One of the most striking aspects of the 2000s is how little happened in the way of guitar and amp innovation. Sure, there's evolution in many products, but there's very little revolution, mostly because today's guitars and amps are in what's known as their "mature" stage. That doesn't mean that nothing of significance has occurred in the past decade, however.

In 2003, while most amplifier manufacturers were dabbling in modeling, Line 6 released the Variax modeling guitar in 2003 (see Figure 2.36), which modeled a host of electric and acoustic guitar models, as well as dobro, sitar and banjo.

In the 2000s, the prices of vintage guitar amps reached all-time highs, due to high demand and product scarcity. As a result, techs and enthusiasts started their own small amplifier-manufacturing companies, in an effort to reproduce the designs of the most sought-after vintage amps. As these boutique manufacturers thrived, they also began to include updated versions, or even completely new offshoots, of those original circuits.

*Figure 2.36: Variax modeling guitar*

Prices also climbed into the stratosphere for vintage Les Pauls, Strats, Flying Vs, 335s and just about anything from the '50s, '60s and even the '70s. As a result, manufacturers began to reissue the most desirable models, with specs as close to the original as possible. Fender took the craze one step further by delivering limited-edition, custom-shop reproductions of the personal guitars played by Stevie Ray Vaughan, Jeff Beck, Rory Gallagher, Andy Summers and others (see Figure 2.37).

*Figure 2.37: Stevie Ray Vaughan-reissue Strat*

With home recording systems getting smaller and less expensive, it was now possible for the average guitarist to own a studio that was more powerful than The Beatles had for only a few thousand dollars. At the same time, software effects and modeling plug-ins from Line 6, IK Multimedia, Tech 21 and others allowed endless modifications of recorded tracks—a boon to the modern guitarist.

After 80 years, the electric guitar is more popular than ever. Read on to learn more about this beautiful, interesting and unique instrument.

# Chapter 3:
# Tonal Characteristics of an Electric Guitar

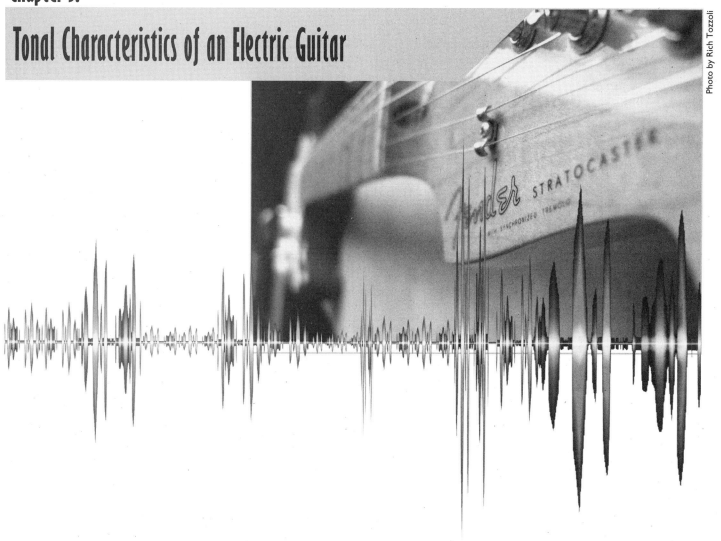

Photo by Rich Tozzoli

As we discussed in Chapter 1, the most important part of a guitar player's tone is the player himself. But let's take him out of the equation for a moment and look at some of the other factors that bring an electric guitar to life.

Why does one guitar sound different from another, even if they're both the same model and were made in the same year? There are a lot more factors involved, even though they may be extremely subtle.

# The Guitar Body

It's easy to look at a Strat, or a Tele, or a Les Paul, or any other guitar model with a body shape that has remained constant over a number of years and think, "The body looks the same. What's different about it?" As you'll see, there's much more going on than you think.

### THE WOOD

Just because a guitar's body looks the same from year to year, that doesn't mean that the guitar is the same, since it may change from manufacturing run to manufacturing run. Let's take a look at everyone's favorite guitar, the Strat, as an example.

When Strats were first manufactured in 1954, they were made of ash until 1956, when they were made of alder, which immediately changed the sound. Why the change to alder? Believe it or not, because they were easier to paint. Since alder trees grow somewhat short, the alder bodies had to be made from two to four pieces rather than the single-piece ash bodies, which again, very subtly alters the tone.

Even though the majority of Strats were made of alder, if you ordered a blond Strat (see Figure 3.1), it would still be made from ash, because of the wood's color and the way it took the yellow stain.

*Figure 3.1: 1956 blond Strat*

In 1963 and 1964, some Stratocaster models were made from mahogany (see Figure 3.2), which imparted an enormous change in the sound, as did a model made from 1981 to 1983 called the Super Strat, which was made out of walnut. In 1990, Fender changed to Basswood for models made in Japan and some models made in the US. If you bought a Mexican-made Strat made after 1992, the body was made out of poplar.

In some cases the change in wood caused only a slight change in the sound (like in the change from ash to alder), and in some cases, the change was huge (like in mahogany, which is rarely used, and maple bodies).

### Tonal Characteristics of Tonewoods

Ash, alder, basswood and poplar have similar sonic properties, but they're not identical; softwood tends to absorb sound, while hardwood reflects it. Let's take a look at some common types of wood used in guitar construction, and their characteristics.

*Figure 3.2: Mahogany Strat*

- **Swamp ash:** Swamp ash (sometimes called "soft ash") is a fairly lightweight wood that usually produces a Strat body weighing under five pounds. It's a very musical wood, offering a balance of brightness and warmth that gives clear, bell-like highs, slightly scooped but very complex mids and strong tight lows. The problem with swamp ash is that the mid frequencies vary a lot from piece to piece, which provides less consistency in guitar sound than most woods.

- **Northern hard ash:** Even though it's still in the ash family, northern hard ash is relatively hard, heavy and dense, producing a Strat body weighing five pounds or more. The wood's density makes it brighter sounding and allows a longer sustain.

- **Alder:** Alder has a balanced tone without much accentuation in any frequency area, aside from a slightly pronounced upper-midrange which improves clarity. It's fairly resonant and complex, with a good dynamic range. An alder Strat body weighs in at about four pounds.

- **Basswood:** The softness of the Basswood attenuates both high and extreme low frequencies. This gives it a pronounced midrange fundamental frequency response. Unlike ash and alder, basswood's tonal response is not particularly complex and the dynamic range is relatively limited. A basswood Strat body weighs about four pounds.

- **Poplar:** Poplar is a bit denser than alder but very similar in weight and tone, coming in at about a half-pound more per body.

- **Walnut:** Walnut is a dense wood that's heavier than all the above woods; a walnut Strat body will weigh five-and-a-half pounds or more. It has a warm low end and a very bright high end, with a mid-range similar to alder.

So, you can see how the sound of a Strat (or any guitar, for that matter) can vary a great deal, depending on the wood used for the body. Add in the fact that wood of any variety varies depending on the environment where it was grown (for example, southern swamp ash and northern hard ash are different), and it's a wonder that they sound as similar as they do.

Gibson guitars are just as diverse. Les Pauls feature a mahogany body with a maple top—both very heavy, dense woods. Over the years, Les Pauls have weighed anywhere between seven-and-a-half pounds to as much as 13. The inexpensive new Les Pauls, such as the Studio model, have even incorporated swamp ash and "chambering" (drilling chambers in the solid body) to reduce weight. Many classic Gibson guitars, such as the original Explorer and Flying V, have been made of korina, which has a grain pattern similar to mahogany, although it is not quite as dense. It has all the good tonal properties of mahogany, but is more responsive, with a sweeter-sounding midrange.

## THE FINISH

The type of paint used, the number of coats and application thickness all contribute to the guitar's tone. For example, in the '50s and '60s, most guitar manufacturers used a nitrocellulose lacquer for all their finishes, and applied it fairly thinly. "Nitro," as it's called, is hard enough to be buffed to a nice, glossy finish, but is still flexible enough to vibrate with the wood and allow it to breathe. One of the problems with a nitro finish is that after four or five years, it begins to yellow, and will wear off under heavy use. This wear is apparent on all Fender guitars from that period (see Figure 3.3).

*Figure 3.3: 1963 yellow "Nitro" Strat*

As a result, in the '70s most manufacturers changed to a thick, glossy polyester finish. It was a lot cheaper and easier to apply, with fewer toxic fumes, but it didn't breathe as well since it was thicker. As a result, the sound changed simply because of the finish. In the '80s and '90s, many manufacturers changed to a polyurethane-based paint, which didn't seal the wood as much, allowing it to resonate a bit more (although not as much as nitro).

Many companies apply an undercoat of filler to hide some of the seams and blemishes of the wood before they paint it, which also affects the tone. Fender bodies were dipped in a yellow stain in the first step in the "sunbursting" process (sunburst was the Strat's primary color at the time). In mid-1964, Fender eliminated the dipped yellow stain and sprayed it on instead, which made the finish less transparent, and let the company use body wood with minor defects as a result. In some cases, Fender even painted a custom color over a painted sunburst finish to save time.

Through the years, every manufacturer has varied the type of paint, the number of coats, the thickness, and the undercoat, sometimes even within the same production run. No wonder guitars sound so wonderfully different!

Today most manufacturers are hip to using thinner undercoats and finishes, and many even offer nitro again, although its chemical formulation has evolved from the one used 50 years ago so it's not exactly the same. That said, it's easy to understand how a guitar body can be affected by something you'd least expect: the finish.

### What Affects the Tonal Quality of a Guitar Body?

The type of wood used

The type of finish

The type of undercoating

The number of coats of paint

The thickness of the paint

# The Neck

The type of wood used for the neck and the fingerboard, and the way the neck is connected to the body, contribute mightily to the tone of the instrument.

## NECK ATTACHMENT
Let's look at the way a neck is attached to the body of the guitar first. There are three primary ways to attach a neck.

**Bolt-on necks** are attached into a fitted slot in the body by means of three or four wood screws running through the back of the body and into the back of the neck (see Figure 3.4). This Leo Fender innovation reduced production costs, which was critical to developing an affordable guitar. Bolt-on necks can be easily repaired, replaced and adjusted, but are sometimes unstable, especially if shims are used, as was the case in many of the early Fenders. Ironically, most of the time bolts are not used in a bolt-on neck.

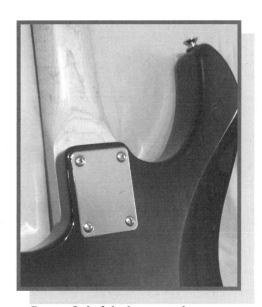

*Figure 3.4: A bolt-on neck*

A **set neck** is glued into the body and sometimes has an extension, called the "tenon," which reaches past the fretboard and deeper into the body (see Figure 3.5). This type of neck is used on Gibson guitars (among many others) and produces a very tight neck joint that freely transfers vibration between the body and neck. The set neck is carefully cut to match its mounting point on the guitar body and the two sections are almost always connected with dovetail joints to maximize the gluing surface and minimize neck wiggle. Gibson Les Pauls are prime examples of electric guitars with set necks. A set neck is more expensive to fashion and much more difficult to repair or change than a bolt-on neck.

**Neck-through** guitars are built around a single column of wood that extends from the tip of the headstock through to the strap button at the tail (see Figure 3.6). This column can either be a single piece or several pieces laminated together side-by-side. The wood body wings are glued to the sides of this central column of wood. Les Paul's early experimental guitar, the "Log," was actually a neck-through guitar, since it began with a 4-inch wood post that ran from tail to headstock, with the sawed-off halves of a guitar body glued onto its sides (an innovation he is not given much credit for).

Neck-through bodies produce the most sustain and have the huge advantage of eliminating the large heel where the neck meets the body, providing easy access to the higher registers. Some players feel that the lower mass of the body wings cuts down on low-frequency resonance, creating a bright, thin-sounding guitar, but the same quality makes neck-through instruments work well when playing in high-volume situations that call for definition and clear low end. The Gibson Firebird, the Parker Fly and the Rickenbacker 425 (see Figure 3.7) are examples of neck-through guitars.

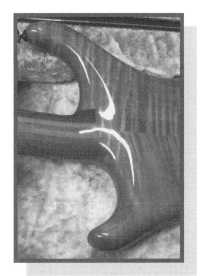

*Figure 3.5: A guitar with a set neck*

*Figure 3.6: Guitar with a neck-through body*

*Figure 3.7: Neck-through Rickenbacker 425*

Regardless of the way the neck is attached to the body, a guitar with a sloppy neck joint will sound weak, because a tight neck joint results in much better tone transference. The guitar will also stay in tune better if the neck is stabilized.

## THE FRETBOARD

Guitar necks are made in one piece, or of two or more sections laminated together to make the neck stronger. As with the body, the neck's wood type greatly determines a guitar's sonic signature. Let's take a look at some of the popular choices.

Ebony is the brightest of the fretboard woods, and is the most desirable from the standpoint that it doesn't require lubrication, other than the oil from your fingers (see Figure 3.8).

*Figure 3.8: Ebony fretboard*

Maple is the next brightest wood, and when serving as the fretboard in many Fender models, has a thin layer of clearcoat, which traps dirt and oil from the fingers but doesn't affect the tone (this coat can wear out over time and heavy use). Maple is medium-hard and medium-weight, which works well without causing the guitar to be neck-heavy (see Figure 3.9).

*Figure 3.9: Maple neck*

Rosewood has a smooth, hard surface that offers a very warm sound. Since it's hardwood, it needs to stay lubricated, which the natural oil from your fingers will do. Remember, rosewood will crack if not lubricated regularly (see Figure 3.10).

Pau ferro is now used as a replacement for rosewood, which is becoming difficult to find.

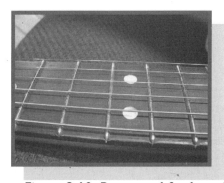

*Figure 3.10: Rosewood fretboard*

## What Affects the Tonal Quality of a Guitar Neck?

The wood

The fretboard

The way it's attached to the body

# Hardware

While there are a number of different types of bridges and tailpieces/string terminations, the characteristic that sets them apart is their effectiveness in transferring string vibrations to the body. Let's look at the different types.

## THE BRIDGE

The bridge supports the strings and sends their vibrations to the body. Although the bridge configuration varies little from guitar to guitar in the same model, there are six types of bridges available.

The Tune-o-matic bridge, developed by Gibson in 1954, was a revelation because it allowed individual intonation adjustment for each string (see Figure 3.11). This system (or some variation) is used on most electric guitars without vibrato arms today.

The fulcrum vibrato used on an SG is attached to a bridge mounted to a plate that extends through the body (see Figure 3.12). The plate is attached to the guitar body with springs. This bridge mounting system allows less vibrational transference than with a Tune-o-matic.

A locking vibrato such as a Floyd Rose is spring loaded and rocks on two bolts on the top of the guitar (see Figure 3.13). The strings are locked at the correct tension on both sides so the tuning stays rock-solid, even with radical use of the vibrato arm. Many guitars that feature a locking vibrato, like even some custom model Jacksons, route the wood to allow the player to pull the notes as far up and down as possible.

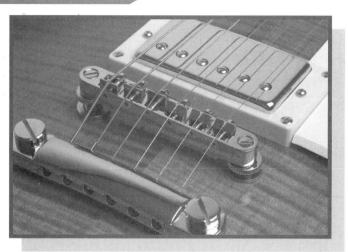

*Figure 3.11: Tune-o-matic bridge*

*Figure 3.12: The fulcrum vibrato*

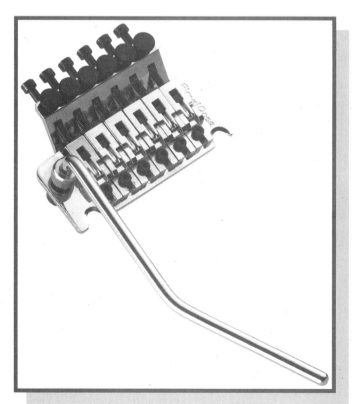

*Figure 3.13: Floyd Rose locking vibrato*

The Bigsby vibrato is the great-granddaddy of all vibrato systems, and is found mostly on vintage or vintage-style guitars (see Figure 3.14). It's a large, heavy device that features a rotating bar where the strings are attached, but it's mounted to the top of the guitar for superior string-body resonance.

*Figure 3.14: Bigsby vibrato*

The six-point rocking vibrato found on the Strat was developed in 1954 by Leo Fender (see Figure 3.15). It's similar to the fulcrum vibrato except that it's attached to the body with six springs, providing greater vibrational transfer.

*Figure 3.15: Six-point rocking vibrato*

Brass-barrel saddles are primarily found on Telecasters of all vintages (see Figure 3.16). They're a pain to adjust and make tuning tricky, but they're also a big part of the bright, twangy tone of the Tele.

*Figure 3.16: Telecaster bridge with brass barrel saddles*

## THE TAILPIECE

The tailpiece, which is where the string ends terminate, is often overlooked for its contribution to tone. There are three main types.

A stop-bar tailpiece, like the one on a Les Paul, bolts to the top of the guitar, allowing the maximum transference of string vibration to the body (see Figure 3.17). This is one of the reasons why a Les Paul has so much sustain.

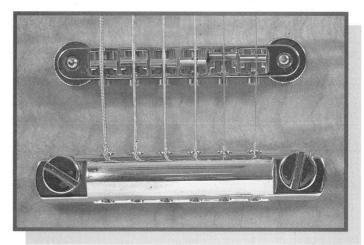

*Figure 3.17: Stop-bar tailpiece*

Trapeze tailpieces are usually found on hollow-body electrics, although you'll find them on some versions of the SG (see Figure 3.18). The string termination swings freely from the tail of the guitar, allowing less vibrational transfer than models with a more solidly connected tailpiece.

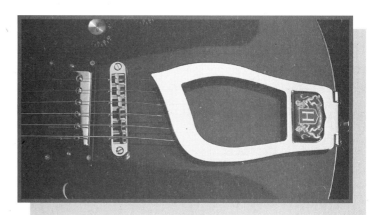

*Figure 3.18: Trapeze tailpiece*

In a string-through body, strings actually mount in the body itself before they run across the bridge (see Figure 3.19). This configuration is what you'll find on most Fender solid-bodies, and has very good vibrational transference.

*Figure 3.19: String-through body*

# Pickups

A pickup turns the vibrations of the strings and body into electrical energy, and allows those vibrations to be amplified (See Figure 3.20). This is accomplished by wrapping a coil of wire around a bobbin that surrounds six magnets, one for each string. The string's vibrations cut through the magnetic field of the pickups, and an electronic signal is produced. There are two common methods for doing this.

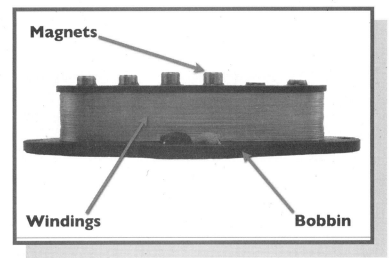

*Figure 3.20: The elements of a pickup*

## TYPES OF PICKUPS

Search the hundreds of electric guitar models available, and on 99.9 percent of them, you'll find only two types of pickups: single-coil or dual-coil (humbuckers). Single-coils, such as the ones found on Strats (see Figure 3.21) and Teles, are bright-sounding, but are susceptible to noise from lights and electrical appliances. Gibson's first pickups, called P-90s, were single-coil as well (see Figure 3.22). They are a bit mellower than the Fender offerings, but still susceptible to outside interference.

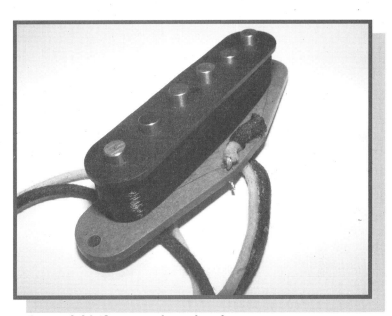

*Figure 3.21: Strat single-coil pickup*

*Figure 3.22: Gibson P-90 single-coil pickup*

Gibson set out to develop a pickup that could reject that outside interference, and came up with the Humbucker in 1956 (see Figure 3.23). The Humbucker consists of two coils of wire with opposite polarity and opposite windings, connected in series, which significantly reduces noise and interference. They "buck the hum," hence their name.

Humbuckers tend to have higher output and less high-end than their single-coil counterparts, thus giving them their unique sound.

*Figure 3.23: Gibson humbucking pickup*

## FACTORS AFFECTING PICKUP SOUND

Like so many things in life, sometimes what seems simple on the outside is very intricate on the inside and a pickup is no exception. The following factors contribute to a pickup's sound.

- **Number of turns or windings.** This is the number of turns of wire around the bobbin (which is the form) of the pickup. The more turns, the louder the pickup, but the worse the high-frequency response becomes. The number of turns determines the electronic resistance of the wire, which is measured in ohms. Humbucking pickups have more resistance than single-coil pickups.

- **Type of wire used.** The diameter and insulation determines the number of windings that can fit on a bobbin, which will determine the resistance, which determines the output, etc.

- **Type of winding method used.** In the early days of the electric guitar, many pickups were wound by hand, which meant that there were often more or fewer than the required number of windings on the bobbin. Also, an uneven wind would affect the capacitance of the pickup, which can cause a peak in frequency response. This problem was virtually eliminated when manufacturers switched to machine winding (see Figure 3.24), but while every pickup now had the same number of windings, some of the magic that occasionally came from a hand-wound pickup also disappeared.

*Figure 3.24: The original Gibson humbucker pickup winding machine*

- **Type of magnets used.** Although alnico (a blend of aluminum, nickel and cobalt) is the alloy of choice for most pickups, occasionally you'll find pickups made of other materials such as ceramic or neodymium. These different materials affect the strength of the magnetic field, and the strength of the magnetic field affects the pickup's output.

- **Magnet strength.** Magnets for pickups are categorized by strength on a scale of two to five, with five being the strongest. A stronger magnet will produce a louder and brighter sound, while a weaker one will produce a warmer sound.

- **Magnet height.** The distance of individual magnets from the strings will determine how loud that string is. As a result, pickups with fixed pole pieces (like a Fender Strat or Tele) can cause a slight imbalance in the string output. As an example, prior to the late '60s, most guitarists used a wound G string, so the fixed height of the magnets on a Strat were different to compensate.

- **Pickup Cover.** Metal covers on humbuckers can cause a resonance that results in feedback problems at high volumes. That's why many of the early rockers removed their pickup covers, and why many guitars and pickups are sold that way today (see Figure 3.25).

- **Pickup potting.** Many pickups are sealed in wax to eliminate vibration induced-signals that make a pickup microphonic. The heat from the hot wax can weaken the magnet if done properly, however, thereby changing the pickup's sound.

*Figure 3.25: Humbucking pickup with cover removed*

- **Potentiometers.** Although not exactly parts of the pickup itself, the volume and tone pots are part of the same electronic circuit and affect the sound (see Figure 3.26). The higher the pot's resistance, the more high end will pass. Fenders use 250k ohm pots, Gibson uses 500k and many other manufacturers use 1-Megohm pots.

Other factors such as winding direction, magnetic polarity and the type of bobbins used all affect tone, but their contribution is subtle at best.

## INTANGIBLE FACTORS

Beyond the known factors that affect pickup tone, consider the intangible factors as well. Most pickups lose their magnetic strength over time due to electrical interference and environmental factors. Pickups can become weakened or demagnetized completely by leaning your guitar against an amplifier with large transformers, or even from taking your guitar too close to the train motor of a subway—which happened to Andy Summers of the Police.

*Figure 3.26: Typical guitar volume pot*

Before the '90s, tolerances of just about every electronic component were much looser. While the difference was indeed subtle, combine enough components at the edge of their tolerances and you suddenly get pickups that sound different even though they're made of the same components and to the same specifications.

Manufacturing intangibles are a whole other story, which is why we're we're going to go a bit into the history of the Gibson humbucker.

### Changes in the Humbucker

The first humbucking pickups on the 1957 models of Gibson guitars had a sticker on them saying "Patent Applied For," because the design was in the patent review queue (see Figure 3.27). These became known as PAF ("Patent Applied For") pickups and are highly sought-after today for their great sound. The problem is, most PAFs sound different from each other due to manufacturing processes of the time.

Until 1961, when it standardized the magnet selection process, Gibson randomly used different-strength magnets (grade 2 through 5) in their pickups, which accounts for some differences in sound. To make matters worse, sometimes a shorter magnet was selected (mostly in gold-plated guitars for some reason), which decreased the power of the magnet as well. In July of 1961, Gibson began to consistently use short Alnico 5 magnets, although occasionally a few Alnico 2s showed up. In 1965, Alnico 5s became standard, which finally brought about a bit of consistency to the process and the sound.

*Figure 3.27: Gibson PAF humbucker*

The number of windings varied enormously as well, especially in PAFs. The early coil-winding machines didn't have an auto shut-off, so workers would shut off the machine when the bobbin looked full, which was at about 5,000 turns. As a result, no two pickups were ever the same.

Even when Gibson bought a winder with an auto-stop, there continued to be problems, even though the pickups did become more consistent. The stop mechanism was controlled by a fiber wheel that would wear out and break, at which point the workers would approximate the number of winds by timing the wind, resulting in more inaccuracies.

Since the humbucker is made up of two coils, sometimes the windings of each coil were different even though the total number of turns were correct. This would cause certain mid-range frequencies to stand out and give the pickup more bite.

By mid-1962, the humbucker patent was granted, and Gibson changed the sticker to read "PATENT NO 2,737,842"—which was actually the patent number for Les Paul's trapeze tailpiece. No one knows for sure if printing the wrong number was merely a mistake or a way to throw off the competition. From 1963 to 1975, these "Patent Number" pickups are very consistent, as are the ones made later when new, more precise winding machines were used (see Figure 3.28).

In the 1990s, Gibson further refined manufacturing and began to make pickups based on the original PAF design. Thanks to precision modern manufacturing techniques, these pickups are remarkably consistent, which also means that a "magic" pickup, a result of loose tolerances, is no longer possible to find. That said, most experts agree that you can now get 90 percent there, soundwise, for ten percent of the cost of a vintage PAF.

*Figure 3.28: Gibson "Patent Number" pickup*

## OTHER TYPES OF PICKUPS

Many other types of pickups have contributed to the sound of great guitars. Fender players wanted to retain the famous Fender tone yet have the advantages of a humbucker, so manufacturers like Seymour Duncan, Lace and Kinman introduced stacked-coil pickups, in which the lower coil provides noise-sensing, while the upper coil senses string vibrations. Although noise is reduced and the sound is good, it's still not the same as a fine vintage Fender single-coil pickup.

Active pickups by EMG (see Figure 3.29) and Seymour Duncan feature a powered electronic gain circuit to keep the noise low by boosting the signal at the coil itself. These pickups do the job well, but have never really caught on, due to what some feel to be a sterile sound. And piezo pickups have recently been fitted to electric guitars to simulate an acoustic guitar sound.

Whichever pickup you choose, each one has its own personality and greatly influences the ultimate sound of your guitar.

*Figure 3.29: EMG active pickup*

### What Affects the Tonal Quality of a Pickup?

The type of pickup

The number of windings

The way the coil is wound

On a humbucker, whether the windings are equal on both coils

The magnet type used

The strength of the magnets

The pickup cover

Whether the pickup is potted

# Strings

String gauge plays a major role in the sound of a guitar. Heavier-gauge strings will be louder and fuller-sounding than thinner-gauge strings. Even though many of today's high-output pickups are made with thin strings in mind, thicker strings will always sound bigger.

String material also contributes greatly to tone. A nickel-wound string, which has nickel plating over a steel wrap, is bright with a good mid-range. Pure nickel strings are smoother and rounder, and more reminiscent of the sound from the '60s (when they were the most common type); while a stainless-steel string is a lot brighter and cuts better. A flat-wound string is very mellow, a half-wound string is a little brighter and a round-wound string is brighter still.

The way a string is made can influence its harmonics. If string winding fluctuates during manufacturing and the mass of the string varies at any point along its length as a result, the harmonics generated will not be true, which can affect the intonation of the guitar as well.

For an inside look at string manufacturing, check out our interview with Jim D'Addario in Part III.

# The Guitar Pick

Although often overlooked as a contributor to tone, the guitar pick has more influence than you might believe. The type of pick should fit with the type of music being played. For instance, many guitarists like to use thin picks because they can provide a range of sounds and produce a "click" that emphasizes the picking attack. This said, thin picks don't work well in genres requiring high gain and distortion, because they tend to produce a muddier, less controllable sound, while a thicker pick makes a more-precise, well-shaped tone. Thicker picks also tend to produce a brighter tone regardless of the genre.

Pick materials also make a difference. Nylon, Tortex, Acetel, Ultem and Lexan picks each have a slightly different sound, as do metal picks made from stainless steel, or even a coin (like the ones Billy Gibbons and Brian May use). Picks have also been made out of agate stone, lignum vitae wood or even tortoise shell.

# Cables

Not many guitarists are hip to the fact that the cable connecting the guitar and amp can make a difference in their sound. In fact, until recently, cables were treated pretty much as an interchangeable commodity, with the general perception being that any one was as good as another. We've come to find that indeed, cable can make a difference in tone, as subtle as it may seem, because there are almost as many cable variables as there are in pickups or body wood. Let's look at some of those factors.

## CAPACITANCE

Capacitance is an electrical parameter that affects high-frequency loss. Low capacitance (below 30pF/ft) cables with a low strand count or solid conductors let more of the signal through, and are more open and defined sounding than those with more strands and capacitance above 40-45 pF/ft.

## CONDUCTOR MATERIAL

A cable's conducting material is also a factor. Copper is the most common cable conductor material, but not all types of copper sound the same. Mass-produced copper has been the standard for guitar and instrument cables as well as speaker cables for the past 50 years, but many companies and players are now keenly aware of the benefits that a higher quality cable can bring. High-purity copper is now the conductor of choice, although many have tried silver, which is an excellent conductor but subject to even greater quality variances than copper.

## STRAND INTERACTION

Cables are stranded to provide flexibility, but every strand in a bundle is carrying the same audio signal as the strands next to it, and strand interaction degrades cable quality. The problem arises from the fact that current running through the strands sets up a small magnetic field, which affects the signal carried in neighboring strands. The more strands a conductor has, the worse the problem. When compared with a solid conductor of equal cross-sectional area, a stranded conductor adds an edge to the sound, similar to the distortion caused by low-purity copper. In addition, mid-bass and lower frequencies lose their sense of impact and articulation. Bass lines sent through stranded conductors are often said to be "fat" and "slow," with obscured harmonics compared to bass conducted through a solid-core cable.

## CONDUCTOR SIZE

Conductor size is a factor in cable signal degradation. It was once thought that the larger the conductor size, the better the signal transfer; now, it is common knowledge that combining several individually insulated smaller conductors is a better solution because there's less strand interaction.

## SHIELDING

Cable shielding protects the signal from external noise. The type of material used and the way it is braided make a big difference in high-end response because of capacitance. Noise can also be mechanically induced by stepping or tapping on it.

## CABLE LENGTH

Cable length can have the biggest impact on sound, regardless of any of the above factors. The rule is, the shorter the better. A shorter cable always has lower capacitance, and therefore more high end (even if the difference is extremely subtle).

# Vintage Versus Modern

One of the reasons that vintage gear is so coveted is that each instrument is unique because many of its components were hand-made to tolerances that were much broader than they are now. As a result, sometimes a drift in tolerance caused by human error (an instrument constructed on Monday morning versus on Friday right before quitting time, for example) resulted in a magical instrument that's difficult to duplicate.

That's not to say that today's gear isn't worth having. Guitars in any price range are far better than they have ever been. In fact, it's difficult to buy something made after about 1985 or so that doesn't perform at a reasonably high level of quality.

Automated manufacturing has driven prices down and raised quality up in a way that couldn't have been imagined in the '50s, '60s and '70s. That being said, the homogenization of manufacturing has also taken what might be called the "character" out of most of today's low-cost instruments, because they're all pretty much exactly the same.

# Evaluating a Guitar

Generally speaking, if an electric guitar has a poor acoustic sound, then it probably won't sound very good amplified, regardless of the pickups or the amp. To hear the tonal influence that the body has on a guitar, turn the guitar around while playing and listen to the back of the body (See Figure 3.30). You will hear more of the body tone with less string, fingerboard and neck influence. Does this matter if you play loud distorted music? You bet! Even KISS's Ace Frehely evaluates his guitars this way.

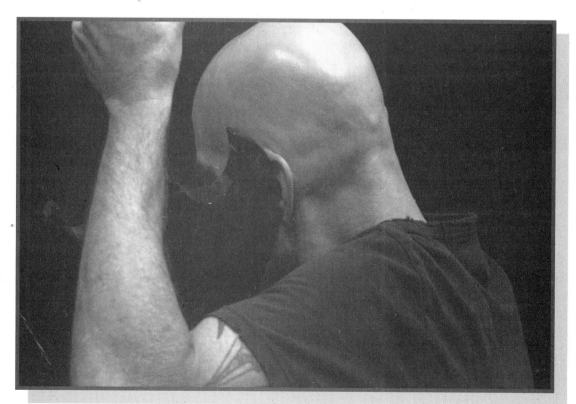

*Figure 3.30: Evaluating the tone of an electric guitar*

## What Affects the Tonal Quality of a Guitar?

The body wood

The bridge

The tailpiece

The pickups

The finish

The way the neck is attached

The neck

The fretboard

The strings

The pick

The cable

# Chapter 4:

## Tonal Characteristics of Guitar Amplifiers

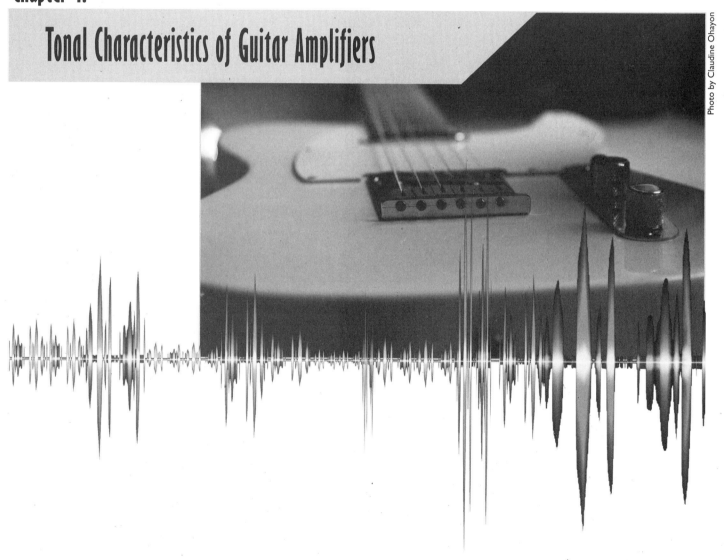

Photo by Claudine Ohayon

Most guitar players obsess over their guitars, but the amplifier is an equal partner in tone. The electric guitar and amplifier form a perfect symbiotic relationship, as they depend upon each other in a closed loop of sound quality. And just like guitars have their own quirks and characteristics, the same goes for amps. Let's take a look at some of the traits that make each amp unique.

In the broadest sense, there are just two types of guitar amps: tube and solid-state (plus a combination of the two called a "hybrid"). While most players will pick the tube amp as their favorite, some—B.B. King, for example—prefer the solid-state variety. Let's take a look at tube amps first.

## Tube Amplifiers

Tube amplifiers are based around those glowing glass cylinders called vacuum tubes, which are electronic amplification components. Tube amps are noted for their big, fat tone, but have many drawbacks. The tubes themselves are getting difficult to find; almost none are made in the U.S anymore, due to government environmental constraints and compliance costs, so they've become expensive. They give off an incredible amount of heat, which eventually degrades the surrounding electronic components. They require a large, heavy output transformer to transfer the amplified electronic energy to the speakers, as well as an equally large, heavy power supply transformer to supply the high DC voltage to the tubes. Tubes wear out, gradually changing in sound quality as they age, and they eventually need to be replaced. Tubes are very imprecise electronic components living in a world of high precision; no two are made exactly alike, and each has slightly different specs. It's best to do an electronic set-up every time you change power tubes, and an audio audition when you change preamp tubes, to be sure everything is optimized.

With all of those negatives, you can see why amp manufacturers have been trying to switch to solid-state guitar designs, going back to 1965 when CBS bought Fender. Regardless of their drawbacks, tube amps have the most important trait required by a guitar player: tone. Let's take a general look at the characteristics that make a tube amp so desirable.

### Tube Amplifier Traits

They're heavy, because of the transformers required by tubes.

They're expensive, because of the tubes and transformers.

Tubes throw off lots of heat, which degrades surrounding components.

Tubes require frequent replacement.

Each tube sounds slightly unique, due to the way they're manufactured.

The sound of the amp gradually changes as the tubes age.

Most amps require a set-up when the tubes are changed.

They're not as reliable as solid-state amps.

They sure can sound good!

## TUBES

A tube-based amplifier incorporates three types of tubes. Preamp tubes boost the guitar's signal level so it can be further amplified. Power tubes do the heavy lifting of amplification by transferring the amplified signal to the speakers. Secondary tubes, such as power amp, reverb and tremolo drivers, prepare the signal for processing at another amplifier stage. Some tube amps also include a fourth category of tube, the rectifier tube, which is found in the power supply section of the amp and has an indirect but very real effect on the sound of the amp. Let's look at them all.

### Preamp Tubes

The vast majority of tube amps use one type of preamp tube, called a 12AX7 (see Figure 4.1). This is a rather small tube whose primary job is to boost the voltage coming from the guitar pickups by a factor of anywhere from 40 to about 100.

*Figure 4.1: A 12AX7 Preamp Tube*

Many tubes, such as the 5751, 12AT7, 12AY7/6072 (the 6072 and 12AY7 are essentially the same) and the 12AU7/6189/5814, serve as a replacememt for a 12AX7 but have a lower gain and each has a different sound as a result (see Figure 4.2). A tube's maximum gain depends upon the way it's set up and the amount of voltage supplied. It's common to substitute a tube with less gain (such as a 12AY7) for a 12AX7 to tame a preamp circuit that distorts too easily. A lot of blues players make tube swaps to try to get less distortion yet keep the sustain. For example, Stevie Ray Vaughan used a 5751 in his Super Reverbs instead of a 12AX7.

### Figure 4.2: Preamp Tube Characteristics

| Type | Maximum Gain | Description |
| --- | --- | --- |
| 12AX7/7025 | 100 | Used mostly for the preamp stage, 7025 is the low-noise version |
| 5751 | 70 | Lower noise than 12AX7 |
| 12AT7 | 60 | Commonly used in driver stages |
| 12AY7/6072 | 44 | Commonly used as a preamp tube in early Fender Deluxe and Bassmans |
| 12AU7/6189/5814 | 20 | Commonly used in driver stages |

The tubes above are known as dual-triodes, which means there are two circuits in a single vacuum-tube package. While the first half of a 12AX7 can act as a preamp tube, the second can act as the tone circuit; both halves can act as the preamp for two channels (although there might be some interference between the two), or even as two gain stages of the same channel. Preamp tubes also are used in the tone control, reverb, tremolo and power tube driver stages.

Preamp tubes, even new ones, can suffer from internal noises like hiss, hums, pops, microphonics (when the tube acts like a microphone and picks up surrounding mechanical vibrations) and radio frequency interference. Nothing can be done to correct these conditions, but a tube with an excessive amount of these flaws may be used in another stage of the amplifier, such as the tone control section, where the gain demands are more modest and noise will be less noticeable.

### Driver Tubes

The driver tube(s) for the output stage of the amp splits the signal to the various output tubes. There's usually very little gain involved at this stage, and it has little to do with the tone of the amplifier, so a low-gain tube such as a 12AT7 is frequently used. Driver tubes are also used for reverb and tremolo, which also require little gain.

### Power Tubes

While preamp tubes boost the guitar's level and shape the tone, and driver tubes prep the signal, power tubes do the heavy lifting of amplification. Amplifiers have long been built around a number of popular power tubes that have unique characteristics (see Figure 4.3). For instance, 6V6s are compact tubes that don't require a very high voltage, so they're perfect for use in smaller, low-power amps. 6L6s were some of the first power tubes made (all the way back in 1936); they were easily available, and were perfect for the amps that Leo Fender wanted to build. Jim Marshal started building amplifiers that were basically Fender Bassman knock-offs that used 6L6s, but had to convert to using EL-34s because they were cheaper and more available in the UK at the time. For serious high-power applications that required lots of clean power (like for bass amps), the 6550 was hard to beat, yet it ended up in some of Marshall's US amps in the mid-'70s because of problems with EL-34s failing in American imports.

Every power tube has its own sonic characteristics, which is why both major and boutique amp manufacturers offer models built around each type (see Figure 4.4). In fact, some manufacturers build amps that either switch directly between different tube sets or allow quick changes between them (which isn't normally possible because of tube socket differences, voltages and other incompatibilities). Manufacturers have changed tube types over the years simply because of available stock, which means that some versions of the same amp model have become more desirable than others.

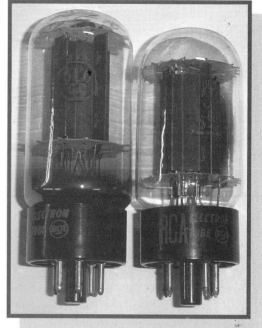

*Figure 4.3: Pair of 6L6GC power tubes*

| Figure 4.4: Power Tube Characteristics | | |
| --- | --- | --- |
| **Power Tube Type** | **Description** | **Used In** |
| 6V6 | Smaller, lower-powered cousin of the 6L6, 10 to 14 watts per pair, good clean tone with noticeable compression when driven hard | Smaller Fender amps such as the early Champ and Deluxe Reverb |
| EL-84 | Miniature power tube, up to 18 watts per pair, darker sounding than other power tubes with good midrange | Vox amps such as the AC-30 (which uses four) and the Fender Pro Jr. |
| 6L6GC/5881/KT-66 | Up to 50 watts per pair, very round and smooth sounding | Fender's main power tube |
| 6CA-7/El-34 | Up to 50 watts per pair, fairly easy to overdrive | Marshall's main power tube |
| 6550/KT-88 | Up to 100 watts per pair, harsher midrange when cranked | Some Marshalls, Ampeg SVTs, tube Leslies |

### Rectifiers

The power supply sends DC voltage to the tubes. Usually, the higher the voltage the tube receives, the more gain or power output it can supply, but the faster the tube ages. The electronic device that converts the AC power from the wall to the DC power used by the tubes is called a rectifier. All vintage amps manufactured before 1965 or so used a special tube for this job, but most modern amps use a solid-state version that's a lot more reliable. That said, the tube rectifier also contributes to the sound of the amplifier (see Figure 4.5).

A solid-state rectifier will give very fast rise time and response, since voltages are produced very quickly. A vacuum-tube rectifier will yield more to a player's touch, and provide compression and sustain in a much different way than its solid-state brother.

With a tube rectifier, when a player initially strikes a loud note or chord, there is a voltage sag—in some cases, a *lot* of sag. As the note or chord starts to decay, the voltage then builds back up, which results in a sound very much like a primitive compressor. Sag has a downside: The more sag there is, the more likely you'll get a "ghost" note that rides just under the note that you play. The note is usually at 120 Hz (because it's a harmonic of the 60Hz line voltage in the US), so it's not necessarily connected to what you're playing, which can really get in the way of what you're hearing.

*Figure 4.5: 5Y3 rectifier tube*

Some of the sound of early Fender amplifiers came because Leo Fender constantly under-designed his power supplies, causing the amp to noticeably distort when driven hard. When CBS took over Fender in 1965, the new designers immediately redesigned Leo's "mistake," causing Fender amps to lose the signature sound that guitar players all over the world were familiar with.

There are a number of types of rectifiers, and they each have a slightly different characteristic and effect on the tone (see Figure 4.6).

| Figure 4.6: Rectifier Characteristics | |
|---|---|
| **Tube Type** | **Characteristics** |
| 5Y3 | Offers a lot of sag and lower headroom |
| 5U4/GZ31 | Less sag than the 5Y3 |
| 5AR4/GZ34 | Least sag with the most headroom, not much different from a solid-state rectifier |
| Solid State | Almost no sag |

### Why All Tubes Sound Different

Two tubes of the same type but made by two different manufacturers can sound quite different. For instance, a 12AX7 made by Sovtek will have a different sonic character than one made from Ei or Tung-Sol.

Most manufacturers supply different models of the same tube, each with slightly different specs. For example, a Sovtek 12AX7WA has a lower gain, a flatter response and a smoother overdrive than its 12AX7WC, while its 12AX7LPS is designed for extra-quiet performance and maximum gain.

Many players still prefer what's known as New Old Stock (NOS), which are tubes that were made back in the '60s or '70s but have never been used. These include tubes from Mullard, RCA, GE, Sylvania, Telefunken and JAN-Philips. Tubes from all of these manufacturers are highly prized and demand top money. Of particular note is the RCA "Black Plate" series, which many players love.

### Tube Suppliers

For a while in the '90s, it was feared that the use of tubes in amplifiers would fall by the wayside as stocks dwindled and major manufacturers like RCA, GE, Sylvania, Mullard, Telefunken and Philips shuttered their plants as solid-state electronics took hold in every industry from medical to military to household appliances. Then it was discovered that tubes were still being made in Russia, China and Yugoslavia, so a few enterprising tube lovers like Mike Mathews (of Electro Harmonix and New Sensor fame) and Aspin Pittman (of Groove Tubes) set about importing, grading and quality checking imported units. Suddenly tube supplies were back and tube amplifiers became a growth industry again. Manufacturers of new tubes now include Tung-Sol and SED (from China), Sovtek, Sino and Svetlana (Russia), Ei (Serbia), and Mullard Reissues (United States). A host of tube suppliers exist online where you can purchase tubes such as NBS electronics (nbs. com), the Tube Store (thetubestore.com), Triode Electronics (triode.com), and many others. It should be noted that companies like Groove Tubes (GT), Ruby Tubes and a host of others normally found in music stores don't actually make their own tubes. They do provide a service by choosing the best ones with the least amount of noise and in the case of GT, even matching them to some degree.

## Tube Amp Circuitry

Surprisingly, most guitar amp circuitry designs come from the same source: the RCA Receiving Tube Manual, which was issued every two years from 1947 until 1973. The manual laid out all of the specs for each tube in RCA's product line, along with suggested circuitry, and most amplifier designers simply copied those circuits.

Make no mistake, those circuits surrounding the tubes do make a huge difference in the sound. It's been proven that you can take an amp that runs on 6L6s (like Fenders) and replace those tubes with EL-34s (like Marshalls) and the amp will sound the same when overdriven. This suggests that there's a lot more to amplifiers than the tubes themselves.

### Gain Stages

The number of gain stages in an amplifier has a great deal to do with its sound. For instance, typical Fender, Marshall or Vox amps all have two gain stages; the difference is that in a Marshall, the first gain stage (the preamp) feeds the volume control, which then drives the second stage (see Figure 4.7). When you turn up the volume control, you begin to overdrive the second stage. You can't achieve this in many Blackface-and-later Fender amps because their tone and volume controls actually decrease the gain so much that it's next to impossible to overload the second stage (see Figure 4.8). In fact, on a Fender the tone controls are effectively out of the circuit when they're all set on 10!

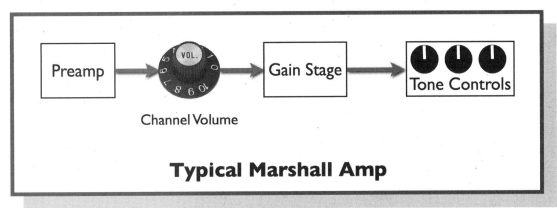

*Figure 4.7: Marshall amp gain stage block diagram*

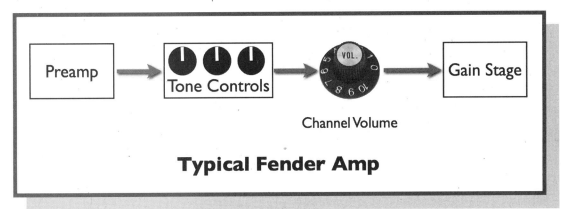

*Figure 4.8: Fender amp gain stage block diagram*

If you add another gain stage behind the tone stage, you suddenly have a lot more gain to work with, which happened as designers answered requests of players looking for more distortion from their amps (see Figure 4.9). Some of the very-high-gain amps, like some Boogies and Soldanos, even have four gain stages. That being said, most traditional amplifiers made before the '90s only use two gain stages, while most of the newer amps use three or four.

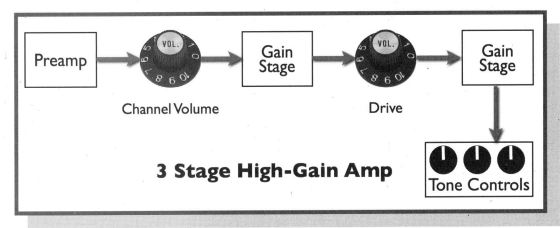

*Figure 4.9: Three-gain-stage block diagram*

### The Output Stage

The output stage of an amplifier is built less around the tubes themselves than the way they function. These are broken down into amplifier "classes."

- **Class A** means, in an un-scientific way, that the output power tubes are conducting all of the time. This class has the least distortion of all the classes, but it offers the least power, and since the tube is conducting all the time, it runs very hot. Amps with one power tube, such as Fender Champs, are Class A, as are most tweed Fender amps and early Gibson and Vox amps.

- **Class B** means that the power tubes only conduct 50 percent of the time. This design is very efficient and produces more power and less heat but a lot more distortion. You might think that's a good thing, but this particular type of distortion is ugly and unusable, not the sweet sustain that a guitar player wants. Class B is virtually never used in guitar amps,except for a few MusicMan models (MusicMan amps were never noted for their tone though).

- **Class AB** design is found in virtually all guitar amps, because it has the best of both Class A and Class B. It's efficient, offers more power than Class A, and can be configured to have a variable amount of distortion. The secret to Class AB is a "push-pull" configuration in which one power tube is on while the other is off; they see-saw back and forth so quickly that you never realize it's happening. Class AB amps always use a pair of power tubes; the more closely-matched, the better.

- **Class D** is used in solid-state amps with output transistors (the solid-state equivalent of power tubes) that operate as switches, turning on and off at a very high rate. This increases the efficiency, making the amp more portable and capable of being battery-powered. Class D designs normally don't provide high enough voltages to work well with tube gear.

- **Class H** is used in solid-state amps where voltage rises as power demand goes up. Like Class D, Class H is very efficient and allows for a very high-power yet lightweight design. It's not an option for tube amps because tubes do not operate well in this environment.

### Bias

Bias voltage sets the operating point of an amplifier's power tubes, and has a huge influence on both the way the amp sounds and the longevity of the tubes. Tubes are nonlinear by nature, and the bias voltage makes sure that the tube is operating in the range that provides the best frequency response with the lowest amount of distortion. Adjustable bias is known as "fixed bias," which sounds contrary, but just means that the bias can be adjusted but stays fixed at one voltage after it's been set (see Figure 4.10).

*Figure 4.10: Bias set-up*

An amp that's biased "cold" will have more headroom and won't break-up as soon, and its tubes will last longer. An amp that's biased "hot" will have less headroom, break-up sooner, and its tubes will burn out a lot faster. Many amplifiers come from the factory biased on the cold side, so the tubes will last longer.

Although not absolutely necessary (especially if you're using the same style of tubes from the same manufacturer), an amp should be biased whenever tubes are replaced to make sure that the bias is set for the sound you want. It also helps if the tubes are electronically matched, which will eliminate a rather nasty kind of distortion called crossover distortion, which occurs when one tube stays on longer than the other (remember, one tube turns off when the other one turns on in Class AB).

Biasing is not a do-it-yourself operation unless you have the right equipment and plenty of experience. The voltages inside a tube amp can be lethal, so it's not a place to play around unless you really know what you're doing. Trust me, all it takes is being thrown across the room once from touching the wrong place inside an amp to make you understand how powerful electricity is (I've been there, and it's really painful).

### Cathode Bias

Cathode bias, also known as self-bias or automatic bias, is the bias usually used in a Class A amp (preamp tubes are also cathode-biased). Cathode bias is noted for its smooth, round distortion that's different from the sound of anything you'll get from a fixed-bias amp. It doesn't require set-up, because it's self-adjusting. The Fender Deluxe Reverb (see Figure 4.11) and the Vox AC-30 amps use cathode bias, and are both prized and unique.

*Figure 4.11: Fender Deluxe Reverb amp*

## THREE WAYS TO TWEAK YOUR TUBE AMP

A tube amplifier is in many ways more tweakable than a guitar, in terms of being able to change the quality of the sound. Here are three relatively inexpensive ways that you can significantly alter the sound of your amp.

1. **Choose your tubes.** Tubes vary a great deal, not only in gain but in tonal quality. Many techs estimate that the very first preamp tube that your guitar signal sees is responsible for 80 percent of the tone of the amp. By selecting a preamp tube that offers an amount of input distortion that feels good to you, then finding one that provides the right tone (some are harsh and some are mellow sounding), you can change your tone more than you think.

   Changing the output tubes also can make a big difference. Some output tubes *break up* (begin to distort) more easily than others (Groove Tubes provides a 1-to-10 rating for this characteristic, with the lower number being easier to overload), while some will sound smooth and others more aggressive. If your amp has a tube rectifier, replacing it with another type may give you some desirable sagging qualities (check with your tech first because these tubes don't necessarily directly substitute for each other). Tubes seem to change with each batch manufactured, so ask your tech or tube dealer for suggestions before you buy something that you might not be happy with.

2. **Set your bias.** The bias setting makes a huge difference in how the amp sounds. A very cold setting can make your amp limp and lifeless, with too much headroom and no distortion or sustain, while a setting that's too hot may be too aggressive for the type of music you're playing. Work with your tech to find the setting that works for you. Once again, DO NOT attempt to do this yourself unless you have lots of experience in high-voltage electronics. The voltage can be lethal, and it's not worth dying over just to save a few bucks and a trip to the tech.

3. **Pull the output tubes for lower output.** A really good trick for those times when you want to turn up the amp to overdrive the output tubes yet keep the volume low is to pull some of the power tubes. If you have a 100-watt Marshall JMC that's just too loud for the studio (they almost always are), pull a couple of the EL-34 power tubes (one from each end) to drop the power to 50 watts. This will not hurt anything, so don't be afraid to do it. It's also possible to pull one of the tubes in a two-power-tube amp like a black- or silver-face Bassman, which will also cut the output power in half (although it might not sound as good as in the four-tube models, where tubes can be symmetrically pulled).

### Power Soaks

Power soaks absorb a portion of your amplifier's power instead of transferring it to the speakers, allowing you to overdrive the amplifier yet keep your volume output at a reasonable level. When they first hit the market in the '80s, power soaks were widely avoided in the studio because they changed the tone of the amp, and their incorrect use lead to frying many an amplifier due to the heat of overloading.

A few decades down the road, the power soak is a respected addition to a guitar player's arsenal. Designers learned to make them react more like a speaker, so the tone has improved as well as their reliability.

One of the main reasons why power soaks led to amplifier trouble is the fact that the player gets seduced by the distortion and sustain of the amp when it's turned way up while the volume stays low. All amps can sustain long periods of maximum use, but cannot continuously deliver beyond their safety zone. The constant overdrive causes the power tubes—or even worse, the power transformer—to fail because of the heat. So be careful when using the power soak. As with most things in life, moderation works best.

The Marshall Power Brake (see Figure 4.12), the THD Hotplate (see Figure 4.13) and the Palmer PDI-03 Speaker Simulator (used a lot by touring guitarists like Phil Collen from Def Leppard) are good examples of modern power soaks.

*Figure 4.12: Marshall Power Brake power soak*

*Figure 4.13: THD Hotplate power soak*

## BAD SIGNS

An amp can give you signs that it's not healthy. Don't overlook these indications, especially if you're in the middle of recording, because not only will the amp not sound as good as it can, but the problem can eventually turn into a costly repair job.

1.  **The amp is noisy, makes popping sounds, or has radio interference.** This is usually a sign that a preamp tube is going microphonic. It won't hurt the amp, but you probably won't get the best-sounding recording either. Try a few tube replacements and see if the problem goes away (you do have extras, right?) Be careful when replacing tubes, because they get extremely hot.

2.  **The amp hums or "motorboats."** Motorboating means that the amp makes intermittent sounds like a motorboat engine, or produces a low-frequency tone (a hum) that won't go away. Both are symptoms of a bad power-supply filter capacitor and mean you're heading for a catastrophic amp failure at some point down the road. How bad? It could be just a blown fuse and a capacitor replacement (you'll have to replace all of them in the power supply at once), or it could mean taking out the power tubes and an expensive output transformer as well, depending upon the the amp vintage. Get it to a tech before it's too late.

3.  **The power tubes are glowing red.** This is another sign of catastrophic failure, and has to be acted on immediately or it will cost you some real money to repair. Most tubes emit a blue glow that pulses with your playing, but if a power tube begins to glow red, it usually means either the tube is about to go bad or the amp has lost its bias (see Figure 4.14). Either way, turn the amp off now and send it to the shop. If you keep playing, you'll blow the output transformer (the large, heavy component that changes impedance for efficient transfer of power to the speakers), which is the most expensive component in the amp.

*Figure 4.14: Healthy 6L6 tubes*

4.  **The amp seems to be losing power and tone.** This is often a problem with vintage amps, and is a sign that the capacitors are growing weak with age. Besides tubes, capacitors are the one electronic component in your amp in which age takes its toll. They contain a moist inner material called the "dielectric," and as they age this dries out from the heat of the tubes and the capacitors change their values. You probably won't hurt anything by continuing to play on an amp with old capacitors, but eventually you'll have to have a tech recap the entire amp to bring it back to life, because if one cap is dying, then they probably all are. Be aware that replacing the caps might change the sound of your amp in a way you might not like.

## WHY DO VINTAGE AMPS SOUND SO GOOD?

Just like guitars, vintage amps have a certain caché about them because of the way they sound. Throwaway practice amps from years past by Silvertone (see Figure 4.15), Supro, Gibson and Fender now bring big bucks on the vintage market. Although many are collector's items, it's the sound that everyone loves, especially in recording.

So why do these relics from the past sound so good? There are three primary reasons.

*Figure 4.15: Vintage Silvertone amp*

### The Design

Most vintage amp designs are rather primitive by today's standards. In the past, amp designers simply copied the circuits out of the RCA Tube Manual, giving little thought to how and why they worked. Although these circuit designs had faults (some of them major), there was also a certain sound in their simplicity that we liked then and like even more now.

Many of the early amps had inadequate power supplies that caused the sound to "sag" when overdriven. When designers "corrected" the mistake, the sag was gone, but so was a sonic characteristic that the player loved. Then as designers began to replace parts with better-made components with stricter tolerances, a little bit of soul went with them.

### Component Tolerances

Just like the electric guitar, the amplifier business really began in earnest in the late 1940s, when the tolerances of the available electronic components were quite wide, especially for non-military applications. Resistors and capacitors had values that varied by as much as 20% (today we're used to using 1% and 2% components), while transformers had winding variances that were every bit as wide as the guitar pickups of the day.

These variations led to some wonderfully magic amplifiers with components so off-spec that they had truly unique sounds. For this reason, many owners of vintage amps are reluctant to replace components as they age, for fear of changing the unique character of the amp.

### Aging

Just as many guitars get better with age, so do some amplifiers. As the internal electronic components age, their tolerances loosen, which sometimes imparts a wonderful sonic character as a result.

# Solid-State Amplifiers

The term "solid state" refers to electronics built completely out of solid silicon material, such as transistors, integrated circuits and microprocessors. Solid-state amps are very light because they don't require large power supplies, high voltages and heavy output transformers. They're very reliable because they have fewer components, no tubes to wear out, and less heat to deal with.

In the '60s, when solid-state amps first came out, they seemed like both a manufacturer's and a player's dream. Easy to build, relatively inexpensive, easy to move and very reliable—what's not to like? Well, all that was great, except the tone. Solid-state amps were sterile sounding, with little of the distortion characteristics that players loved. While that might've worked for bass players and jazz guitarists (who loved the solid-state Polytone amps, for example), it just didn't cut it for the majority of guitar players.

Although the first solid-state amps suffered from terrible reviews, manufacturers never gave up, and soon created amps that earned some high-profile fans. Perhaps the first came in 1975 with Roland's Jazz Chorus-120 (see Figure 4.16). This amp was (and still is) unique in that it was stereo, with two 60-watt channels, and had the wonderful Roland chorus effect built in. While it was never much for an overdrive sound, the JC-120 had a clean sound that dominated for many years.

*Figure 4.16: Roland Jazz Chorus-120*

In 1979, the Norlin Company introduced the Lab Series, and the L5 became a favorite of B.B. King, Allan Holdsworth and later, King's X's Ty Tabor (see Figure 4.17). The L5 had a unique feature in that it had both a built-in compressor and distortion circuit, which was a sign of things to come in later solid-state amps.

Through the years, every major manufacturer has dabbled in solid-state amps, to the point where many guitarists are now quite accepting of them. Perhaps the biggest breakthrough came in 1996 from Line 6 with its AxSys 212 modeling amp. While the amp never caught on in a big way, the amplifier world was changed, thanks to the arrival of modeling technology.

*Figure 4.17: Lab Series L5*

## AMPLIFIER MODELING

Modeling amplifiers digitally emulate the sound of various well-known guitar amps, speaker cabinets, types of speakers, and effects, right down to even how the cabinets of these amps are miked, through digital signal processing (DSP). Although Line 6 remains a leader in modeling technology, most other amplifier companies, including Fender, Marshall, Vox, Tech 21 and Roland, have now incorporated modeling into several amp models. In fact, most small, low-power practice amps are now solid-state modeling amplifiers.

## SONIC ATTRIBUTES

Solid-state amps, especially the ones that use modeling, have a lot going for them sonically. They offer a huge variety of sounds to choose from, effects that used to require external stomp boxes can be built in, have relatively small and light packages that can have high output power, and the sounds can be selected almost instantly.

Perhaps the biggest complaint about solid-state amps in general is that elusive "feel" that comes when you combine a guitar and amp. The movement of the air, the attack when you hit the strings, and the imperfections of the amp itself are often missed by a player who is used to using vintage, boutique or high-end tube amps.

Experienced players often consider imperfections important. The sag of the amp when it goes into overdrive, the low-frequency "thunk" from a leaky power supply that happens every time you pick a note, and even some of the tube hiss, are considered to be a big part of the overall amp sound and are missed when they're not there. Amp manufacturers have listened, though, and are beginning to incorporate these imperfections into their models in order to improve the realism.

Another big complaint about solid-state amps has been the sound of their distortion, which never sounded close to that of a tube amp until recently. A tube amp emphasizes even-order harmonics when overdriven, which the ear perceives as smooth and pleasing. Solid-state amps, on the other hand, emphasize odd-order harmonics, which are edgy and far less pleasing to the ear. As manufacturers have become aware of this difference, they have taken great pains to more closely simulate the distortion of a tube amp, with varying degrees of success. But since modeling has become a staple in the typical amplifier toolkit, the sound of the overdrive and distortion has become much less of an issue.

In the studio, a small modeling amp can sound so much like the amp it's modeling that no one ever misses the real thing, especially if it's mixed a bit back in the track. In fact, a generation of guitar players have never been exposed to anything other than modeling amp or software, and really don't have a reference point for what a real tube amp sounds like. That's okay though, they've been getting along just fine in the digital world of tone.

Finally, there's no way to alter the sound of the amplifier other than through its front-panel controls, and there's almost no way to modify the amp like a tube amp, other than factory updates. This is either a blessing or a curse, depending upon how you see the amplifier world.

**Solid-State Amplifier Traits**

Lightweight—there's no need for heavy transformers

No tubes to wear out

Low heat, and low component degradation

Inexpensive, no tubes and transformers

Very reliable

The sound is consistent

Higher power potential than most tube amps

# Hybrid Amps

Hybrid amps combine tubes and solid-state components to get the best of both worlds in terms of tone and convenience. The first hybrids made by MusicMan in 1976 used a solid-state preamp section with a tube output section. Although Leo Fender (who was one of the founders of MusicMan) understood that guitar players like the sound of an overdriven output stage, he soon determined that the solid-state front end felt lacking to many players, and that the tube preamp had as much to do with an amp's sound as the output section of the amp.

In the '80s, when rack-mounted studio effects were all the rage, many guitarists switched to a large switching interface, such as the type made by Bob Bradshaw or Pete Cornish (see Chapter 7). In order to minimize noise and properly match impedances, Bradshaw designed a rack-mounted, 3-channel tube preamp (see Figure 4.18) that would feed into a solid-state power amp (the preamp was first

*Figure 4.18: Soldano X88 3-channel preamp*

produced by Soldano, then by Bradshaw's Custom Audio Electronics). To meet the high demand for this new hybrid set-up, many manufacturers made their own tube preamps and separate tube and solid-state power amps. Modern amps such as the Marshall Valvestate amps (see Figure 4.19) and Vox Valvetronix also use this hybrid scheme.

*Figure 4.19: Marshall Valvestate amp*

Line 6 has taken yet another hybrid approach in its Spider Valve II, which features a modeling front end that's combined with a tube preamp and a tube output section.

## Boutique Amplifiers

Not that long ago, if you liked the sound of a particular vintage amp, you had to search everywhere to find a used one and then pay a premium price for it. Today, there are so many boutique amp manufacturers that make a reasonable facsimile of just about any vintage amp that it's difficult to count them all. You can even classify boutique manufacturers by whether they copy old amps, such as JMI and Victoria, or build modern amps based on classic amp circuits, such as Blankenship, Divided By 13, Top Hat (see Figure 4.20) and Fargen. In fact, most companies now do both.

Generally speaking, most of these companies are centered around three designs, based on the Vox AC-30, early Marshall Plexis or Bluesbreakers, and early Fender Tweed amps.

One advantage to a new boutique amplifier is that it should last for many years without a major failure, while providing a fairly consistent tone. While the sound may not be a 100% accurate reproduction of a vintage model, it will probably be close enough to use in the studio to get the sound you need. In many cases, the amps have been upgraded for easier servicing and more tonal variety.

*Figure 4.20: Top Hat Super*

## What Affects the Tonal Quality of an Amp?

Tightness of component tolerances

Whether it's tube or solid-state

The preamp tubes

The power tubes

The type of rectifier

The number of gain stages

Its operating class

Whether it is fixed or cathode biased

The amount of biasing

# Chapter 5:

## Speakers and Cabinets

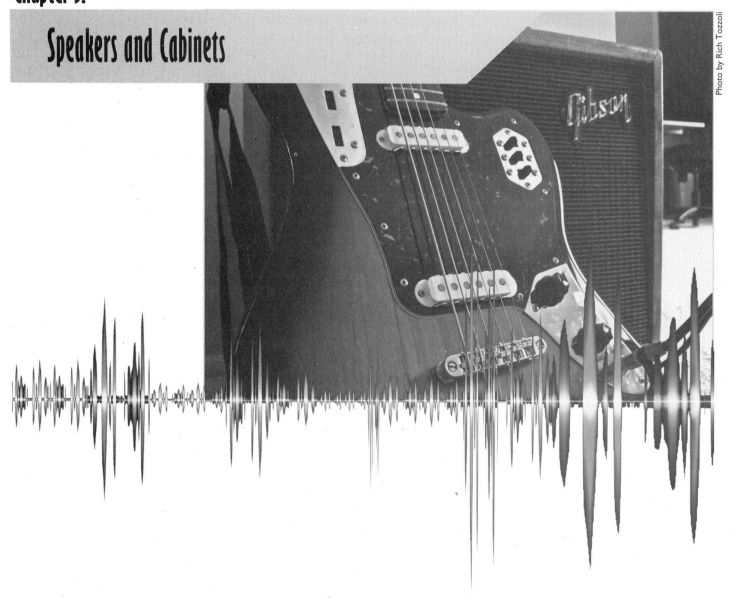

Photo by Rich Tozzoli

While most players are aware of the role that the loudspeaker has in an amplifier's tone, many don't realize that the cabinet shares much of the influence. An ideal combination of the two leads to a thing of sonic beauty, while anything else can lead to endless searching and experimenting. Here are the major items to look for in both speaker cabinets and the speakers themselves. Please note that many parameters aren't mentioned here because they really get down into the academia of the subject. We're looking to impart real-world differences that can easily be heard and defined.

# Speaker Cabinets

The speaker and cabinet combination can have as much effect on the tone as the amplifier itself, which is why we must take a close look at their design and construction elements.

## TYPES OF SPEAKER CABINETS

Almost from the beginning of guitar amplifier time, the controversy has raged about which sounds better, an open-back combo amp or a closed-back cabinet. Let's take a look at both.

### Open-Back Cabinet

The typical combo amp has an open back (see Figure 5.1) where the speakers are exposed at the rear, which affects the sound in a number of ways. An open-back cabinet will spread the sound around the room, but will decrease low-frequency response. The sound will be a bit more harmonically complex, a bit more open and often even louder than a comparable closed-back cab, because the sound from the back of the cabinet is reflecting off the room behind the amp and mixing with the sound coming out its front.

*Figure 5.1: A typical open-back combo amp*

Not all speakers work well in an open-back combo amp. A Celestion G12M Greenback, which is considered a wonderful speaker in a Marshall cabinet, will break up in a rather unpleasant way in an open-back cab because it has a stiff cone meant to handle the back-pressure of air in a sealed cabinet. As a result, it will flop around a lot more than a speaker such as a Jensen P12N, which has a cone designed for an open-back environment. Stick that G12M in a closed-back cab, however, and it just sings.

An open-back cabinet gives you more miking possibilities than a closed back, since you're able to mic the rear of the cabinet (watch the phase when miking both sides). You can also change the sound of the cabinet by placing it on a chair or flight case, or in the center of the studio, away from the walls.

### Closed-Back Cabinet

A closed-back cabinet (see Figure 5.2) seals the air inside the cabinet, which compresses the sound coming from the rear of the speakers, affecting the tone.

*Figure 5.2: Typical closed-back cabinet*

A closed-back cabinet, such as a Marshall 4x12 or Fender 2x12, has a tight, punchy sound with extended bottom end. It's a lot more directional sounding than the open-back because the sound is more focused. This causes the sound to be a bit thicker, less airy, and harmonically simpler. Most closed-back cabinets have a resonance point of about 120 Hz, the equivalent to an open A string, which makes them seem like they're made for rock (although they're not as good for other types of music).

## CABINET COMPONENTS

A number of factors go into the sound of a cabinet, from size to materials to contruction method. Let's consider some of these parameters.

## CABINET SIZE

The size of the cabinet determines the lowest frequency that can be reproduced; the larger the internal space, and therefore the larger the cabinet, the lower the frequency response. This is why bass cabinets are always larger or deeper than guitar cabinets. Bass cabinets don't work well for guitar, however, because they accentuate the bass frequencies, making the guitar sound boomy. If, on the other hand, the cabinet is too small, bass frequencies can be all but non-existent. Cabinet designs have developed over the years so just about any cabinet that you buy is the optimal size, more or less, but there's more to the cabinet's sound than the size. The type of material and speakers used, whether the cabinet is sealed or ported, its bracing, and the type of internal damping material used (if any) all have a bearing on the sound.

## CONSTRUCTION MATERIALS

The type of wood used for building a cabinet contributes to its tone. Cabinets, like guitars, can be built out of just about any kind of wood. But like guitars, amps are generally made from only a few kinds of wood due to their sound or cost.

Marshall cabinets are built out of 11-ply Baltic birch, a wood that's known for its strength and low weight. This is one of the reasons—besides its speakers and closed back—that nothing else sounds quite like a Marshall cabinet. Other manufacturers also use birch, but some use cheaper and thinner 3- or 5-ply, which compromises the sound. Others use 13-ply birch, which makes the cabinet more robust for transport, but heavier as well (see Figure 5.3).

*Figure 5.3: 13-ply Baltic birch*

Early Fender cabinets were made of pine (see Figure 5.4), which is light and has a unique tone. Pine was inexpensive and easy to obtain, but it wasn't very strong, which was a negative for the gigging musician. Like most manufacturers, Fender slowly but surely changed their cabinet wood, first to marine plywood, then to particleboard known as MDF (medium-density fiberboard). MDF is very strong and inexpensive, but sounds somewhat neutral at best, and harmonically dissonant at worst.

Today, most manufacturers—even Fender and Marshall—use MDF in their inexpensive cabinets, and birch or birch composite in their more expensive or vintage cabinets (see Figure 5.5). As a result, two cabinets from the same company, loaded with the same speakers, can sound completely different.

*Figure 5.4: Pine plywood*

Plywood and MDF have lower cabinet resonance than solid woods such as pine, cedar and birch. The resonance contributes to the "warmth" of the sound, but can also be responsible for blurring notes because of the slight sound absorption. That means that a pine cabinet may sound full and round, but it won't project as well as a plywood cabinet. Baltic birch is chosen for its musicality, but it's not quite as resonant as pine, although it does have a harder sonic edge. The resonance that occurs with MDF is often described as "dead" and "atonal."

Sometimes cabinets were designed out of necessity, instead of a grand tonal design. In the case of the famous Marshall 1960 4x12, the cabinet was built to contain four Celestion G12 speakers, which were cheap and plentiful at the time. These speakers were rated at just 15 watts and were prone to flapping on hard-hit low notes, so the closed-back cabinet helped limit cone travel through air suspension, and having four speakers kept the amp from blowing them out.

*Figure 5.5: Medium-density fiberboard (MDF)*

## CONSTRUCTION METHODS

A cabinet's construction method makes a difference in its strength and the way it vibrates. Most quality cabinets use finger or dovetail joints to solidly connect pieces together (see Figure 5.6), while some even use reinforcement to hold everything secure. A cabinet without these type of construction techniques will be fragile and subject to rattles as the joints loosen.

*Figure 5.6: Cabinet with dovetail joints*

### The Baffle

One of the most overlooked parts of a cabinet is the baffle (see Figure 5.7), which is the board that the speaker is directly mounted on. The baffle has more tonal influence than perhaps any other single piece of the cabinet. Its material (pine, birch, MDF), thickness, and mounting method all contribute to the sound.

*Figure 5.7: Typical speaker baffle*

- **Material:** Thin plywood tends to be louder and have better low-end response than pine of the same thickness. ¾-inch birch projects more of the speaker sound and less of the cabinet itself. Closed-back cabinets with birch baffles are tighter and have a slight edge than those using other materials.

- **Thickness:** The baffle's thickness has a great deal to do with its sound. Most tweed amps from the '50s used either ¼-inch or ⁵⁄₁₆-inch pine, which sounds open and loose. Amps made in the '60s generally have a thicker baffle and impart a tighter, cleaner sound as a result.

- **Mounting method:** The way the baffle is connected to the cabinet makes a big difference in its sound. Fender used a "floating baffle" for a long time, which provided a bigger, more "organic" tone. A floating baffle is attached to the cabinet at two points: either top and bottom, or side and side. The 1959 Fender Bassman is a good example of a top-and-bottom floating baffle, while the Super Reverb is a good example of a side-to-side floating baffle. On the other hand, the Bandmaster 2 x 12-inch speaker cabinet does not have a floating baffle; it is attached on all four sides to be very rigid and tight. A thin baffle makes the best floating baffle because it vibrates more and those vibrations blend with those of the speakers.

If you open up a closed-back cabinet, you'll notice that a piece of wood in the center of the cabinet connects the baffle to the back panel (see Figure 5.8). This design allows the baffle and back panel to resonate in phase. Without it you'd have a lot of phase cancellation and a cabinet with a lot of peaks and dips in frequency response.

*Figure 5.8: Wood piece in the center of a closed-back cabinet*

## MANUFACTURING INCONSISTENCIES

Just like with guitars, pickups and amplifiers, cabinets also suffered from wobbly tolerances in the '50s, '60s and even into the '70s. Not all cabinets of that time period are perfectly straight and their sizes slightly vary. These factors can contribute to the variation in sound among cabinets from that era. Thanks to advanced CNC (Computer Numerically Controlled) woodcutting machinery, modern cabinets are made with a precision that hardly wavers.

## CABINET BUZZES

An invisible problem that often plagues speaker cabinets during recording (especially cabinets that are also used for playing live) is loose hardware that causes buzzing. Certain notes will cause the loose component to vibrate, sometimes so much that it can sound just like a blown speaker. Handles (especially on Marshall cabs; see Figure 5.9), input jacks, wheels and anything improperly secured are the usual suspects. It's always a good idea to take a powered screwdriver and tighten up all the screws before you record. In the event that a cabinet uses rivets instead of screws (like on a Marshall cabinet), the best thing you can do is shim the loose area with a piece of foam rubber or a cut-up mouse pad. When you're under the microphone microscope, you'll be glad you did.

*Figure 5.9: The Marshall side handle is prone to rattling*

# Speakers

You probably never thought that there'd be so many cabinet variables, but speakers are another level of variation altogether. Whatever the application, there are a number of speakers designed for it. The problem comes when speakers are used in applications they're not meant for, or they're substituted indiscriminately. Let's look at some factors that contribute to a speaker's sound, as well as some popular manufacturers and their speakers.

## SPEAKER PARAMETERS

Many parameters make speakers unique. Keep in mind that there are a lot more than the ones mentioned here, but these parameters are the ones that the average player needs to know.

### Size

The size of a speaker has a great deal to do with the way it sounds. As you've probably noticed, an 8-inch sounds different from a 10-inch, which sounds different from a 12-inch, which sounds different from a 15-inch speaker. The reason is simple physics: The larger the cone, the more energy it takes to get it moving, so the high-end response and the attack time won't be as good as a speaker that's smaller. Conversely, a smaller speaker has poorer low-frequency response because it has less cone area to move the air.

As a result, you'll notice that an 8-inch speaker won't have nearly as much bottom end as a 15-inch speaker, and the 15 will not have quite the top end of a 10-inch speaker. Guitar rigs mostly use 12-inch speakers since they're a nice compromise between the two.

### Number of Speakers

The number of speakers in a cabinet affects both the overall volume level and the low end. The more speakers that acoustically couple together, the more effective the cone mass. As a result, a cabinet with two 12-inch speakers gives you 24 inches of cone mass, while a a cabinet with four 10s (such as Fender's original Bassman; see Figure 5.10) gives you 40 inches. Of course, other factors such as resonant frequency are involved, but this is a simple way to look at it.

### Cabinet Type

The type of cabinet that a speaker is mounted in makes a big difference in the way it sounds. A speaker made for a closed-back cabinet such as a Marshall, will sound bad in an open-back cabinet because the cone is too stiff to accommodate the air compression on the inside of the cabinet. Likewise, a speaker designed for an open-back cabinet won't work too well in a closed-back cab because its cone isn't stiff enough to handle the air pressure bouncing at it from the back of the cabinet.

*Figure 5.10: An original Fender Bassman amp*

### Speaker Wattage

Contrary to what you might think, lower-wattage speakers usually sound better than high-wattage ones. High-wattage speakers have heavier cones that change the reaction time of the speaker, and therefore the tone. Because the cone is heavier, it responds slower than a thin cone when a signal is applied, so its high-frequency response isn't as good.

In a higher-watt speaker, the diameter of the voice coil and the type of wire it uses are usually larger, which change the speaker's response. A heavier magnet is also required because the voice coil is heavier to move.

As a result, you have a speaker that's harder to blow up, but doesn't break up as easily and has a different frequency response.

### Magnet Structure

There are three different types of materials used in speaker magnets: Alnico, ceramic, and neodymium. Each material has a distinctly different effect on the speaker's tonal characteristics.

- **Alnico**, an alloy of aluminum, nickel and cobalt, is a magnetic material used in the original speakers in all of the vintage amps. It produces a classic tone that's warmer and sweeter at lower volumes than other materials, and many players feel that a speaker with an Alnico magnet reacts faster to the touch. Alnico was used for decades because of its strong magnetic field, but once the alloy became a bit pricey, many manufacturers opted to build speakers with less-expensive ceramic magnets.

- **Ceramic** magnets were developed as an inexpensive alternative to Alnico and have the advantage of being more versatile with a wider range of tones. Speakers with ceramic magnets tend to weigh more than speakers with other magnets, but generally handle more power and sound better at high volumes.

- **Neodymium** is the latest development in speaker magnet material. It's less expensive than alnico but costs more than ceramic magnet speakers. It weighs about 50 percent less than other materials and has stronger magnetic properties. Speakers made with neodymium magnets respond to a player's touch similar to alnicos and have a well-balanced frequency response.

## SPEAKER MANUFACTURERS

Traditionally, a number of companies have supplied speakers to amplifier manufacturers. Here's a brief overview of some of their most revered products.

### Jensen

Jensen speakers were used mostly by Fender from 1946 until 1961. When Leo Fender asked for some speaker modifications and Jensen wouldn't comply, Fender switched to Oxford speakers as standard in his amps. In late 1965, Fender, then owned by CBS, switched back to Jensen again  (adding a tag saying "Fender by Jensen") until 1967, when Jensen stopped making speakers altogether.

The original Jensen company, which manufactured speakers in Chicago, is long gone and the Jensen name is now owned by Audiovox, which makes speakers in Italy. The speakers are said to be made to the same specifications as the classic speakers used by Fender, Ampeg and Gibson.

The most famous Jensen speaker was the P12N (see Figure 5.11), whch was used in most early amps requiring a 12-inch speaker. The P10R was a 10-inch speaker used in Super Reverbs, while the first large cabinet Bassman amps were loaded with P15Ns.

## Celestion

It can be said that both Celestion and Marshall are responsible for the "British tone," since both are known for their unique sound to begin with, and their synergy makes it even more pronounced. Celestion has been making speakers since 1924, and while the company has gone through numerous ownership changes over the years, it hasn't drastically changed the sound of its products unlike so many other companies.

Celestion has a number of loudspeakers that have become quite revered over the years. The Alnico Blue is a 15-watt speaker with a smooth response and the same mild break up found in the original Vox AC-15 and AC-30 (see Figure 5.12). The G12M Greenbacks are the sound of British rock and roll and can be found in the original Marshall 1960 Series cabinets (see Figure 5.13). The Vintage 30 is a new version of the G12M with higher power handling. It's now found in many Marshall, Mesa Boogie and Orange amps.

*Figure 5.11: Jensen P12N*

*Figure 5.12: Celestion Alnico Blue*

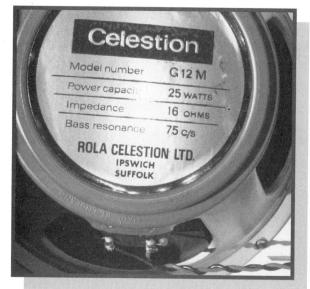

*Figure 5.13: Celestion G12M*

### Weber

One of the most interesting speaker manufacturers today is Weber, who makes a reasonable knock-off of just about any vintage speaker you can think of, as well as a few modern variations (see Figure 5.14). Weber is also one of the few manufacturers that will allow you to "roll your own" limited run of custom speakers. Check it out at https://taweber.powweb.com/weber/

*Figure 5.14: Weber AlNiCo Blue Dog*

### Other Manufacturers

While many players love the sound of the speakers in older amps, remember that there were a lot of manufacturers that contributed. Oxford, CTS, Utah, Eminence, Fane and Electro-Voice can often be found inside amps (many times with the amplifier manufacturer's label on them) and JBLs were always available by special order.

**What Affects the Tonal Quality of a Speaker Cabinet?**

An open- or closed-back cabinet

The size of the cabinet

Speaker cabinet tolerances

The speaker baffle

The cabinet wood

The speakers

The number of speakers in the cabinet

# Chapter 6:

## Electric Guitar Miking Techniques

Photo by Rich Tozzoli

Your guitar is tuned, your amp sounds great and your chops are up; now it's time to capture that terrific sound. If it were as easy as just placing a mic in a standard spot, recording great guitar sounds would never be much of a challenge, but we all know that's not the case. Capturing the sound of an electric guitar can often be frustrating, because unfortunately, recording that perfect sound that you hear in the room is not always as easy as it seems. Sometimes something that sounds great when you stand next to the amp doesn't work at all when heard in the mix, while sometimes a sound that's, shall we say, less than amazing in the room fits it perfectly. That's the fun and mystery of recording.

This chapter is about learning tried-and-true miking reference points, and knowing how to adjust them when they don't seem to work as well as you'd like. Let's begin with the basics.

# Microphone Technique 101

Before we get into the nitty-gritty of proven microphone methods, we have to look at recording issues that are often overlooked. Regardless of the instrument you're recording, here are a few things to consider first.

## CHOOSING THE BEST PLACE IN THE ROOM

As we discussed in Chapter 5, the room can make a big difference in the sound of a guitar amp, especially if the amp has an open back. It's best to find the place in the room that's acoustically beneficial to the sound.

When you're tracking with other players (especially a rhythm section), finding the best room placement is secondary to leakage concerns and player sight lines, unless you can place the amp in an iso booth. Try to capture the sound as best as you can, but there's a good chance that you might have to replace it later.

That brings us to overdubs, where we concentrate on the sound of the guitar the most. Here are some considerations in finding the best placement in the room. Keep in mind that the following ideas work equally well for amps or acoustic instruments.

- **Look for a spot where the amp or acoustic instrument sounds relatively live**, without the environment acting as a detriment to its sound.

- **It's usually best to stay out of a corner.** Corners normally cause "bass loading," meaning that low frequencies will build up, causing low notes to boom. When you're tracking with a drummer, this can also lead to sympathetic tom ringing and snare buzzing on the drum kit.

- **Test the room by walking around and clapping your hands.** That's a good way to find a place in the room that has a nice, even reverb decay. If the clap has a "boing" (a funny overtone known as flutter echo) sound to it, then so will the your amp or acoustic instrument, so it's best to try another place in the room where it will hopefully sound smoother. If you can't find a place without a boing, place the amp where it sounds the smoothest and try putting some padding or something soft on one side wall to break up any standing waves.

- **You don't want to be too close to a wall.** The reflections (or absorption, if the wall is soft) can change the sound of the amp or acoustic instrument, especially if you're using an open-back combo amp. The middle of the room usually works best.

- **Ideally, place the amp in the part of the room where the ceiling height is the highest.** If the ceiling is vaulted, try placing your amp or acoustic instrument in the middle of the vault first, then adjust it as needed.

- **Whatever you do, stay away from glass if you can.** Glass creates more unwanted reflections than just about any material. If you have no choice, try setting up the amp at a 45° angle to the glass.

- **Try putting a rug under the amp or acoustic instrument.** A rug diminishes reflections off the floor, which can sometimes have a negative impact on the overall sound. On the other hand, sometimes the reflections from a hard floor can enhance the sound as well. Try it both ways.

- **Try placing your amp on a chair or road case.** Since the amp isn't coupling with the floor, there are fewer phase cancellations in the low end, so the sound will be more direct and distinct. Placing the amp on acoustic foam from manufacturers such as Auralex works as well.

## CHOOSING THE RIGHT MIC

Choose your microphone after considering the sound of the amp or instrument. If you have several mics to choose from, go through this list before you make your choice.

- **Choose the mic for the right reasons.** Just because a mic is considered an industry "standard" choice for a particular application doesn't necessarily mean that it'll work in your situation. Just because your favorite engineer or guitar player uses a particular mic doesn't mean it will also work for you. There are so many variables that you can never count on anything other than your ears in your particular situation.

- **Select a microphone that compliments the instrument or amp.** If your sound is edgy or has a lot of top end, you wouldn't want to choose a mic that emphasizes those frequencies. On the other hand, a mic that emphasizes the upper midrange a bit might make a mellow-sounding amp step out of the mix.

- **Consider the pickup pattern of the mic.** A directional mic is not always the best choice for the sound you're trying to capture. When leakage is not a consideration, an omni or figure-8 pattern might provide a smoother sound with better ambiance (providing you're recording in a good-sounding room).

- **Understand the proximity effect.** The closer a directional mic gets to the sound source, the more the bass response increases. This isn't always desirable, so either move the mic back a bit from the source or change its pattern to omni (where it picks up from all directions). However, some players also use proximity effect to their advantage to gain extra bass.

- **Large-diaphragm condensers are not necessarily better than small-diaphragm condensers.** Contrary to popular belief, small-diaphragm condensers reproduce low-frequencies better (if that's what you're after), and are generally less colored off-axis than large-diaphragm mics. Large-diaphragm mics are less noisy, however.

## MIC PLACEMENT

A common recording situation has an engineer trying to capture a sound by EQing, compressing and adding multiple mics, yet never actually taking into account what the sound is like at the source out in the tracking room. It's imperative that every engineer use the following steps when placing mics:

1. **Go out into the room, stand in front of the amp or acoustic guitar player, and listen to him or her play the part from the song you're about to record.** Playing the song is important because you might be deceived if your reference is another song or just random playing. Listen to the tonal balance from the amp or instrument, as well as the way the room responds. Listening to the amp or acoustic guitar in the room will give you an accurate reference point so you have a better idea of what you're trying to capture.

2. **Find the sweet spot.** There are several ways to find it:

   » To place an omnidirectional mic, cover one ear and listen with the other. Move around the amp or player until you find the spot that sounds best.

   » To place a cardioid mic (a mic with a heart-shaped pickup pattern), cup your hand behind your ear (don't cover it) and move around the player or amp until you find the place that sounds best.

   » To place a stereo mic or stereo pair, cup both ears and move around the player or amp until you find the place that sounds best.

   » As an alternate method, crank the amp and listen to the noise, then put on headphones and listen to the mic as you move it around until the sound has the best combination of highs and lows.

3. **You can't place a mic by sight.** The best mic position must always be found, not predicted. It's okay to have a starting place, but that spot doesn't usually end up being the best spot.

4. **Change the mic position instead of reaching for the EQ.** Chances are that you can adjust the sound enough by simply moving the mic. The EQ will add at least a small amount of unwanted phase shift at some frequency, which can't be undone later. Moving the mic (which amounts to acoustic EQing) will usually make things sound smoother and more pleasing to the ear.

5. **Give the mic some distance.** Remember, distance creates depth. The guitar and amp will sound more natural than if you use artificial ambience. If possible, leave just enough distance between the mic and the source to capture a bit of room reflection.

6.  **Be careful when miking multi-speaker cabinets.** 4x12 cabinets like the typical Marshall 1960 pose a special challenge in that at a certain distance you will pick up phase anomalies from the multiple speakers. The cabinet will sound fine when close-miked somewhere between right against the grill cloth to approximately three inches away from the best-sounding speaker in the cabinet, but between there and a distance of 18 inches, where the sound of all the speakers converges, you may capture some unpleasant speaker interaction (this distance varies with the make and model of speaker cabinet).

**Microphone Technique 101**

Choose the place in the room that sounds best

The middle of the room is usually best

Choose a mic that compliments the sound of the amp

Listen to the sound of the amp before placing the mic

Find the sweet spot

Move the mic instead of using equalization

Microphone distance equals depth

# Electric Guitar Miking Set-Ups

While many believe there's only one accepted way to mic an amplifier, you'll be surprised to learn that there are as many techniques as there are guitar and amp sounds. Let's look at some.

## SINGLE-MIC TECHNIQUES

It's amazing what you can do with a single mic if you experiment a bit. Here are a number of techniques that have been used on popular recordings since the '50s. They all work, but remember that a method that works for one recording may not work for another. It's good to always have an alternative in your pocket when you need one.

### Classic Set-Up #1: A Shure SM57 on the Cabinet

Place a Shure SM57 about one inch away from the best-sounding speaker in the cabinet, about three quarters of the way between the edge of the speaker and the voice coil (away from the voice coil). If you need more high end, move the mic toward the voice coil. If the sound needs more body, move it toward the outside edge of the speaker. Make sure that the mic does not touch the speaker cone when the loudest passages are played (see Figure 6.1).

Figure 6.1: The classic set-up—an SM57 on a guitar cabinet

### Classic Set-Up #2: Miking Where Speakers Converge

In the '60s and '70s, the most common amp-miking technique was placing the mic between one and two feet away from the center of the speaker or speakers (see Figure 6.2). This configuration allows the sound from the speakers and the cabinet to develop, but also captures some of the room, which can be a nice bonus. The ideal miking distance on a cabinet with two speakers is the point where the output of both speakers combines. If more high end is required, move the mic to the side to capture more of one of the voice coils.

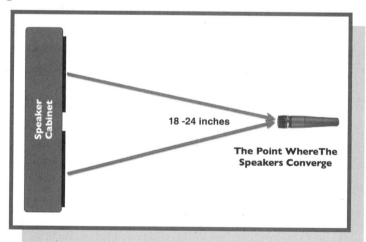

Figure 6.2: Classic Set-up #2—miking the point where speaker sounds converge

### Single-Mic Variation #1: Miking a Marshall with a Single Mic

If you're recording a Marshall cabinet, position a single mic between 12 and 24 inches from the cabinet, dead-center to all four speakers, aiming for the logo plate (see Figure 6.3). You can use this technique on other closed-back cabinets as well, except their logos might not be in the same position. On a typical 4x12 speaker cabinet (such as the standard Marshall 1960 model), the four speakers usually become additive at a distance of 15 to 24 inches from the cabinet center (depending upon the speakers).

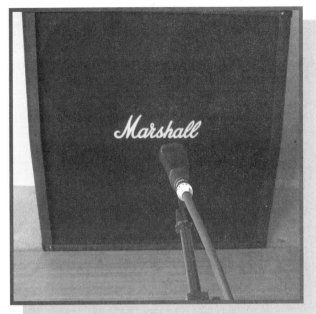

*Figure 6.3: Miking a Marshall cabinet with a single mic*

## TWO-MIC TECHNIQUES

Over the years, engineers discovered that they could more closely capture the sound that they were hearing in the room by adding a second microphone. You can get a lot of variety with one mic, but you'll get a lot more with two. Here are some examples of multi-microphone techniques.

### The Classic Two-Mic Set-Up: a 57 and a 421

Place an SM57 near or against the grill cloth, as in the Single-Mic Classic Set-Up #1 above. Add a Sennheiser MD 421 just to the right of the 57, but aimed at a 45-degree angle pointing toward the voice coil. Many sounds can be achieved from this set-up by summing the mics at different levels and by flipping the phase on one of them (see Figure 6.4). Of course, you can use any mics you choose, but the classic set-up uses the 57 and 421.

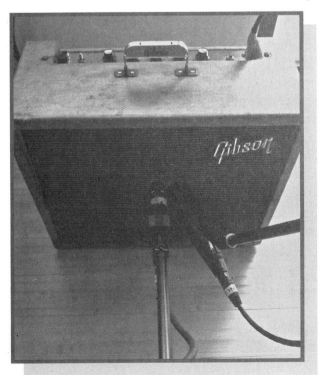

*Figure 6.4: Shure SM57 and Sennheiser MD 421 on guitar cabinet*

### Two-Mic Variation #1: Miking the Rear of an Open-Back Cabinet

When miking an open-back amplifier (such as a typical Fender), place one mic about a foot away from the rear of the amp, off-center from one of the speakers, while using any of the single-mic set-ups on the front of the cabinet (see Figure 6.5). Usually you'll have to flip the phase on the rear mic, but try both switch positions and use the one that has the most low end.

*Figure 6.5: Miking the rear of an open-back cabinet*

### Two-Mic Variation #2: a Close Mic and a Distant Mic

Using the Single-Mic Classic Set-Up #1, set the mic close to the grill of the cabinet and add another mic at the point where the sound of the speakers converges, 18 to 24 inches away (see Figure 6.6). This distance can be increased as far as 6 feet, depending on the size and sound of the room, to capture additional ambience.

*Figure 6.6: Distance mic added to close mic*

## THREE-MIC TECHNIQUES

The high end of a guitar cabinet sound has never been a problem to capture; it's the low end that has always been difficult. As a result, many engineers have resorted to using three microphones, in an effort to record a bigger sound. Here are some of the most common methods.

### Three-Mic Technique #1: Bundling a 421, R-121 and a 57

After finding the cabinet's sweet spot, as mentioned above, bundle SM57, MD 421 and Beyer M160 (or another ribbon mic such as a Royer R-121) microphones together. Aim the three mics directly at the best-sounding speaker in the cabinet and mix together to taste. The 57 will provide the bite; the 421, the mids; and the 160, the body (see Figure 6.7). Be aware that this technique only works with a 57 and 421, although any ribbon mic will work as the third mic.

*Figure 6.7: Sennheiser 421, Royer R-121 and Shure SM57 bundle on guitar cabinet*

### Three-Mic Technique #2: Adding a Distant Mic to a Two-Mic Set-Up

To any of the two-mic methods, add a third mic about six feet back from the cabinet (see Figure 6.8). Large-diaphragm condenser mics work well, as do figure-8 ribbon mics, or condenser mics configured with a figure-8 polar pattern. Make sure that you have plenty of space in the room to place the mic and that the mic isn't close to the wall, since it could pick up unpleasant-sounding room reflections. Remember, this technique only sounds as good as your room sounds.

### Three-Mic Variation #1: Aim One at the Wall

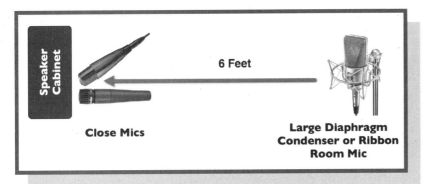

*Figure 6.8: Three-mic technique, using a distant mic*

To any of the two mic methods, add a third mic facing a hard wall in the room (do not aim it at the amp). Listen to the sound of each of the hard walls, and find the one that has the most pleasing reflections. Place the mic about three feet from the wall. The three mics can be mixed together to create many different tonal effects (see Figure 6.9). Once again, the success of this method depends upon the sound of the room.

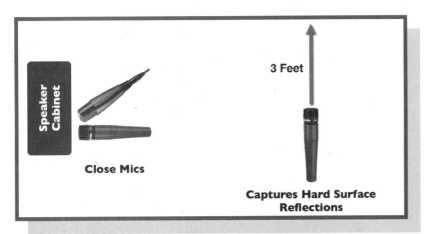

*Figure 6.9: Three-mic technique, using a mic aimed at a hard wall*

**Bonus—For Marshall Cabinets Only**

It's common for engineers to complain that they can't seem to capture the low end of a Marshall cabinet. It might sound great in the room, but it just never comes across the same when recorded. Fortunately, there is a trick to help capture that big Marshall sound, although it may appear a bit unorthodox.

Along with any of the above miking methods, place a ribbon mic two inches away from one of the cabinet's rear corners (see Figure 6.10). This only works with Marshall cabinets due to the type of wood they contain and their construction technique, but it works really well! Ribbon mics seem to work best for this trick, but you'll still capture a nice, round low end, regardless of the mic you choose.

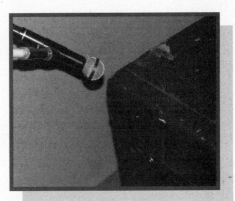

*Figure 6.10: Beyer M160 on a Marshall cabinet corner*

## MORE COMPLEX TECHNIQUES

In an effort to capture the ultimate guitar sound, engineers have tried variations of all of the above miking techniques, some using all of the techniques at the same time. Sometimes multi-miking techniques yield spectacular results, and sometimes they don't work at all. Perhaps the best example of a great sound from a sophisticated multi-mic set-up is the one that legendary engineer/producer Eddie Kramer developed for Jimi Hendrix, which combines a few of the above miking techniques.

### Jimi's Sound

Eddie started with a microphone bundle combining an SM57, MD 421 and Beyer 160 at the cone of the best speaker of a Marshall cabinet. Then he placed a Neumann U67 about three feet back from the cabinet, and finished it off with a stereo mic approximately six feet away from that (nine or ten feet away from the cabinet).

But wait, there's more. Eddie would then bus all of the mics into a tape-delayed EMT-140 plate reverb and bring the stereo returns back to the console. Between the mics and the reverb, that's a total of eight channels for a single guitar sound. The proof, of course, is in the listening, as Jimi's guitar sound is still emulated to this day.

### A Caveat

While it may be tempting to throw up every available mic in an attempt to record the ultimate electric guitar sound, this type of set-up can prove counter-productive due to acoustic phase cancellation between the mics. If you choose a mic set-up this complex, make sure that you check the phase between the mics every time you add or move one. This means flipping the phase selector switch on your console, mic preamp or DAW on every mic. Choose the position that provides the most low end.

### Miking the Strings

This technique seems like something right out of the acoustic guitar chapter (it is), but it will give you that little extra zing of interesting top end when nothing else seems to work. Place a condenser mic between three and six inches from the point where the guitar neck meets the body to capture the sound of both the strings and body (see Figure 6.11). Mix this with the amp mic tracks for a most unusual sound. This only works if the guitar is isolated from the amp, there's no other sound in the room, and you're listening on quiet headphones.

*Figure 6.11: Miking the strings of an electric guitar*

**Electric Guitar Miking Techniques**

Find the best-sounding speaker in the cabinet.

With a single mic, move closer to the voice coil for more high end, or toward the edge of the speaker for more bottom.

Placing the mic a foot or two away from the cabinet allows the sound to develop.

Two mics can be used for more variation in the sound.

Use the three-mic technique for a bigger, more ambient sound.

The more mics, the greater the need to check the phase.

# Recording Direct

Once upon a time, direct recording of a guitar was the last thing a player wanted to do. The sound suffered as the high-end rolled off, and the output was just so wimpy that virtually no one thought it was usable.

That thinking began to change in the '80s when better direct boxes, mic preamps and direct recording techniques were developed. With the advent of multi-effects devices in the '90s (especially Line 6's Pod), direct recording became totally acceptable, and in some cases even preferable to using an amp. Certainly from the convenience and sound variety perspective, there's no comparison since so many guitarists record direct. Let's take a look at some of the direct recording methods.

## USING A DI

Recording direct with a DI (direct injection) box became possible with the advent of relatively inexpensive active direct boxes that featured very high impedances so they would not affect the high-frequency response of the instrument. Any DI with an impedance above about one Mega-ohm (which is the same input impedance of most tube amps) works well. Guitar output impedances are fairly high compared to keyboards, the other instrument that DIs are usually used on.

## DI Types

Direct boxes come in two types: active and passive. Active boxes require either AC or DC power, while passive boxes do not. A passive box is based around a transformer, so its input impedance is lower than that in an active box. If you want to go direct with a traditional DI, choose an active box such as the Countryman Type 85 (an old standard), the Radial J48 (see Figure 6.12) or the very high-end Avalon U5.

*Figure 6.12: Radial J48 active direct box*

### Direct from the Amp

While many of the newer amps have facilities for direct recording, don't connect to them if you're expecting the same sound that you get from the speakers. You'll get the sound of the preamp, but not the amp's output section, so the amp will sound considerably different than if you simply miked it. However, if you treat the direct output sound as a slightly-effected, clean direct signal, you might find the sound very pleasing to work with. Keep in mind that your normal amp settings might have to be changed in order to get a usable direct sound.

Another way to record direct, especially with an amp that doesn't have a direct output feature, is to feed a signal from the extension speaker jack of the amp into a direct box that has the ability to accept this type of input (see Figure 6.13). Usually the DI will have two inputs: one labeled *Instrument* and the other labeled *Amp* or *Speaker*. Make sure that you only connect to the *Amp* or *Speaker* input, since the voltage coming from the extension speaker output is high enough to destroy the direct box if it's plugged into the *Instrument* input, and may even damage the amp as well. As with the direct output from the amp, this sound will not be the same as the sound that you experience out of the speakers, so you may have to adjust the amp's controls in order to get a sound that you find useful.

*Figure 6.13: Direct box speaker switch*

### Compression—The Secret Ingredient

The real secret to getting a great-sounding direct recording is compression, and plenty of it. A compressor reduces a signal's audio level once it rises above a set threshold level. The amount of gain reduction is determined by the compression ratio. A guitar amplifier has some natural built-in compression between the circuitry, the tubes and the speakers. Unfortunately you don't have the benefit of any of this help when you are recording direct. That's why it's important to always use some compression to keep the sound at a relatively consistent volume level. Without compression, the sound will be weak.

Start with the compressor set to either a 4:1 or 8:1 compression ratio, with both the attack and release controls set to medium. Set the threshold so there is about 5 or 6 dB of compression occurring. Depending upon the type of rhythm that you're playing, you may want to decrease both the attack and release time so they react faster, but be aware that the sound will begin to dull if the attack is set too fast, and you'll begin to hear the compressor work if the release time is too short.

### Benefits of Recording Direct

A direct signal has sort of an '80s sound to it (that's when it was really popular), but there's a lot more that you can do with that direct signal than keep it clean.

One of the advantages of a cleanly recorded sound is that you can change it or add effects later. By reamping (we'll discuss this in depth in Chapter 7), you can send the signal from your DAW back out to an amp of your choice and record the resulting sound, over and over. You can also use your favorite amp simulator to change the sound to anything that fits. An interesting guitar device is the Creation Audio Labs MW1 Studio Tool (see Figure 6.14), which acts as both a direct box and a reamp tool, giving the guitar player or engineer a lot of options during the recording process. Thanks to direct recording, we're no longer locked into the sound we recorded.

*Figure 6.14: Creation Audio Labs MW1 studio tool*

## RECORDING THROUGH AN EFFECTS BOX

Many effects boxes on the market are capable of acting as an optimized preamp for recording. Starting with the Pod in 1998, just about every manufacturer now offers an inexpensive guitar box capable of direct recording. IK Multimedia has even launched the iRig, which allows recording directly to your iPhone (see Figure 6.15).

Whichever unit you use, keep the following in mind:

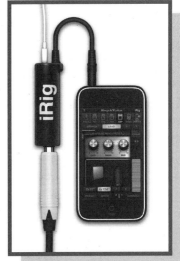

- **Be judicious with distortion and sustain.** As stated many times in this book, lots of distortion and sustain is fun to play with, but they aren't always appropriate for the song. Be prepared to dial it back to make your part fit better in the mix, especially if you'll be adding other guitar parts later.

*Figure 6.15: the IK Multimedia iRig*

- **Be judicious with effects.** One of the cool things about modeling and multi-effects boxes is that you can get a wide variety of sounds, some with over-the-top effects. Just like with distortion, think about what's appropriate for the song, not what feels fun to play with. Once again, take into account the way everything will fit together in the mix, especially if you add parts.

### Recording Direct

Active DIs will provide better high-frequency response for a guitar recorded direct.

The amp's direct output won't sound like what comes out of the speakers.

Moderate compression is key for direct recording.

Recording direct allows you to change the sound afterward.

Be judicious with distortion and effects when using a multi-effects box.

# Recording

You may or may not have a lot of recording experience, so here's a brief overview of some of the principles.

## THE SIGNAL PATH

The typical recording signal path goes like this: the sound source (in this case, the amplifier) into the microphone, into the microphone preamp (either internal or external), into the recorder (see Figure 6.16). Sometimes a compressor is inserted after the mic preamp, but you might not always need it when recording electric guitar. Generally speaking, the more distorted the sound, the less likely you'll need that compressor, since a distorted sound is compressed by nature.

## RECORDING LEVELS

For the most part, you do not have to record the level close to 0 dB these days. In the early days of digital recording, this

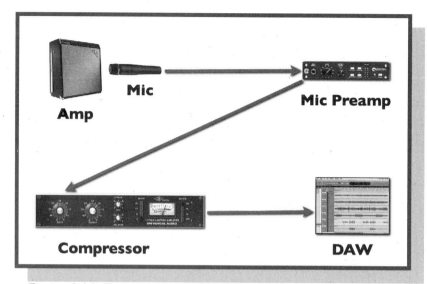

*Figure 6.16: Typical recording signal path*

practice was a necessity in order to get the least amount of noise, but modern 24-bit recording doesn't have this limitation. If your signal peaks between -6 and -10 dB or even lower, it will sound fine.

### If It's Distorting...

If something in your signal path other than your guitar sound is distorting, go through the following list to track it down:

- **Is the microphone preamp overloading?** Does the red overload LED light up, or is the meter peaking into the red? If so, decrease the input gain or select the input pad.

- **Is your signal path overloading somewhere else?** If you're using a console (regardless of the size) or an outboard compressor, check to see if any overload LEDs are lighting up and if the meters are peaking into the red. If so, decrease the output level of the stage before the overload.

- **Is your DAW overloading?** Once again, check to be sure that no overload LEDs are lit. This shouldn't happen if you keep your input level between -6 and -10 dB. If it does, decrease the input level on the DAW, or the output level of the previous stage.

- **Is your playback signal path distorting?** Are you listening back through a console? If so, are the input channels overloading? Are the monitors turned up too loud? Are there any overload lights lit anywhere in the signal path? If so, decrease the level from the DAW first, or turn down any input level controls in the playback signal path.

- **Is it a mic or cable?** Replace the cable first. Is the sound cleaner? If not, try a different mic. Any better?

- **Is it your amplifier?** Sometimes a recording picks up something that you can't hear live unless you're really listening for it. For instance, a buzz coming from a loose amp handle can sometimes be interpreted as distortion. Go out into the room and listen to the amp extra close, but be sure to play the exact same part as you played when you heard the distortion. Sometimes the sound will come from a single note or string, so by playing the same part you ensure that it can happen again so you can track it down.

- **Does the amp hum?** Hum is not exactly an overload but a form of distortion nonetheless. On vintage tube amps, simply flip the *Ground* or *Polarity* switch on the rear panel of the amp and choose the position with the least hum. That being said, the biggest cause of hum these days comes from when you have your amp plugged into an AC outlet on one side of the room, and your effects plugged into a different one that's connected to a different circuit on the other side of the room. If you plug your amp and effects into the same outlet via a power strip, the hum should either go away completely or diminish.

### Recording Overview

You don't need to get close to a 0dB meter reading.

Peaks of -6 to -10 dB are okay.

If something is distorting, check the overload LEDs and meter peaks.

If still distorting, replace the mic cable and microphone.

Is the distortion coming from your amp?

# Chapter 7:
## Electric Guitar Production Techniques

Photo by Claudine Ohayon

In many ways, recording was much easier back in the days of magnetic tape recorders and limited tracks. The sound coming from your amp was the sound that you heard in the recording, and if you were lucky, you might have an extra track left for a double or a lead.

Today we have almost unlimited tracks at our disposal, which allows for an assortment of layers, doubles and thickeners, and soon becomes a very convenient excuse for over-production. You could even say we're encumbered by the possibilities of workstation recording because of its vast potential. That being said, having these possibilities also enables us to create soundscapes never envisioned by our musical predecessors. This chapter explores modern production techniques that every guitarist should know in order to best take advantage of the power available in recording.

## Production from a Player's Perspective

There are a number of things a player should be aware of before a sound hits a microphone. Make sure you understand the following before you begin recording.

### THE REASON FOR TONE CONTROLS

So often, players are confused by the tone controls on their amps (see Figure 7.1). What do they really mean? What's the best way to set them? In order to get the most out of them, it's best to understand the reasons why they're there in the first place.

*Figure 7.1: Amplifier tone controls*

Tone controls let you make sure that all of the frequencies of your instrument speak evenly and no particular range is louder or softer than any other (unless, of course, you want them to be). Shortly after the first amps were developed with only a single tone control, manufacturers noticed that players might be using guitars with different types of pickups with their amps, so more sophisticated tonal adjustments were necessary. A guitar with a humbucking pickup might sound too boomy through an amp, but if you roll off the low end with the bass control, the frequencies even out. Likewise, a Strat might be too light on the low end or have too much top end, but a simple adjustment makes all frequencies come out at roughly the same level.

Tone controls come in handy when a particular frequency really jumps out, either because of the way the amp is overdriven or because of a pedal effect. Often a slight adjustment of the *Treble*, *Middle* or *Presence* control can alleviate the problem, although these controls will also adjust all the frequencies around the offending one as well.

Tone controls are especially effective in regards to the way the guitar fits within the context of the mix of the song. You want to be sure that every instrument is distinctly heard, and the only way to do that is to be sure that each one sits in its own particular frequency range. The tone controls will help shape this. It's especially important when two guitar parts are played on similar instruments and amps (such as two Strats through two Fender Super Reverbs). If this occurs, it's important to be able to shape your sound so that each guitar occupies a different part of the frequency spectrum. To make this example work in the mix, one guitar would occupy a higher-frequency register while the other would be in a lower register, which would mean that one guitar has more high end while the second guitar is fatter sounding, or that both guitars have different mid-range peaks.

Not only do guitars need to stay out of the way of each other, but they have to sit in a different frequency space than the bass and drums (and vocals, keys, percussion and horns). To separate them, either adjust the tone controls on your amp or try another guitar that fits better in the sonic space with everything else. While the engineer can do this with equalization either during recording or mixing, it's always better if you get as close to the desired sound as possible in the tracking room because it will save time and sound better.

The best way to get an ear for how guitars are sonically layered is to listen carefully to a number of hit songs in almost any genre and really dissect how everything fits together. Of course, the producer, engineer and artist (if you're playing on someone else's recording) will have specific ideas as to the sound they're looking for in the track, and will guide you in that direction.

## USING A VARIETY OF GUITARS AND AMPLIFIERS

One of the easiest ways to achieve a variety of sounds is by using different guitars and amplifiers during the recording, which is why studio musicians usually bring such a huge assortment of gear to a session (see Figure 7.2). Although you can alter the sound of your main axe by selecting a different pickup, changing to a different amp channel or using a different pedal, sometimes that's not enough of a meaningful difference in the context of the song.

In an ideal recording situation, a player has at least one guitar with humbucking pickups and another with single-coil pickups, and a variety of amp options from Marshall-like to Fender-like to even Vox-like, which are all distinctly different sounding. While sometimes you might be asked to play because of your unique sound, if you're an artist, you probably want a variety of sounds to help you develop

*Figure 7.2: A variety of guitar and amps*

a more varied sonic landscape. Remember that the idea is to make each track sound different, so the engineer doesn't have to spend a lot of time trying to do the same thing later (even if you're the engineer).

### Small Amp for a Big Sound

In an odd paradox, smaller amps and speakers tend to sound bigger than large amps and speakers when recording. One of the reasons is that at low volume, a 12-inch cone has a relatively shallow excursion (the distance it travels from its resting spot), while the same voltage from an amp to an 8-inch speaker will produce a larger cone excursion, causing it to pump more air to which the microphone reacts.

As an example, if you've ever listened to the guitar sounds on Eric Clapton's seminal recording of "Layla," both Clapton and Duane Allman used small Fender Champ and Princeton Reverb amplifiers (the Champ is 6 watts into an single 8-inch speaker, and the Princeton Reverb is 12 watts into a 10-inch speaker; see Figure 7.3), but the guitar sounds are huge.

*Figure 7.3: Fender Princeton Reverb amp*

### Large Amp, Small Cab

It's common for players in the studio to power small speakers (8 and 10 inches) with a larger amp (20 to 50 watts). If you want an overdriven sound that requires you crank it to 10, small speakers are going to pop in no time, so you're better off with your normal amp and cabinet combination. But if you're just looking to add some edge to a clean sound, a large amp with a small speaker is the way to go in the studio.

### Small Amp, Large Cab

Another frequently used combination is a low-wattage amp, such as a 5-watt Epiphone Valve Junior (see Figure 7.4), and a large speaker cabinet such as a Marshall 4x12. As long as the impedance of the cabinet matches the impedance that the amp is looking for, you can get an unbelievably big sound.

Using a low-wattage amp with a large speaker (or speakers) allows you to turn the amp up to the point where it's overdriven without blowing down the studio walls. It's an effective technique for getting unique sounds.

## THE IMPORTANCE OF WELL-MAINTAINED EQUIPMENT

Well-maintained gear is essential for the guitar player who's serious about recording. Everything is expected to work perfectly, with no tuning problems, no extraneous noises and no "intermittents" (unexplainable signal drop outs, crackles and deviations in sonic character). Not only does your gear have to work, but it has to be in tip-top condition as well. The better everything works and sounds, the better the recording will sound.

*Figure 7.4: Epiphone Valve Junior*

When you're recording, having gear that works perfectly is not only expected but required in order to give your best performance and create the best sound. First and foremost, your instruments must sound great.

In this context, a guitarist's signal chain can be a huge help or a big hindrance. Typically, it's best for a player who is new to the studio to keep the signal chain on the simple side, without lots of processing happening before the amp. That being said, some effects are integral to a player's sound and have to be in the chain for the player to be comfortable.

You'll usually get a warmer yet aggressive guitar sound by decreasing the amount of distortion from pedals, and turning up the amp's volume instead to obtain the sustain and distortion from the amp and speaker.

## LAYING IN WITH THE RHYTHM SECTION

All guitar players play rhythm guitar sooner or later, so it's important that you're aware of your interaction with the rhythm section. While it's possible to fix a shaky rhythm part with a software program such as Beat Detective or by cutting and pasting in the DAW, edited tracks just never seem to compare with a part that's played well while locked with the bass and drums. Playing rhythm well and locking in with the rhythm section is an essential part of your studio playing technique and an essential part of getting the track to sound great, so let's take a look at just how it's done.

Locking into the rhythm section means that you're playing with the exact pulse of the drummer. It doesn't mean that you're playing exactly the same rhythm as he's playing, but it means you're with him on every beat of the part that you're playing. Metallica is a really good example of a band that plays these parts together in a lot in their music, especially in a song like "Master of Puppets."

The easiest way to lock in with the drummer is to watch him as much as you can if you're tracking together. Whenever he hits the snare drum, you have to strum with him as closely as possible. Playing even a small amount before or after isn't close enough; it has to be exactly on to really sound tight!

If you're lucky enough to play with the same drummer for a while and you're to the point where you each know how the other plays, you'll naturally lock into each other's rhythms and watching all the time might no longer be necessary. That being said, it's still important to watch him during recording since it's the absolute easiest way to lock in as closely as possible.

If you're tracking with the drummer, try to set up so that you can watch his feet and hands as well as listen to him. Sometimes, if you watch his body and his face, you can almost anticipate what he's going to play before he plays it. If he grimaces, for instance, it might be a cue for you to emphasize a note because that's what he's about to do.

So that takes care of beats 2 and 4. How about beats 1 and 3 with the kick drum? The kick drum usually isn't very easy to hear, whether it's live on stage, in rehearsal or recording. One trick that experienced studio players use is putting a foot against the kick drum so they can feel the vibration and play to that.

What if you're overdubbing? The best thing to do is bring the snare drum up high in your headphone mix, then do your best to lock to it. Playing rhythm is tougher when you're overdubbing because you can't actually see the drummer, but if you concentrate on the snare, you should be able to lock in after a few passes (as long as the drum track is steady, that is).

**Production From a Player's Perspective**

Amp tone controls can make all frequencies speak evenly on your guitar, and shape the sound to fit better in the mix.

Using a variety of guitars and amps helps differentiate the parts.

When recording, small amps can sound better than large ones.

Listening to the snare drum is the easiest way to lock into the rhythm section.

# Common Guitar Production Techniques

Modern digital audio workstations have brought us new production techniques, thanks to the almost unlimited tracks, the variety of plug-ins available, and new ways to record directly. Here are some of the typical techniques that you should understand.

## DOUBLING

Doubling is an important technique for making a simple part sound bigger. A double means that you're playing the same part exactly the same way twice. For a rhythm guitar, the two parts are usually spread left and right in the stereo spectrum, but on a lead guitar part, you might pan them both up the middle. A double usually uses the same guitar sound for both parts, unless a specific type of layered sound is desired.

### Doubling Tricks

There are a number of tricks you can use to make a double sound either bigger or fatter, or just make the whole process of doubling easier.

- **Slightly detune the double.** Want a bigger-sounding double part? Then ever-so-slightly detune a couple of the strings on the second guitar. This technique works like a champ, but be sure you don't detune too much or it will begin to make the rest of the track seem a little sour.

- **Move the mic back.** This trick is used a lot with background vocals, but it can be equally effective on guitars. Before you record the second guitar track, move the mics on the guitar amp back a foot or two, then adjust the microphones' gain until the level on the meters is the same as it was for the first guitar. This will give the double part a bit more ambience, and make the two parts sound bigger together.

- **Use a delay.** You can sometimes produce a very acceptable double part just by adding a very short delay to a guitar part. This delay could be anywhere between about 25 and 100 milliseconds and even timed to the track, which makes it pulse with the music and sound bigger as a result. This technique is used frequently by Alex Lifeson of Rush.

- If a $\frac{4}{4}$ song tempo is 120 beats per minute (bpm), then the length of time it takes a quarter-note to play would be half a second (60 seconds/120 bpm = .5 seconds). Therefore, a quarter-note delay should be .5 seconds or 500 milliseconds (.5 x 1,000 ms), which is how almost all delay devices are calibrated.

- A 500ms delay might be too long and set the track too far back in the mix. To shorten to the next rhythmic subdivision, divide that number in half for an eighth-note delay (500 ms/2 = 250 ms). Divide in half again for a sixteenth-note delay (250 ms/2 = 125 ms), again for a thirtysecond-note delay (125/2 = 62.5 ms, rounded up to 63), and again for a sixtyfourth-note delay (62.5/2 = 31.25 or rounded to 31 ms). Divide again for a one hundred twentyeighth-note (31 ms/2 = 15.625, rounded up to 16 ms).

- **Copy and delay the track in your DAW.** If you don't want to use a delay, another way to achieve the same effect is to copy your original track, paste it onto another track, then move it back in the timeline until it starts to sound bigger. Be aware that if you don't move the track back far enough, you will hear it phase, which is probably not the effect you're looking for.

## LAYERING GUITARS

Layering parts gives your whole mix depth and richness. Where a double makes one part sound larger and fatter, layering makes the entire track more sonically expansive. When layering, guitar parts are treated to sound different from each other in order to stand out rather than blend together.

### The Secret to Guitar Layering

The real secret to layering guitars is to use a variety of instruments and amplifiers. Using two guitars (a Les Paul and a Strat, for instance) and two amplifiers (a Fender and a Marshall are the classic combination), combined with varied pickup settings, allows for quite a number of guitar tracks to effectively live in the mix together (see Figure 7.5).

*Figure 7.5: Recording set-up with multiple amps*

During mixing, you can create layers by equalizing various parts, but it's so much easier to create unique parts during recording by using different instruments or amplifiers. Layers can be created in the song arrangement, as we'll see in the next section.

### Using Alternate Tunings

Changing guitar tunings is a great way to layer tracks. While we'll cover the various types of tunings in Chapter 12 (they're pretty much work the same for acoustics and electrics) , it should be noted that common alternate tunings on electric guitars include *open E* (E–B–E–G♯–B–E) and *open A* (E–A–E–A–C♯–E) for slide, and *dropped D* (D–A–D–G–B–E), *double dropped D* (D–A–D–G–B–A), and *open G* (D–G–D–G–B–D— the sound of the Stones) tunings.

## BATTLE OF THE GUITAR TRACKS

These days, most recordings have many guitar tracks, so it's important to learn how to refine your sound so that each track compliments the others instead of fighting for the same sonic space.

Your amp tone controls are a starting point for molding your sound for the track, but when a recording has multiple guitar tracks, you have to make sure that the songs are arranged so that the guitars stay out of each other's way. If you listen closely to just about any guitar-rich recording in almost any genre, you'll hear the following.

- **Each guitar plays something completely different.** In order to differentiate their parts, one guitar might play full chords while another plays a line, or they both play different lines. A good example is Lynyrd Skynyrd's "*Sweet Home Alabama,*" where the first guitar plays the signature intro line, the second guitar plays the lead line in the middle of the neck, and when the entire band comes in, a third guitar plays a line that contrasts the first. Lynyrd Skynyrd is a great example of interplay between three guitars, and just about all of their songs are worth studying.

- **Each guitar plays in a different register or voicing.** This means that if one guitar plays an A chord on the 2nd fret, the second guitar plays the A chord up on the 5th fret. If one guitar plays a line on the 3rd and 4th strings, the second guitar plays the same thing up an octave on the 1st and 2nd string. For a good example of this technique, listen to Lenny Kravitz's "Are You Gonna Go My Way," where the signature line is played in the open E position and a second guitar plays the line one octave higher on the 12th fret. Another way to accomplish the same thing is to have the rhythm guitarists use a capo and play the same chord progression as a first guitar, since combining the different chord shapes creates a more interesting sound.

- **Each guitar plays a different rhythm.** In this arrangement, one guitar plays long, sustained chords (sometimes called power chords or "footballs," because they're whole notes that look like footballs when transcribed), while a second guitar plays a quarter- or eighth-note rhythm. This is a signature arrangement trick in hard rock and metal music.

If you have a lot of ideas for different guitar parts, using these techniques will help the parts lay in the track better and better support the vocals and rhythm section. It will make the song a lot more interesting as well.

## CLEAN GUITARS

As we mentioned in Chapter 6, direct clean guitar tracks now are held in the same esteem as gritty, amplified ones. Don't underestimate the value of a clean guitar recording, even if you have an array of great-sounding amps.

### *The Sound of the '80s*

During the '80s, many of the hit songs by Wang Chung, The Fixx, and others in the New Wave genre featured a distinctive-sounding clean guitar. The archetype for that "L.A. clean rhythm guitar sound" is a DI'ed guitar, compressed by about 6 dB, with a 25ms delay on the left side and a 50ms delay on the right. It might have been the sound of the '80s, but it still works in many situations today.

### Sympathetic Vibrations

There are a number of ways that you can use sympathetic vibrations from the sound of another instrument to enhance a clean guitar sound. Here are a couple of things to try:

- **Tune an acoustic guitar to the key of the song in open tuning, then place it on a stand near your amp.** The sound from the amp will make the strings resonate, and if you mic the acoustic as you normally would (see Chapter 11), the sympathetic vibration of the strings gives you an instant tuned reverb chamber, and a very interesting sound.

- **Place the amplifier or speaker cabinet under a piano and put a heavy weight on the piano's sustain pedal to keep it depressed.** Have someone hold down all of the roots and fifths in the song's key, so that the piano strings ring sympathetically with sounds from the amp. For example, if the song is in the key of E (major or minor), then hold down all E and B keys. Mic the piano as you normally would, and you'll have a wonderful, big sound that can't be achieved any other way.

## REAMPING

In recent years, reamping has become a popular technique for engineers and producers. The reason is simple: Don't like the sound? Change it by reamping.

Reamping means sending a recorded signal from the DAW or recorder back out to an amplifier and recording it again in order to capture a new sound that hopefully fits better in the track. In practice, it's a little more involved than that because the signal level from the DAW, recorder or console is far too high for your amp, and the cable used is usually a balanced XLR, which has to be changed to an unbalanced line such as a guitar cable.

There are special boxes that will do this for you though, such as the box called the Reamp (made by the biggest proponent of the idea, engineer John Cuniberti; see Figure 7.6), the Little Labs Red Eye Recording Tool and the Radial Pro RMP.

You might think that you can get away with using a direct box in reverse for this technique, but because the box isn't made for this application, the impedances usually won't match, and there's no way to dial back the level so you're left with a lot of hum and distortion. Do yourself a favor and invest in a reamp box if you feel the technique fits into your production style.

*Figure 7.6: John Cuniberti's Reamp*

### Amp Simulator Plug-Ins

A great variety of modeling plug-ins and amp simulators are available today. If your sound isn't too distorted (which is key), a simulator can transform it. Popular amp simulators include Line 6's Amp Farm, IK Multimedia's Amplitude (see Figure 7.7), Native Instruments' Guitar Rig and Vintage Amp Room by Soft Tube, among others.

Once again, the cleaner the recorded signal, the more variety you can get from an amp simulator plug-in. If your signal is already over-the-top distorted, a simulator can still shape the sound, but it can never take it back to clean.

### A Few Tips

Although amp simulators are pretty much plug-and-play, a few tricks will help you make the most of them.

*Figure 7.7: IK Multimedia's Amplitude amp simulator*

- Use an impulse-response reverb, such as Altiverb or TL Space, to find a good spring reverb or room setting to make your track sound a bit more realistic.

- If you're recording directly into a computer first, then into an amp simulator, use a short cable to minimize hum and buzz.

- Most amp simulators work best when hit with a hot signal, so Les Pauls often sound far better with them than Teles or Strats. The hotter the pickups, the better the amp simulators will sound. Try driving the input stage to the edge of distortion, then back off a bit.

- If you're recording directly into the computer, listen to the way your pickups react to the computer monitor and move around the computer until you find a sweet spot with the least amount of noise.

- Try doubling your parts with two different amp sounds, or use the same amp sound for both, while altering its settings on one track for a bigger sound.

---

**Common Guitar Production Techniques**

Doubling makes guitar tracks sound bigger.

Layering guitars builds a bigger mix.

Using a variety of guitars and amps is the secret to layering.

Keep multiple guitars out of the same frequency range.

Playing different rhythms, different lines, or in different registers keeps guitar parts from fighting each other.

Clean guitar sounds are easy to change after they've been recorded.

# Guitars in the Mix

Guitars, especially overdriven ones, can be harmonically complex, and often require a special mixing approach. It's common for a guitar track to blend so well with the other instruments that it disappears into the rhythm section—which is okay, if that's what you're looking for. But if you are looking for a distinct guitar track, here are some tricks to pull that guitar out of the din and place it where it belongs: front and center of the mix.

## COMPRESSION

Compression is an important mixing component, not only for maintaining a consistent signal level, but for shaping the tonal quality of the sound as well.

### Using Compression on Clean Guitars

Generally speaking, the cleaner the sound is, the more compression is required during mixing (assuming that little or none was applied during recording). On the other hand, the more distorted the sound is, the less compression is required because of the built-in compression in an overdriven or distorted signal.

For a clean guitar track, start with the compressor set to either a 4:1 or 8:1 compression ratio, depending on how consistent the performance was. If the track has a lot of transients and level variations, use an 8:1 ratio, otherwise, 4:1 works fine.

Set both the attack and release controls to medium. Depending upon the rhythm that was played, you can decrease both the attack and release time so they react faster, but be aware that the guitar will begin to sound dull if the compressor attack is too fast and cuts off the transient part of the signal. If you shorten the release time too much, you will hear the compressor "pumping." This means generating rhythmic gain fluctuations, which can be a desirable effect if it pulses with the rhythm of track. The best way to do this is to solo the guitar and the snare drum, and set the compressor's release time so the compression level returns to normal at the same time as the end of a snare drum hit.

Set the threshold to the desired amount of compression, which might only be a dB or two, or as much as 10 dB, depending upon the sound you're looking for.

### Using Compression On Distorted Guitars

Distorted guitars don't need much compression to level out the signal, but compression can help bring the guitar out in the mix, especially during a solo.

Start with the compressor set to either a 4:1 or 8:1 compression ratio, although the more distorted or overdriven the sound, the more likely that the 4:1 setting will work best.

Set both the attack and release controls to medium. Most distorted or overdriven guitars don't have many transients left in the signal and the volume envelope is already long, so medium settings work fine.

Set the threshold to the desired amount of compression, which is usually somewhere between 3 and 6 dB. If the guitar begins to sound lifeless, you've gone too far and you'll have to back off the compression a bit.

## EQUALIZATION

Equalization can be very confusing to musicians who are trying to engineer their own recordings, but if used judiciously, it can make almost any guitar blend into the mix better, or jump out for everyone to hear. Here are a couple of simple EQ techniques, followed by some specific tips for EQing guitar.

### EQ Techniques

It's important to remember that you can't just solo a guitar track and EQ it until you think it sounds good. The first secret to EQing is to do it while you are listening to the entire mix so you can hear how the instruments blend together. The second secret is to juggle the frequencies so that each instrument has its own dominant frequency range.

- Make sure that equalizers used on different instruments don't boost the same frequencies. If they do, adjust one so it affects frequencies a little higher or lower than the instrument it's competing with.

- If an instrument is cut at a certain frequency, boost the same frequency on another instrument. For example, if you cut one guitar at 500 Hz, boost the second one at 500 Hz.

- Add the rest of the elements into the mix one by one. As you add each instrument, check it against the previous elements, going through the steps above.

There are a lot of other EQ methods that are beyond the scope of this book, which you can read about in *The Mixing Engineer's Handbook* (Mix Pro Audio Series).

### Guitar EQ Points

Learn these important points in the frequency spectrum and how they pertain to guitars.

| Figure 7.8: Electric Guitar EQ Points | |
|---|---|
| **Frequency** | **Description** |
| 20 to 100 Hz | Nothing of importance in this region. Roll it off. |
| 100 to 300 Hz | The meat of the guitar tone. The exact frequencies depend upon the guitar and amp combination. |
| 300 to 1k Hz | The mids of the guitar. Some engineers attenuate the 300 to 500Hz or 600 to 800Hz ranges. |
| 1k to 3k Hz | The pick range. Boosting will make the guitar jump out of the mix, but it might clash with the snare or vocal. Adjust EQ settings of competing frequencies. |
| 3k to 6k Hz | High end of the guitar. Too much emphasis can make a distorted guitar sound frizzy. |
| 7k to 10k Hz | "Presence" and "air" range of a clean guitar. A little boost goes a long way. |
| 10k to 20k Hz | Nothing of importance in this region. Roll it off. |

### The Highpass Filter

The highpass filter (sometimes called "low cut") is one of the most valuable processors in a mixer's toolkit (see Figure 7.9). Here's why.

- The low frequencies of many instruments (especially guitars) just get in the way of each other and don't add much to the overall sound. If you roll off the frequencies below 100 or 200 Hz on instruments other than kick and bass, the mix will begin to clean up.

- Rolling off low frequencies can eliminate rumble that mics pick up from sources such as trucks and machinery that are so low that you can't hear them, yet they muddy up the mix.

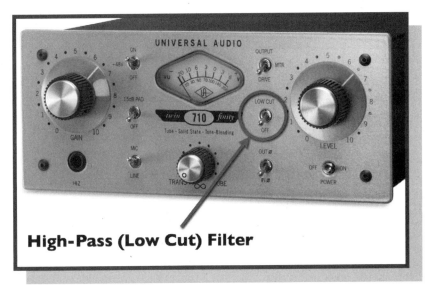

**High-Pass (Low Cut) Filter**

*Figure 7.9: Highpass filter*

Get in the habit of using the highpass filter. It's a mixer's secret weapon.

## STUDIO EFFECTS

Effects like reverb and delay are often added to tracks without any real plan, but there's a reason for everything in a mix, so it's important to understand why these effects are used in order to apply them effectively.

There are four reasons to add effects to a track:

- To create an aural space, like a room or hall, around the instrument.

- To add excitement. Sometimes a delay or modulation effect can be just the thing to make a guitar the hook or a major focal point of the song.

- To make a track sound bigger, wider or deeper.

- To move a track back in the mix (giving the impression that it's farther away).

## Effects Tips

So now that you know why you add effects, let's look at a strategy for doing it. Here are some considerations that can help you choose the best effects for each track.

- Before adding an effect such as a delay or reverb, picture the guitar in an acoustic space, and then try to match it.

- Delays can sometimes be more effective than reverb. When in doubt, try the following settings:

### Delay Settings

| Delay Time | Effect |
|---|---|
| 50 milliseconds | Gives a slap-back effect |
| 175 milliseconds | An all-around good starting place when in doubt |
| 350 milliseconds | Gives a long delay with distinct repeats |

- Use shorter delays (less than 100 ms) and reverb times (under one second) to make tracks sound larger.

- Longer delays (more than 100 ms) and reverb times (more than one second) make tracks sound farther away if they are prominent in the mix.

- A delay or reverb that's timed to a track will blend into the track and add depth without being noticeable. If it is not timed to the track, it will stick out more. See the section on doubling for directions for timing the delay.

### Guitars In The Mix

The cleaner the sound, the more compression is required.

EQ while listening to the other instruments to be sure they blend.

Be sure that each instrument has its own predominate frequency range.

Sometimes a delay works better than reverb.

# Chapter 8:

# Effects

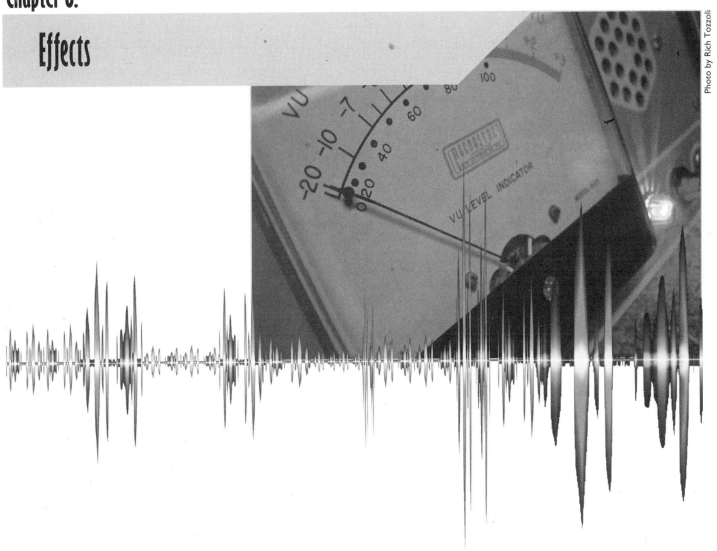

Photo by Rich Tozzoli

Ever since the first stomp box appeared in 1963, pedals have been both a fascination and a curse to most guitar players. Guitar players are drawn to stomp boxes, because with a minimal investment they're instantly able to change their sound. Yet players always seem to be on a never-ending search to find better ones. As soon as you think you've found the ultimate pedal, another one suddenly appears.

This chapter will answer some of the major questions that players frequently have about pedals. But first, a little background.

# Basic Effects

Guitar effects come in four main categories: volume, overdrive/distortion, ambience and modulation. Let's take a look at each.

### VOLUME

Volume effects vary the level of the guitar or amplifier. They come in several flavors.

#### The Volume Pedal

Although you can easily adjust your guitar's volume with the volume control, a pedal allows you to change the volume without using your hands, which can create a great effect. Pedal steel and lap steel players consider a volume pedal to be an essential part of their arsenal.

*Figure 8.1: Ernie Ball VP Junior volume pedal*

Like guitar volume controls, a volume pedal can also affect your sound by rolling off some of the high end, which is why an active pedal is sometimes preferred over a simple passive one. The best volume pedals change volume evenly across the entire treadle action, hold the pedal where you set it, and don't suck any of your tone away. A good active pedal should have the same qualities as a good passive pedal, and its active electronics should not contribute extraneous noise. The Ernie Ball VP Junior (see Figure 8.1) is one of the most popular passive volume pedals, while the Morley Little Alligator is one of the most popular active pedals.

#### Signal Boost

If you have an amplifier that's difficult to distort or a guitar with a low output, a signal booster can sometimes work wonders for your sound. By adding gain to the signal, you can overdrive the preamp of the amplifier, or bring your level up if some level is sucked up by other pedals in your signal chain. You can also use a signal booster to add a bit of level on solos. The MXR Micro Amp (distributed by Dunlop) is an example of a popular signal boost pedal (see Figure 8.2).

*Figure 8.2: Dunlop Micro Amp signal boost pedal*

### Tremolo

A tremolo is a cyclic variation in volume, like the effect you'll find on Fender amplifiers (even though it's incorrectly labeled "vibrato"). Don't confuse tremolo with vibrato; vibrato is a pulsating change in pitch, while tremolo is a pulsating change in volume.

With the exception of Fender amps, most amps don't come with tremolo built-in, so you'll need an outboard pedal if you want that effect. The Voodoo Lab Tremolo is a good example of a tremolo pedal (see Figure 8.3).

*Figure 8.3: Voodoo Lab Tremolo pedal*

### Compressor

Many guitarists like to use a compressor pedal to keep their signal steady and improve their sustain, especially on clean sounds. A compressor reduces a signal's level once it rises above a set threshold. The first pedal compressor was the MXR DynaComp, which is still made today. Many players love the JangleBox, which was designed to reproduce the sound of Roger McGuinn's 12-string on the original Byrds records (see Figure 8.4).

*Figure 8.4: JangleBox compressor pedal*

### Noise Gate

Noise gate pedals (or rackmount devices) are frequently used to clean up noise that is sometimes induced by long signal chains and multiple noisy pedals. A gate works in the opposite way that a compressor works—by reducing the level of a signal when it drops below a set point. Unlike gates made for studio use, many guitar noise gates also include noise-reduction circuitry. The ISP Decimator is an example of a noise gate that can be found in both pedal and rackmount form (see Figure 8.5).

*Figure 8.5: ISP Decimator noise gate pedal*

## OVERDRIVE AND DISTORTION

Distortion and overdrive pedals seem to be the most elusive pedals for most guitar players. These pedals all sound different and interact differently—not only with a player's gear, but with his feel and touch as well. Let's break down the difference between distortion and overdrive.

When a clean guitar signal starts to overdrive, sine waves begin to square off (see Figure 8.6). The more the waveform resembles a square, the more distorted it sounds. An overdrive pedal boosts the signal until it gradually begins to distort. It's like a signal booster that's intentionally designed to distort as you turn it up. The Ibanez Tube Screamer (see Figure 8.7) is an example of a pedal that has become a go-to overdrive pedal in guitarists' toolkits over the years.

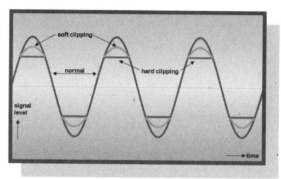

Figure 8.6: Clean signal waveform being overdriven

Figure 8.7: Ibanez TS-9 Tube Screamer pedal

A distortion pedal, on the other hand, uses internal electronics to change the waveform as soon as it hits the pedal. The only adjustment that you can make is the amount that the original signal is distorted. The Boss DS-1 is an example of a popular distortion pedal (see Figure 8.8).

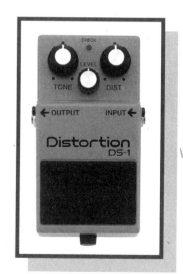

Figure 8.8: Boss DS-1 distortion pedal

In some cases, if an overdrive pedal's controls are turned all the way up, it becomes a distortion pedal. If the overdrive function is kept relatively low and the output is turned up, it becomes a signal booster pedal. Likewise, if the level on a distortion pedal is turned down, the pedal acts more like an overdrive pedal (depending upon the unit), and can also act like a booster pedal. Some pedals, such as Creation Audio Labs' Holy Fire pedal (see Figure 8.9), combine overdrive, distortion and clean boost into one compact package.

Figure 8.9: Creation Audio Labs' Holy Fire pedal

## TONE

Changing the guitar's tone is always at the forefront of a guitarist's playing. You can make changes dynamically while you're playing by using a wah-wah, during a solo by using a treble booster, or even make a permanent change to the signal with a graphic EQ pedal. Let's look at all of these options.

### Treble Booster

A treble booster pedal simply boosts the high-end frequencies of the guitar to give it a little more bite so it can cut through a mix at a critical point in the song, such as a solo. The treble booster was one of the first widely used pedals, and many of today's treble boosters are based on the extremely rare vintage Dallas Rangemaster (see Figure 8.10), used by Eric Clapton (during his Blues Breakers days), Tony Iommi, Brain May and Rory Gallagher. Modern treble boosters based on the Rangemaster include the Fryer/Brian May Treble Booster, the BSM BM-Q (see Figure 8.11) and Scott's Crispy Creme from Snake River Guitar Works.

*Figure 8.10: Dallas Rangemaster*

*Figure 8.11: BSM BM-Q Treble Boost Pedal*

### Wah

Originally made for wind instruments in 1966 so they could emulate the sound of a trumpet with a Harmon mute, the wah pedal instantly became a must-have for every guitar player, both for the wah effect and the pedal's versatility.

While everyone knows the wah sound ("The Theme From *Shaft*" by Isaac Hayes comes immediately to mind), the wah is also an excellent device for shaping your tone. This is done by switching it on, setting it to a particular point in the pedal's travel, and leaving it there. Although not exactly the same as the original pedal produced in the late '60s, the Vox V847a (see Figure 8.12) is still the top of the line in terms of sound, along with the Dunlop Crybaby, although the Teese Real McCoy 3 is thought by many to be the closest thing to the original wah pedal on the market today.

*Figure 8.12: Vox V847 wah pedal*

Two things differentiate one wah pedal from another; the frequency range which it operates and the depth of its tonal notch. Even though many new wahs let you adjust both of those parameters, quite a few guitarists feel that vintage wahs sound better because many of the parts that were used to make them back then aren't available today, although re-issue models try to closely duplicate the originals.

## EQ

Many guitar players include an EQ pedal (sometimes called "tone modeling") in their signal chain, usually because the amp just isn't getting the sound they're looking for. An EQ pedal becomes a convenient temporary fix, but usually it comes at the expense of increased noise. The Boss GE-7 is a popular graphic equalizer pedal (see Figure 8.13).

Some EQ pedals are similar to a treble booster, but have controls for bass, treble and mid frequencies instead of individual frequency sliders.

*Figure 8.13: Boss GE-7*

## AMBIENCE

Ambience pedals such as delay or reverb have become popular guitar pedal accessories, although in most cases, delay seems better than reverb for placing the guitar in an artificial space. Reverb usually gets lost because it's less distinct and tends to push the guitar further back in the mix and wash it out, at least on stage.

### Delay

Guitarists have always liked the sound of delay and have gone to extraordinary lengths to use it on stage, even back before the days of simple pedals. In the '60s, the only way to get a delay was to employ a reel-to-reel tape machine, which players like Ritchie Blackmore and Robert Fripp did with Revox machines. Soon, dedicated tape delay units such as the Maestro Echoplex and Roland Space Echo (see Figure 8.14) came on the market, eliminating the need to transport a large tape machine. Nevertheless, these new units were still bound by the limits of magnetic tape.

*Figure 8.14: Roland Space Echo*

Soon enough, inexpensive digital processors became available, and in 1984, the guitarist's dream of having a delay unit in a pedal became a reality with the debut of the Boss DD-2. Today, delay pedals are some of the most common guitar effects, rivaling overdrive pedals for the most choices in the market. Popular units include the Boss DD-7 (an updated version of the DD-2), the Electro-Harmonix Memory Man and the Line 6 DL4 (see Figure 8.15).

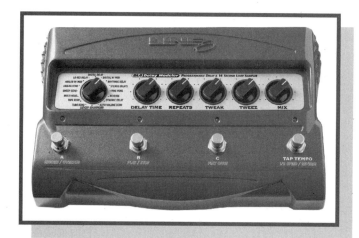

*Figure 8.15: Line 6 DL4 pedal*

### Reverb

Reverb pedals usually cost more than delay pedals because they involve more sophisticated technology. Most reverb pedals often offer tone controls, as well as other effects such as chorus or flanging. While some reverb pedals emulate studio reverb programs, other pedals model revered classic reverbs, such as the reverb in a vintage Fender amplifier, emulated by the Boss FRV-1. (See Figure 8.16.)

**Figure 8.16: Boss FRV-1 reverb pedal**

## MODULATION

Modulation effects such as phase shifting, flanging, and chorusing are a standard parts of a guitar player's sound arsenal today, but not many players know the difference between these modulation effects, or how they affect their guitar sound.

### Different Types of Effects

There are three types of modulation effects: phase shift, chorus and flange. The main difference between them is that a chorus and flange effect are generated by a modulated delay that's mixed back into the original signal. Another difference is that while a flanger uses a shorter delay than a chorus—usually a second or less—a phaser uses no delay at all (see Figure 8.17).

Flangers, phasers and choruses work by producing a series of notches that are slowly swept across the guitar's frequency spectrum. You don't really hear the notches themselves, but you hear what's left in the frequency spectrum, which is a series of peaks. Phasers generate a small number of notches, spaced evenly across the frequency spectrum, while flangers and choruses generate many notches that are spaced harmonically.

### Figure 8.17: Differences Between Modulation Effects

| Effect | Delay | Description |
|---|---|---|
| Phase Shift | None | Cancels different frequencies to create the effect. Frequency notches spaced evenly across the guitar frequency range. |
| Flanging | <1 to 5 ms | Deepest depth, with greatest frequency cancellations. Frequency notches spaced harmonically across the guitar frequency range. |
| Chorus | 5 to 25 ms | Sounds similar to a doubling effect, while widening the sound. Used to thicken the sound and create a stereo image. Frequency notches spaced harmonically across the guitar frequency range. |

### Phasers

Phasers don't sound very dramatic, so they're not found very often in a guitarist's array of effects. Back in the '70s before the introduction of inexpensive digital delay electronics, using an analog phaser was the only way to get any sort of modulated effect. At the time, the Maestro PS1A Phase Shifter (see Figure 8.18) was the unit to have, but since it offered very little control over the effect, guitarists were constantly on the lookout for something more usable and adjustable. The solution came the late '70s with the introduction of Boss and Roland chorus devices.

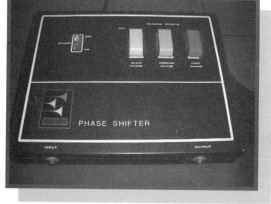

*Figure 8.18: Maestro PS1A Phase Shifter pedal*

### Flanger and Chorus Devices

Flangers are dramatic effects that are used sparingly because they're not very musical, but that's not the case with choruses. It's very easy to fall in love with a chorus effect, since it's lush sounding, and if used in stereo, can widen the sound of a guitar quite a bit. Popular chorus pedals include the Electro-Harmonix Small Clone (see Figure 8.19) and the MXR Stereo Chorus. The Danelectro Fab Flange and Boss BF-3 are best-selling flanger pedals.

Since the chorus and flanger are so closely related, many pedals, such as the popular TC Electronic Stereo Chorus Flanger, can create both effects. The MXR Phase 90 and Phase 100 are also best sellers, even after many years on the market.

*Figure 8.19: Electro-Harmonix Small Clone chorus pedal*

### Pitch Shifters

A pitch shifter combines your original signal with a duplicate played back at a different pitch, letting you play harmonies with yourself. The first pitch shifter pedal, made by Jimi Hendrix tech Roger Meyer, was called the Octavia (see Figure 8.20), and it pitched the sound you were playing up an octave and mixed it with your original. You can hear this effect at the end of the solo on "Purple Haze." Today, Dunlop produces the JHOC1, a copy of the Octavia. Other devices such as the MXR Blue Box shift the sound down one or two octaves.

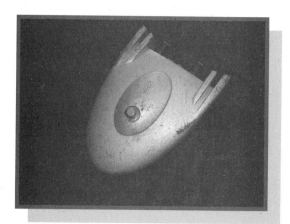

*Figure 8.20: An original Octavia pedal*

While playing in octaves is a nice effect, the Holy Grail of pitch shifting is the ability to play harmonies with yourself—which is a lot more difficult than you'd think. Sound quality is critical; you can hear harmony notes better than octave intervals, which means that you can also hear artifacts more readily, especially in a cheaply designed circuit. To generate correct harmonies, the unit must be able to process the key and harmonic mode you're playing in, which is up to the player to dial in—an exercise that usually requires some musical background to do properly.

Today, pitch shifters such as the Digitech Harmony Man (see Figure 8.21) and Boss PS-5 Super Shifter sound great and make modal choices a lot easier.

Although you're always better off just playing the harmonies as an overdub in the studio, a pitch shifter may get you some interesting effects along the way, so it's worth checking out.

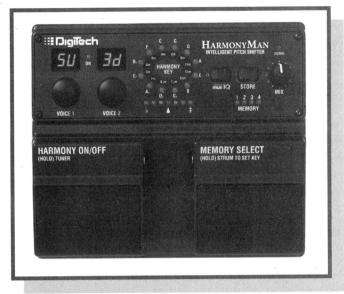

*Figure 8.21: Digitech Harmony Man Intelligent Pitch Shifter*

## Basic Effects

Chorus is the most pleasing modulation effect to the ear.

Overdrive pedals boost the signal; distortion pedals process it.

The difference between wahs is defined by the points of the guitar's frequency range in which they work.

Many guitarists use the wah as a tone control.

# Effects Interfacing

Even if you have only a basic array of effects, you must know how to put them together in a way that sounds best and is also convenient to set up and move. Here are a number of concepts and ideas.

## TYPICAL EFFECTS-PEDAL PROBLEMS

As long as there have been effects, there has been the question, "Which order should I put my effects in?" Two things happen when you put a number of effects into your signal path: tone suck and noise build-up. Let's look at both.

### Tone Suck

Tone suck means the tone of your guitar changes when you insert a pedal between your guitar and amp, even if the pedal isn't turned on. The reason this happens is because your guitar signal still runs through some of the pedal's circuitry, even without the effect switched in. That circuitry degrades the signal, either by changing the frequency response or by decreasing the volume. Either way, you need to avoid tone suck if you want to maintain that great tone you started with. There are two solutions for this problem:

- **Use an effect with "true bypass."** True bypass means that when the effect is switched off, the signal completely bypasses all of the circuitry, so the pedal has zero influence on the guitar sound. This feature is a rather recent development (since the late '90s), but just about all boutique pedal manufacturers use true bypass as a selling point these days.

- **Bypass via a switching network.** Sometimes you have an effect that you just can't live without, but you hate what it does to your tone when it's bypassed, so the only thing to do is bypass it externally with a switching network. These systems can be small and relatively inexpensive or highly sophisticated, so we'll devote an entire section to them later in the chapter.

One of the problems with true bypass is that it creates an illusion that the volume and tone of the guitar signal won't ever change, but that's not necessarily true. If you have a 15-foot cable from your guitar to your pedalboard, a one-foot cable between each of your 15 stomp boxes and another 15-foot cable to your amp, that's 45 combined feet of cable, which will degrade your signal! You can get around this problem with buffers (unity gain amplifiers) and loop-switching systems, but many players never consider the consequences of simply connecting up all of their pedals.

### Noise Buildup

Noise buildup occurs whenever you switch an effect on (or even while they're switched off, if they don't feature true bypass). The level can be anywhere from a slight escalation in the noise floor to the sound of a full-on hurricane, depending upon the gain of the device or devices. Buildup occurs for three reasons:

- **Each device adds its own inherent noise.** Some devices are designed better than others (they're usually more expensive as a result). Keeping the noise floor down is one of the elements of a good design.

- **The type of power used affects noise.** Although many effects can run on a 9-volt battery, they're actually designed for 12-volt use. If you use an external AC power supply, the noise level can drop considerably. In some pedals, the noise floor can rise as the voltage drops from a weak battery.

- **The input stage of the amplifier matters.** Most amp input stages are designed for the relatively low signal coming directly from a guitar, which they will then boost up as much as 50 times. If the gain from a pedal is cranked up, that signal will still be boosted by 50 times, regardless of the amp's volume control.

## THE EFFECTS CHAIN

Two things directly affect the way your effects interface with your amp: the effects order and gain staging. There are several schools of thought on effects order, and they each have a different result.

### School of Thought #1

The following effects chain is the order generally recommended by most pedal gurus. There are several rules that make up this order regardless of if you're playing live or in the studio.

- A distortion pedal comes first, right after the guitar. The exception is if you're using a compressor pedal, which will be first in the chain. Do not put a volume pedal first because it can alter the sound of a compressor or distortion pedal that comes after it.

- Modulation or tone devices such as wahs come next. This configuration lets you preserve the sustain from your distortion or overdrive devices, and alter an already harmonically rich signal.

- Delays come near the end of the chain, since you want to delay an effected signal.

- A volume pedal comes either last in the chain, or directly in front of any delay.

- In situations where a pedal is providing a lot of clean gain, put that pedal last in the chain so you won't overload any of the other pedals.

---

**The Sound of Batteries**

A battery's effect on a pedal's sound has long been debated. While you might think that 9 volts is 9 volts no matter where it comes from, it turns out there really is a difference between batteries, though it's a small one.

Guitar golden-ears like Eric Johnson have advocated that stomp boxes sound better with old-style zinc-carbon batteries than with today's manganese dioxide "heavy duty" batteries. In fact, old-style batteries can produce an effect similar to a power-supply "sag" (see Chapter 4) when they're under load and a bit past their prime. This effect happens mostly because the rate that they supply current under load is different from that of today's batteries.

Older stomp boxes seem to sound better with old-style batteries because they were designed for them, but just like vintage guitars, amps and pedals, zinc-carbon batteries are difficult to find these days.

A typical effects order might go something like: compressor, distortion, wah, chorus, delay, volume pedal (see Figure 8.22). Although this might not be the quietest effects order, it sounds really good because distortion, overdrive, and sustain modify the effects that come behind them.

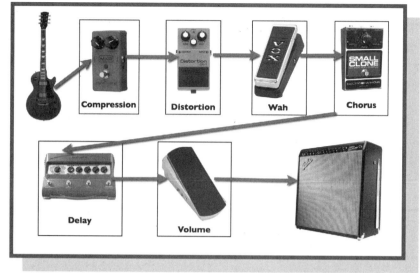

Figure 8.22: Typical effects order, school of thought #1

### School of Thought #2

When recording, we want the least amount of noise going into the amp. With that in mind, there are two rules:

- The noisiest pedal goes last in the chain before the amp.

- The pedal with the most gain goes last before the amp.

The reason for both of the above points is simple: If the noisiest pedal is first in the chain, that noise will be altered and amplified by every other pedal in the chain that you switch on. The same goes for the pedal with the most gain; if it's at the beginning of the chain, it could overload any other effect that comes after it, since most pedals are designed to handle a typical guitar signal, nothing greater (see Figure 8.23). Also, noise caused by increasing a pedal's gain will be amplified downstream by any other pedal that is switched on.

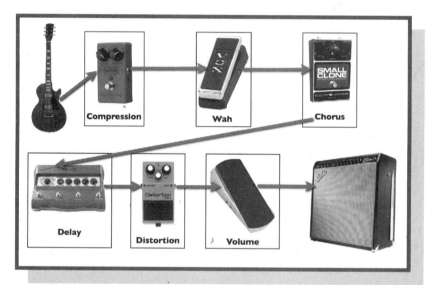

Figure 8.23: Effects order #2

In general, keep the same basic order as in School of Thought #1 (page 114) to ensure that distortion or sustain is processed by the effects placed later in the chain. That said, playing through effects in this order won't sound the same as playing through order #1, especially if a distortion pedal is placed last in the chain (which isn't recommended), so it might not be for everyone.

### Proper Gain Staging

Proper gain staging means adjusting the gain of each effects device to keep the noise at its lowest and prevent overloading of any device after it. Since almost all pedals have output gain controls these days, the best way to approach gain staging is to adjust all the output controls so the gain is exactly the same whether they're switched on or off. If you're running a distortion or overdrive pedal, put that last in the chain, and increase its output level until you get the sound that you like (see Figure 8.24).

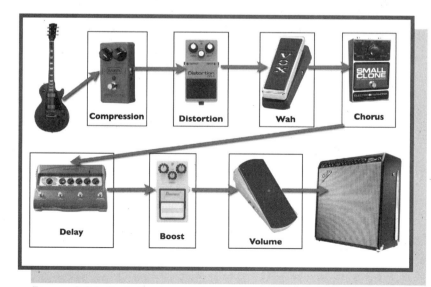

Figure 8.24: Pedal gain staging

## Amplifier Effects Loops

It's common for modern amplifiers to have an effects loop built in. This means the amp has an output from the preamp and an input to the power amp section so that you can patch your effects in without boosting the noise from the preamp section of the amp. Many effects loops also provide the ability to select between -10dB level for pedal effects and +4dB level for rackmount studio effects. There are two problems with using the amp effects loop:

- Most guitar pedals want to see the impedance of a guitar, not an amplifier preamp output, so they won't sound the same when placed in the effects loop.

- Most guitar effects simply sound better connected in front of the amp, for the reasons explained in the effects order section.

That said, reverb and delay effects, especially the rackmount studio versions, work well in the amp effects loop.

### Problems With Effects Pedals

Tone suck changes the sound of the guitar, even when the effect is off.

True bypass and bypassing with a switching network counter tone suck.

Sound can degrade even with true-bypass pedals if cables are too long.

Configuring the correct gear order and proper gain staging quiets the effects chain.

Put the distortion pedal first and the pedal with the most gain at the end.

Amp effects loops work best with reverb and delay.

# The Pedalboard

As guitar players began to collect a huge array of pedals, set-up became long and tedious, as did finding enough floor space for them—not to mention having to do a dance to switch them on and off during a performance. They needed a new way to deal with all of these effects. Enter the pedalboard.

## MULTI-EFFECTS UNITS

The first pedalboards were pretty do-it-yourself; they were basically wooden boards with effects mounted to them, so they still had all the traditional noise and gain problems. Manufacturers were quick to realize that an opportunity existed, and multi-effects units were created.

A multi-effects unit essentially combines various categories into one streamlined package, such as the Korg AX1500G (see Figure 8.25). All of the multi-effect's modules are designed and interfaced to be optimized with each other, so noise is kept low. Eventually, logic was built in, which let guitarists program the units so that one switch could automatically accesses custom effects presets.

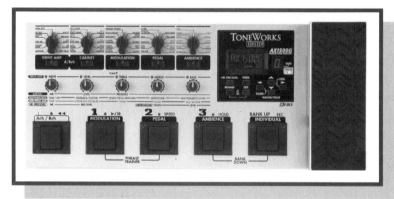

Figure 8.25: Korg AX1500G multi-effects unit

The downside to a multi-effects unit is that if you don't like the sound of some of the onboard modules, or want to use additional pedals, you are back to the same problems as before. Also, if the unit goes down, you're left plugging directly into the amp with no effects at all. With a chain of individual pedals, if one fails it's easy to patch around it and still keep most of your effects intact.

## THE BRADSHAW SWITCHING SYSTEM

In the beginning of the '80s, guitarists playing on high-budget, major-label records became frustrated because they couldn't easily produce those same studio sounds live. Usually the sounds were a result of various high-end rackmount outboard devices from manufacturers such as Lexicon, Eventide and TC Electronic. Many guitarists purchased these same devices to interface with their live rigs, only to find that the impedances and level demands were totally different, which resulted in severe hum and noise problems. Bob Bradshaw, a young electronics tech in Los Angeles, formed Custom Audio Electronics to develop a solution to the problem.

Bradshaw's first system properly interfaced the rackmount studio gear with guitarists' beloved pedals and amplifiers in order to minimize noise, and included a series of switches that would allow each device to be seamlessly turned on or off in true bypass fashion to maintain the tone. Later, he designed a MIDI switching system that included device presets that could be switched instantly during a song (see Figure 8.26). Soon every major guitar player from Eric Clapton to Steve Lukather to the Edge was using his systems.

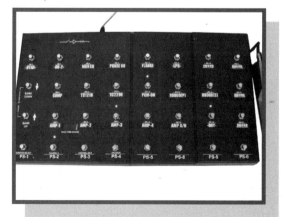

Figure 8.26: Custom Audio Electronics/ Bob Bradshaw Switching System

Bradshaw's systems are built on the premise that the cleanest, quietest effects are a result of the effects being inserted between an amp's preamp section and power amp section (which is why many amps have "Preamp Out–Power Amp In" jacks and level controls). As a result, he designed a rackmount 3-channel preamp that had one Fender-type channel, one Marshall-type channel, and one high-gain channel that would allow the guitarist to easily obtain the sound of each style of amp (his systems also work with all existing amps and make it easy to switch between them). These switching systems have become standard on the LA studio scene, as it allows a player to easily deliver an excellent, quiet guitar sound complete with studio quality effects.

Other suppliers of custom switching systems include Pete Cornish (the UK equivalent to Bradshaw), Pedal-Racks and Rack Systems Ltd.

## LESS-SOPHISTICATED SYSTEMS

Custom Audio Electronics switching systems are custom-designed for each client and as a result, are generally priced out of the range of most guitarists, but many lower-cost systems have appeared on the market to meet the demand for programmable switching systems.

The GigRig Pro14 offers 10 true bypass effects loops, 14 programmable presets and an A/B amp switcher (see Figure 8.27). Similar products include the Voodoo Lab Pedal Switcher, Commander and Ground Control, the Carl Martin Octaswitch, and the TC Electronic G-System, among others.

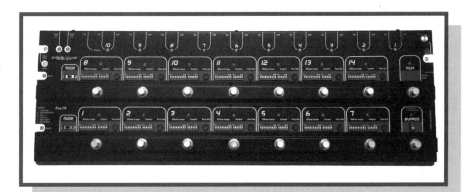

*Figure 8.27: GigRig Pro 14*

### Pedalboards

Multi-effects pedals combine effects from one manufacturer.

Custom pedalboards interface studio effects with pedals and amps.

Programmable pedalboards allow for preset effects set-ups.

Ready-made programmable pedalboards are available.

# Part Two
## Acoustic Guitars

**Chapter 9:**

# A History of the Acoustic Guitar

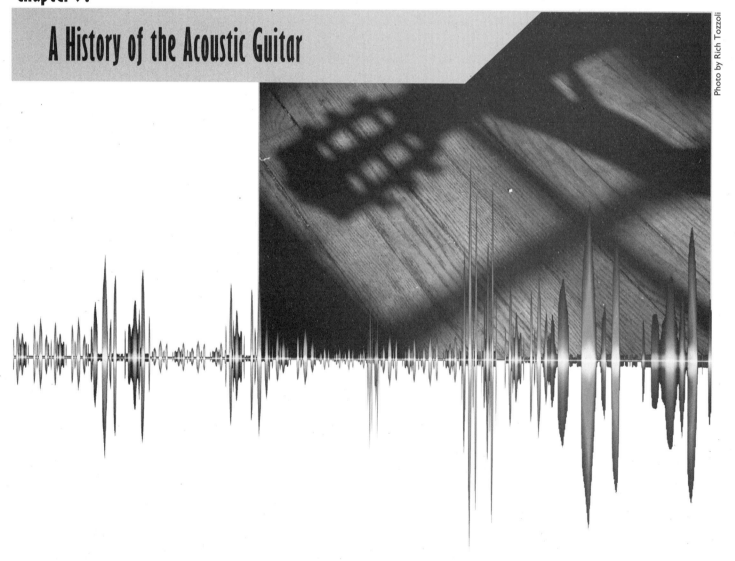

Photo by Rich Tozzoli

While the history of electric and steel string guitars reaches back only into the early 1900s, the acoustic guitar goes back thousands of years. Images from ancient Egyptian, Roman and Babylonian cultures depicted musicians playing stringed instruments that resemble guitars, and similar instruments pop up repeatedly throughout the ages.

While we could devote a very long chapter to the complete history of the guitar and guitar-like instruments, you're probably most interested in the evolution and development of the guitar as we know it today. We'll get to that in a bit—but first, some backstory…

## From the Beginning

Guitars are members of the *chordophone* family, meaning they feature plucked, vibrating strings supported and amplified by a body that helps develop the sound. Various chordophones throughout history have been referred to as guitars, as the English word guitar evolved from the Roman word "cithara."

Stringed instruments from the Renaissance and Baroque periods usually featured four or five *courses*, or pairs of strings. These strings, made from animal gut, were usually tuned either in octaves or in unison. Instruments such as the Spanish and Mexican Vihuela featured five or six courses, which were tuned in fourths.

The modern guitar appears to have evolved from several instruments around the world, including the four-string oud, the Scandavain lute, the Persian sehtar, and more directly, the four-course Moorish guitar (*guitarra moresca*) and the Latin guitar (*guitarra latina*). Eventually, around the 14th century, these instruments were simply called guitars.

## The Originators

Today, many luthiers and companies build wonderful-sounding acoustic guitars. With a variety of incredible tonewoods from around the world, modern technology and historical hands-on techniques, great acoustic instruments are produced in virtually every price range.

There have been many guitar innovations and contributions to the art by many luthiers, but we're going to focus on the three who had the greatest influence on making the acoustic guitar (and the electric) what it is today.

### THE FATHER OF THE MODERN GUITAR

According to guitar history, in 1779, Italian luthier Gaetano Vinaccia created the first single-course six-string guitar with modern tuning. However, Spanish guitar maker Antonio Torres is often credited as being the "Father of the Modern Guitar" because sometime around 1850, he introduced "fan" bracing inside the instrument, which gave it the strength that enabled him to build a larger instrument than was previously possible. Today's modern Spanish and classical guitars still retain much of the same specifications as the original Torres instrument.

## C.F. MARTIN

In 1883, luthier Christian Frederick Martin established the C.F. Martin & Company. He and his company are perhaps the most influential designers of the modern guitar.

Based on the work of Martin's mentor, the famous Austrian luthier Johann Stauffer (see Figure 9.1), Martin's company was responsible for a number of innovations still in use today. Around 1850, Martin & Company began using X-bracing on its instruments to make them stronger. To accommodate the public's demand for louder guitars, the company began building guitars with steel strings on them in the early 1900s. The company also developed the famous dreadnought body around 1916, which was revolutionary because its larger size enabled it to produce more volume, allowing it to compete with other instruments of the time period.

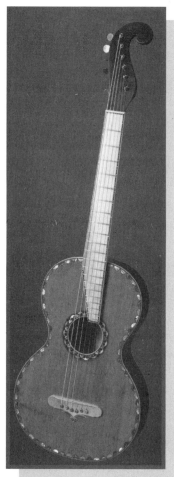

*Figure 9.1: 1830 Martin Stauffer-style guitar*

Another Martin innovation was the 14-fret neck, developed in the late 1930s. Until that time, 12-fret necks were common on guitars, and the 14-fret guitar provided access to more notes on the instrument.

## ORVILLE GIBSON

Luthier Orville Gibson changed the course of guitar history when he founded the Gibson Mandolin-Guitar Mfg. Co., Ltd. in 1902. Gibson was granted a patent on his a guitar design that featured a top shaped like that of a violin, carved and arched from a single piece of wood. This design is known today as the "archtop" acoustic guitar.

The archtop also featured such innovations as f-holes and a movable, adjustable bridge. In 1922, taking the design a step further, the company developed the famous L-5 design, which would influence both acoustic and electric guitars thereafter. The L-5 was electrified in the 1936 (the electric version was named the ES-150), and numerous variations of its style still remain popular.

# Modern Acoustic Guitar Milestones

With all due respect to the many great artisans and innovators that aren't mentioned, here are just a few of the milestones in the development of the evolution of the modern acoustic guitar.

**1833** C.F. Martin arrives in the United States from Austria and builds his first guitars, patterned after designs by his mentor, Johann Stauffer.

**1850** Martin begins producing his own designs and introduces X-bracing and flat-top guitars.

**1894** Orville Gibson begins making his own instruments.

**1902** C.F. Martin introduces the Style 45 and 000 size. The Gibson Mandolin-Guitar Mfg. Co., Ltd. is formed.

**1918** Gibson builds its first flat-top guitar, which would not begin serious production until 1926.

**1917** Martin builds its first steel-string guitar.

**1922** Gibson launches the groundbreaking L-5 guitar and F-5 mandolin. The L-5 implemented designer Lloyd Loar's theory that the body should be tuned to a specific pitch (see Figure 9.2).

**1928** Gibson introduces the first signature-model guitar with the Nick Lucas model (see Figure 9.3).

**1927** Epi Stathopoulo's Epiphone company releases its "recording guitars." Hawaiian music influences guitar construction as the slide, slack-key and open tunings are introduced. National introduces the first resonator guitar, aimed at coaxing more volume from an acoustic instrument.

*Figure 9.2: 1924 Gibson L-5*

*Figure 9.3: 1928 Gibson Nick Lucas Signature Guitar*

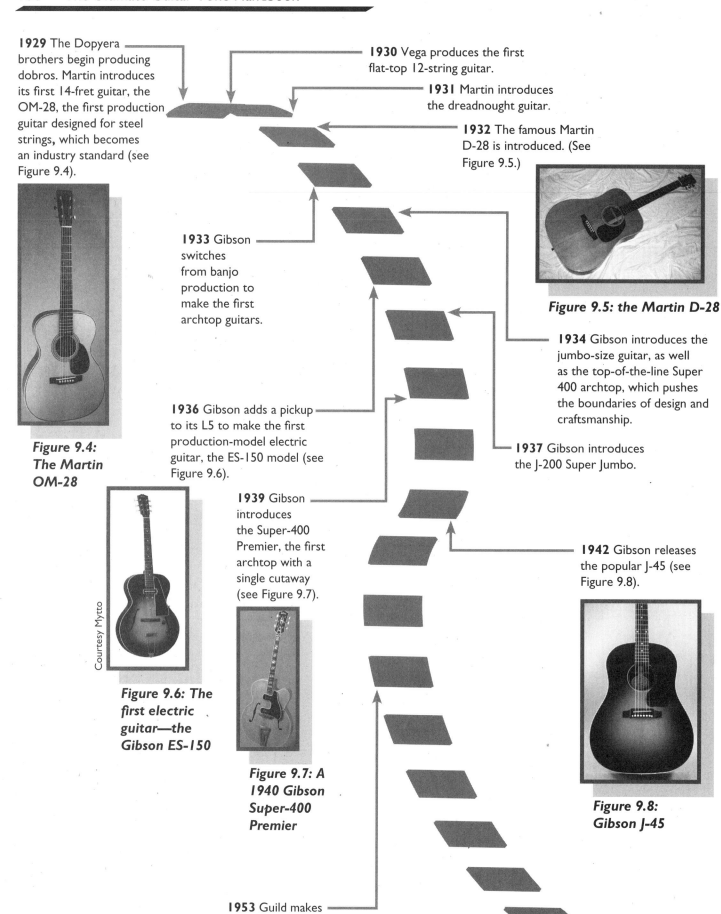

**1929** The Dopyera brothers begin producing dobros. Martin introduces its first 14-fret guitar, the OM-28, the first production guitar designed for steel strings, which becomes an industry standard (see Figure 9.4).

**1930** Vega produces the first flat-top 12-string guitar.

**1931** Martin introduces the dreadnought guitar.

**1932** The famous Martin D-28 is introduced. (See Figure 9.5.)

*Figure 9.4: The Martin OM-28*

**1933** Gibson switches from banjo production to make the first archtop guitars.

*Figure 9.5: the Martin D-28*

**1934** Gibson introduces the jumbo-size guitar, as well as the top-of-the-line Super 400 archtop, which pushes the boundaries of design and craftsmanship.

**1936** Gibson adds a pickup to its L5 to make the first production-model electric guitar, the ES-150 model (see Figure 9.6).

**1937** Gibson introduces the J-200 Super Jumbo.

Courtesy Mytto

**1939** Gibson introduces the Super-400 Premier, the first archtop with a single cutaway (see Figure 9.7).

**1942** Gibson releases the popular J-45 (see Figure 9.8).

*Figure 9.6: The first electric guitar—the Gibson ES-150*

*Figure 9.7: A 1940 Gibson Super-400 Premier*

*Figure 9.8: Gibson J-45*

**1953** Guild makes its first flat-top models: the F-30, F-40 and F-50.

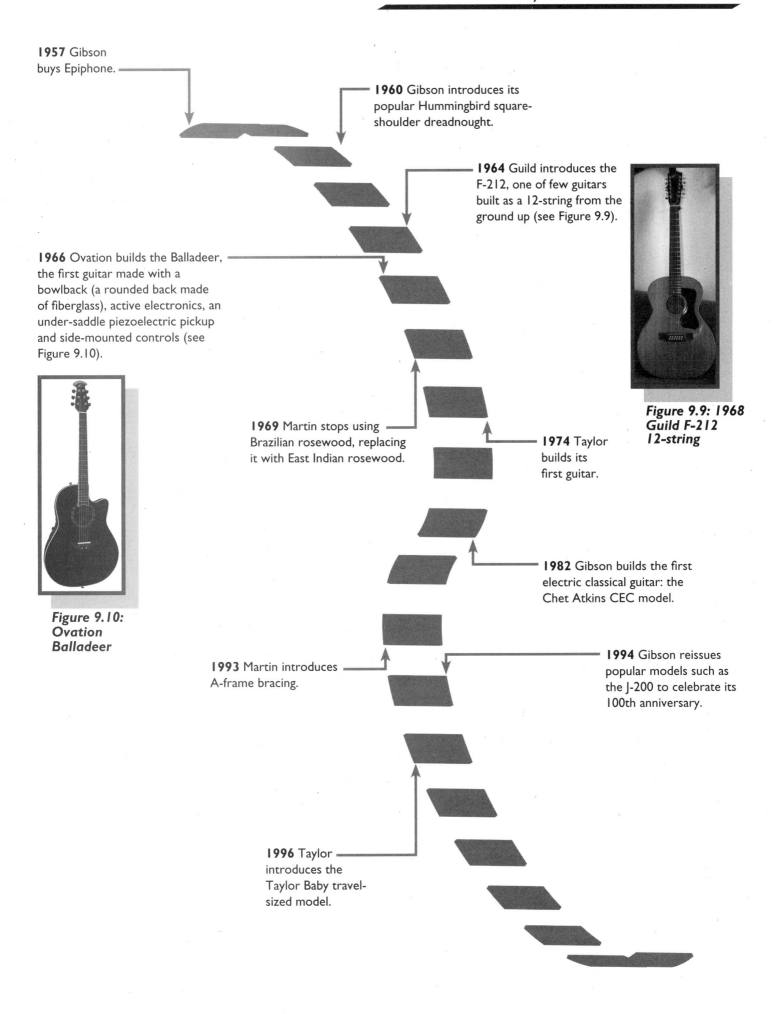

**1957** Gibson buys Epiphone.

**1960** Gibson introduces its popular Hummingbird square-shoulder dreadnought.

**1964** Guild introduces the F-212, one of few guitars built as a 12-string from the ground up (see Figure 9.9).

**1966** Ovation builds the Balladeer, the first guitar made with a bowlback (a rounded back made of fiberglass), active electronics, an under-saddle piezoelectric pickup and side-mounted controls (see Figure 9.10).

*Figure 9.9: 1968 Guild F-212 12-string*

*Figure 9.10: Ovation Balladeer*

**1969** Martin stops using Brazilian rosewood, replacing it with East Indian rosewood.

**1974** Taylor builds its first guitar.

**1982** Gibson builds the first electric classical guitar: the Chet Atkins CEC model.

**1993** Martin introduces A-frame bracing.

**1994** Gibson reissues popular models such as the J-200 to celebrate its 100th anniversary.

**1996** Taylor introduces the Taylor Baby travel-sized model.

# Chapter 10:

## Tonal Characteristics of an Acoustic Guitar

Photo by Rich Tozzoli

It's difficult to describe the sound of an acoustic guitar. Luthiers have attempted to define the elements that comprise a "great" sound, and while there are no definitive answers to this great question, there is a set of considerations.

Before we look at the tonal factors that make up an acoustic guitar, here's a brief overview of how it works (see Figure 10.1). Think of an acoustic guitar as a drum; the back and sides are the shell, and the top is the head. Plucked or strummed strings transmit vibrations through the bridge and saddle to the soundboard (the top) of the instrument. The back and sides project and amplify the sound outward through the top. Sound bracing provides resonation and strength necessary to absorb stress applied by the strings. With that in mind, let's look at how each component affects the guitar's tone.

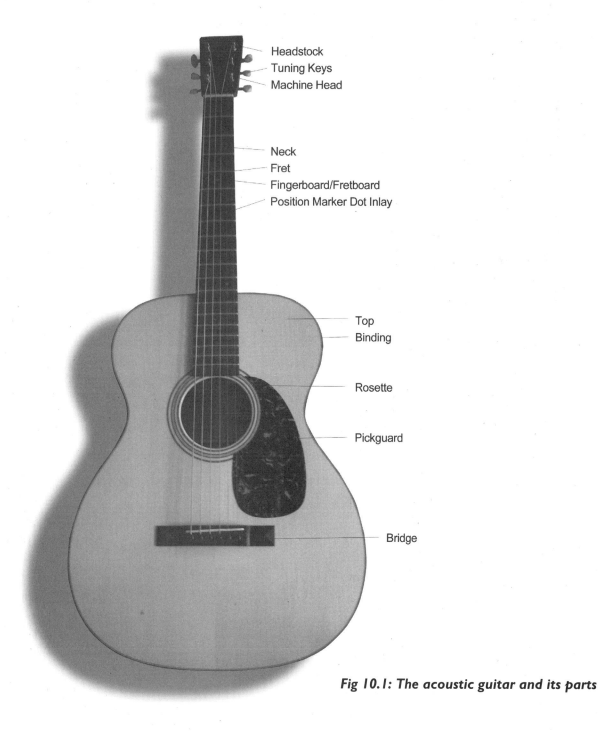

*Fig 10.1: The acoustic guitar and its parts*

# Acoustic Guitar Types

There are three basic types of acoustic guitars: nylon-string, steel-string, and archtops. Each has unique characteristics.

## NYLON-STRING

Nylon-string guitars are categorized as either classical guitars (also known as Spanish guitars) or flamenco guitars. Both use nylon strings and differ from other acoustic guitars in that they do not have a truss rod. For the most part, the flamenco and classical styles are more alike than different. Let's take a look at them.

### Flamenco

Flamenco guitars typically have shallower bodies, lower action, less bracing and thinner soundboards than their classical counterparts. This construction, along with wood choice, contributes to that bright, percussive sound that flamenco guitarists seek. Flamenco bodies are usually made of maple, cypress or sycamore, with spruce or cedar tops. Some models also feature a *golpeador*, a large tap plate used as a finger rest (see Figure 10.2).

*Figure 10.2: Flamenco guitar with golpeador tap plate*

### Classical

The Spanish-style nylon-string guitar has become known as a classical guitar primarily because the repertoire played on it is classical in nature (see Figure 10.3). Classical guitars are typically made with rosewood or mahogany back and sides, and spruce or cedar tops. Its action is usually set up higher than a flamenco guitar, and it often features classic fan bracing inside, in which a center piece of light wood such as spruce is glued to the soundboard along with braces fanning out on either side (see Figure 10.4).

*Figure 10.3: A typical classical guitar*

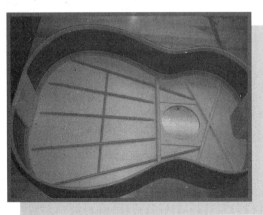

*Figure 10.4: Center fan bracing inside a classical guitar*

## STEEL-STRING

Steel-string, or flat-top guitars, are direct descendants of Spanish/classical guitars. Early Spanish guitars with gut strings did not project enough volume to compete with other instruments of the the early 1900s, so around 1921, manufacturers such as C.F. Martin began outfitting guitars with steel strings to make them louder (see Figure 10.5).

*Figure 10.5: A typical steel-string guitar*

To compensate for the increased tension on the guitar body, Martin needed to enhance and strengthen the internal bracing, and developed the X-bracing that's used today in most steel string guitars (see Figure 10.6).

With the advent of these 'new' steel-string guitars, players began to experiment with new playing techniques such as bending strings and playing with slides, which contributed to entirely new forms of music. Eventually, the steel-string guitar became popular in musical genres ranging from blues to country to folk and beyond.

*Figure 10.6: X-bracing inside a steel-string guitar*

### The Archtops

Archtop guitars were developed in the 1890s by Orville Gibson (of Gibson Guitar fame) and featured a carved or pressure-laminated arched wooden top, constructed from a single piece of wood and featuring f-holes instead of a traditional single soundhole (see Figure 10.7). The back of the guitar was also often carved out of a single piece of wood.

Archtop guitars feature a tailpiece and a floating bridge, traditions (along with the f-holes) borrowed from violin makers. Archtops became so popular with jazz musicians in the '20s and '30s that companies like Gibson began outfitting archtop guitars such as their L5CES model with a pickup, which could then be plugged into an amplifier to compete with louder instruments in a band.

*Figure 10.7: Archtop guitar with f-holes*

### 12-Fret

A 12-fret guitar simply means that its 12th fret meets the edge of its body. Most guitars were 12-fret models until the early 1900s, when many players asked luthiers to build instruments that let them access extended higher notes on the fretboard. As a result, Martin developed the 14-fret model in 1929.

*Figure 10.8: Martin 000-18 Norman Blake 12-fret*

12-fret guitars are the same scale length (the distance between the bridge saddles and the nut; see section below) as 14-fret guitars, but they alter the position of the bridge and the soundhole, which become more centered in the top. For example, models such as Martin's 24.9-inch scale-length 000-18 Norman Blake guitar features a body shape like the 14-fret 0000 model, but the neck is joined at the 12th fret (see Figure 10.8). This design allows its bracing to be shifted forward so it crosses just below the sound hole. The bridge is offset as well, which increases the guitar's vibration and projection. 12-fret guitars tend have an open, bright and airy sound, which often makes them preferred instruments of fingerstyle players.

### Notes on Acoustic Guitars

Flamenco guitars have shallower bodies, lower action and thinner tops than classical nylon-string guitars.

Steel-string guitars were created to project more volume than nylon-string guitars.

An archtop's tailpiece, floating bridge and f-holes are borrowed from the violin.

Finger pickers prefer 12-fret guitars for their bright, airy sound.

# Basic Tonal Factors

Beyond the basic body style, many elements contribute to an acoustic guitar's sound. We'll look at a few major components.

## WOOD

A guitar's size, types of strings used, style of picks, finger technique, soundboard, nut material and even bracing structure all have an effect on its sound. However, the woods used to build the top and body are arguably the most important factors in determining the tone.

Most acoustic guitars are primarily made of wood, and every type of wood has a sonic character and soul. Rosewood-bodied guitars will sound different from mahogany, which will sound different from koa. Wood comes in many varieties from different parts of the world, and even different species of the same wood sound different from each other.

### Back and Sides

The wood used to construct a guitar's back and sides must be resonant and effective at reflecting sound. Rosewood has always been considered the best wood for this application because of its ideal bass response, with Brazilian rosewood being the most desirable sub-species. It's hard, dense and resonant, colors the tone in a pleasing way and absorbs the vibrations from the top. Brazilian rosewood is now extremely rare, however, and its use is restricted, so other types of rosewood are used instead.

East Indian rosewood is softer than Brazilian rosewood, but it's the most widely available rosewood and offers a rich bass response, while Cambodian, Amazon and Madagascar rosewood have many of the same tonal properties as Brazilian and are sometimes used as a substitutes. Tulipwood and Kingwood are also members of the rosewood family, but they have problems with availability and quality, and are difficult to find in sizes large enough to build guitar bodies.

Each wood type has strengths and weaknesses. Rosewood makes for wonderful live guitars, but will not always be appropriate in the studio because they offer additional bass response. Mahogany, on the other hand, has a very crisp, crystalline and glassine tone that works well for recording because it's an extremely light wood without the reflectivity of rosewood. Of course, both can be used successfully in the right studio recording situation.

Hawaiian Koa is a popular wood for guitar making, since it has a density that falls between mahogany and rosewood. Maple is a traditional choice for violins and many other instruments because it's extremely hard, it doesn't have the resonance of rosewood and its tone is sometimes considered harsh for guitars. A maple body can be tempered with the right soundboard wood, however, sometimes resulting in a very projective, powerful sound. Ovankol (also called shedua or African teak) isn't as dense as rosewood, so its tone is somewhat dark.

### The Soundboard

The soundboard's job is to be light enough to vibrate, yet be strong enough to withstand string tension. Spruce has the highest strength-to-weight ratio of any of the woods, which is why it's a typical choice for a guitar top, although cedar, redwood, mahogany and koa wood are also used (none of them are as light as spruce, however, so they produce totally different tones).

Adirondack spruce is known for its great tone, but much of it grows in protected forests, so supplies are very limited. Sitka spruce from Alaska is very strong and easily available, and has become a popular choice for most guitar tops. Engelmann spruce has a very light weight and produces a very open sound, but because it's not as strong as the others, there's a potential problem with its longevity (which is also true of cedar).

Carpathian and Italian alpine spruces from Europe fall somewhere between Sitka and Adirondack in tonality, but they're rare and come at a premium price. Mahogany is sometimes used for soundboards but it has less projection and fewer overtones than spruce, which produces a punchier sound with less bass.

### Necks and Fretboards

Mahogany or cedar are typical woods used in necks. Cedar is a little lighter in weight but mahogany is extremely stable and easy to carve. Ebony is often used for the fingerboard and bridge because it's very dense and durable, although rosewood is also a good material for fingerboards and bridges as well. For a more in-depth look at tone woods, check out the interview of Martin Guitar's Dick Boak in Part 3 of this book.

| Woods and Their Tonal Qualities | |
| --- | --- |
| **Wood Type** | **Description** |
| **Rosewood** | Great projection and balanced tone with excellent bass response |
| **Mahogany** | Fewer overtones, crisper and less bass than rosewood. Necks are warm sounding. |
| **Spruce** | Lightweight, yet stiff; used for tops. Good projection and clarity. |
| **Ebony** | Lowest projection of all woods; used mostly for necks. |
| **Koa** | Low projection and lots of mid-range; used for soundboards. When used for back and sides, behaves like mahogany with more mid-range. |
| **Maple** | Low projection, few overtones, can be harsh sounding. |
| **Cedar** | Lightweight but stiff, used for tops and necks. Rich in harmonics and crispness. |

## BODY SIZE

Both nylon- and steel-string acoustic guitars come in various body sizes and shapes. Although a guitar's size impacts overall tone, sensitivity and volume, the relationship between big guitars and loud volume is not a black and white issue. Much depends on the type of wood used for the back, sides and top, the instrument design and construction method, and the skill and technique of the luthier or company building it. That said, there are many standard guitar sizes, and they all have an affect on tone and volume.

*Figure 10.9: Martin D Series dreadnought guitar*

### Dreadnought

Dreadnoughts, made famous by the Martin Guitar Company in 1916 and named after the legendary World War 1-era English battleships of the early 1900s, are the most popular large guitar size (see Figure 10.9). Although Martin was the first to produce dreadnoughts, many other guitar makers such as Bourgeois, Alvarez, Collings and Taylor make guitars in this size. Some guitars, such as Gibson's classic J-45, are referred to as a "rounded-shoulder" dreadnought (see Figure 10.10), due to the instrument's rounded upper bout, or outward curve in the body.

*Figure 10.10: Gibson J-45 rounded-shoulder dreadnought*

### Jumbo

A jumbo guitar is even larger than a dreadnought, and projects a slightly rounder and deeper sound. Jumbo guitars are also referred to as concert- and auditorium-size guitars, but many manufacturers have their own names for guitar sizes. For example, Paul Reed Smith calls its jumbo model a "Tonare Grand." Other examples of jumbo guitars include the Guild F-50 (see Figure 10.11), Gibson J-200, Goodall Concert Jumbo, Lowden 023 series Jumbo and the Wechter 5714 Elite Jumbo.

*Figure 10.11: Guild F-50 jumbo guitar*

### Mini-Jumbo

A mini-jumbo is slightly smaller than a jumbo, and is a style available from builders such as Seagull and Hohner (see Figure 10.12). These large instruments have more wood both on the top, back and sides than a dreadnought, so they project a lot of volume, and tend to offer extended bass response.

### Small-Body

Smaller-bodied guitars are inclined to offer crisper highs and a smoother midrange, but offer a bit less bass than jumbos or dreadnoughts. Guitars such as the Martin OM-1, Guild F-30 and Larrivee OM-5 are revered by folk and blues players for their compact size and smooth tone. Over the years, many small-body guitars have been produced, such as the Classic, Parlor, Salon, Steels, 00, 000, Artist, NEX, Folk, and many others.

*Figure 10.12: Seagull Mini-Jumbo*

## Cutaways

Some guitar bodies feature cutaways on their lower bout. While this style slightly reduces the bracing design and the amount of sound a guitar projects, it does allow easier access to the higher frets. For example, Ovation's popular Adamas Series (which features a semi-parabolic body made of aerospace composites) includes several models with deep cutaways for easy high-fret access (see Figure 10.13).

*Figure 10.13: Ovation Adamas Series cutaway model*

### Figure 10.14: Guitar Sizes

| Guitar Sizes | Characteristics |
| --- | --- |
| Jumbo | Rounder and deeper than a dreadnought. |
| Mini-Jumbo | Loud with better bass response. |
| Dreadnought | The most popular guitar size. |
| Small-Body | Crisper highs, smoother mid-range, but less bass than a dreadnought. |
| Cutaway | Easy high fret access but a little less volume as a result. |

## THE NECK

Like on an electric guitar, an acoustic guitar neck features a fretboard, frets, headstock, truss rod (on a steel-string guitar) and tuning pegs. Typically, the neck on an acoustic instrument is attached via a "set-in," in which the neck joins the body in a dovetail or mortise-and-tenon-style joint with adhesive. Taylor guitars are unusual in this respect since they use a custom screw system instead of glued set-in necks.

Necks are typically constructed from hardwoods such as mahogany, but other woods, such as ebony or cedar, can be used. The fingerboard (sometimes called fretboard), which sits on the neck, is typically made of a different material, such as ebony or rosewood. Some neck fretboards may be scalloped, which creates a "U" shape between each fret to make string bends easier, as preferred by guitarists such as John McLaughlin.

Acoustic guitar necks are under a huge amount of tension, especially when using heavy-gauge strings, so they incorporate a truss rod for stability, to maintain stable tuning and pitch. Nylon-string guitars typically don't suffer from this problem because they have less tension on the neck. Although the fretboard wood doesn't contribute much to the guitar's tone, a rosewood or ebony fretboard can feel different to the player, which may alter how he or she plays the instrument.

### Radius

A fretboard's radius is the arc to which the fingerboard is sanded, which has a big effect on the way the neck feels in your hands. The radius can affect response traits that are important to players, such as finger comfort, chord fingering and note bending.

If you think of the neck as a cylinder, the fretboard radius is simply a segment of that circle. The typical steel-string acoustic has a fretboard radius anywhere from 12 to 17 inches or so, measured with a tool called a radius gauge.

Mathematically, the value of the radius number represents the distance to a center point of the theoretical circle that its arc runs along, but simply put, it's the actual curve of the fretboard.  Smaller numbers represent rounder necks and larger numbers represent flatter necks. Many classical guitars have flat fretboards, with a zero radius measurement. A typical Martin steel-string acoustic might have a radius of 16 inches, a Gibson acoustic is typically 12 inches and a Fender Strat has a radius of 9.5 inches. Classical guitars are almost totally flat. Usually, the flatter the radius, the easier it is to lower the action of the guitar by lowering the strings towards the frets.

### Nuts

As with an electric guitar, the nut of an acoustic guitar guides the strings from the tuning pegs to the fretboard. Positioned where the fretboard meets the headstock, it can be made of bone, stainless steel, graphite, Micarta, plastic or other materials.

Nuts aid in the vibration and tuning of the strings, and some guitarists employ the trick of using pencil lead to lubricate the area where the strings slide through the nut's individual grooves. This helps smooth the friction caused by a moving string, especially when players bend notes. Some guitars also use roller nuts, or even what's known as a "zero fret" (which is higher than the other frets, so the strings directly rest on it) just in front of the nut itself. Different nut materials create slight differences in tone, so guitarists frequently experiment by changing the type of nut on their guitar.

### Scale Length

The scale length of an acoustic guitar is simply the distance between the bridge saddles and the nut. The strings will vibrate and create sound within that measured length, with the 12th fret positioned exactly at the midpoint. Scale length directly affects string tension, which therefore affects the way a guitar plays and feels.

Typical scale lengths depend on the guitar model, but classical guitars typically have a scale length of 25.6 or 26 inches, while a Martin 000 is 24.9 inches and a Taylor acoustic is 25.5 inches (see Figure 10.15). As a comparison, a Strat is 25.5 inches and a Les Paul is 24.75 inches.

Longer scale-length guitars require more tension on the strings than a shorter scale-length guitar to play the same pitch. They tend to feature tighter strings and have a crisper, punchier feel as a result. In addition, they produce a louder volume and tend to have more clarity, especially in the bass.

*Figure 10.15: A 25.5-inch scale-length Taylor 210CE acoustic*

The classic scale-length comparison is that of a longer-scale Fender Strat, at 25½ inches, and the shorter-scale Gibson Les Paul, at 24¾ inches. Most would argue that the Les Paul, strung up with the exact same set of strings as the Strat, has a "looser" or "slinkier" feel, and is a bit easier to play. The Strat tends to have a more defined sound with a tighter bottom, which is due in part to the fact that the shorter-scale Les Paul needs less tension on the strings to reach the same pitch. As a result, it's easier to bend notes on short-scale guitars, depending of course on the string gauge used. Shorter-scale acoustic guitars tend to have a lighter, more expressive sound than longer-scale models, which feature a louder, more bass-heavy sound. Think about what happens when you capo your acoustic guitar: If you place a capo on the third fret and then tune the guitar to concert pitch, the strings will have less tension on them. The capo is changing the scale length, and therefore, not only the feel of the instrument, but the tone as well.

## GUITAR AGING

Although a guitar should sound great freshly made coming off the line, it improves with age. According to Martin's Dick Boak, the aging process happens in three stages:

- In the first three to six months, the guitar's lacquer hardens and shrinks, which begins to open up the sound with more high frequencies and fewer mids.

- Within three to five years, the finish shrinks even more, down to about half of its original thickness. The simple act of playing the guitar causes the lacquer and the wood to vibrate as a single unit, which further opens up the tone.

- Over an extended period of time, the guitar expels much of the wood's moisture weight. This makes the guitar dryer and lighter, which affects the way all the parts vibrate together, further improving the tone.

## STRINGS

Whether your acoustic guitar uses nylon or steel strings, their thickness, type, gauge and age will have a profound impact on the instrument's sound and tuning.

### Nylon Strings

Strings were historically made from the intestines of animals such as sheep and goat, and were called catgut or gut strings. Today's modern strings for classical or flamenco guitars are made of advanced polymer materials, primarily nylon filament and plastic threads, wound with bronze or silver wire. However, few companies still make original gut strings as well.

### Steel Strings

Steel strings were first developed in the early 1900s to provide a brighter tone and more volume than nylon. There are many different kinds of steel strings available, each with its own character. They range from the popular phosphor bronze-wound style to unique blends of bronze and steel or silk and steel. Typically, the heavier the string gauge, the more volume an acoustic guitar will have. However, heavier strings will also apply more stress to the guitar's neck.

Several companies coat their acoustic strings with durable materials to make them last longer, such as Elixir strings with Nanoweb Coating and D'Addario's EXP coated strings.

## FINGERS AND PICKS

Whether you're playing steel or nylon strings, playing with your fingers or a pick will produce a variety of different tones. Fingerstyle players strike strings with their fingernails, fingertips or a set of picks attached to their fingers; many feel that playing this way provides more tonal control and expressive dynamics than using a traditional pick, since they touch the strings directly. This is especially true with classical and flamenco players.

Playing with a pick (plectrum), often referred to as flat picking, creates more attack; this style can be used either on individual notes or chords. Some players use a hybrid style of fingerpicking and flatpicking.

Today's picks are made out of many kinds of materials including plastic, tortoiseshell, felt, wood, rubber, stone and others. Each type of pick, depending on its thickness, shape and material, will provide a different sound, so it helps to have various kinds on hand, depending on your needs.

### Factors Affecting Tone

The wood used to build the guitar's top and body is the biggest contributor to tone.

Rosewood offers more bottom end, but mahogany sometimes records better.

The dreadnought is the most popular guitar size.

Larger-size guitar models are often louder, and may offer more bass.

The fretboard wood and radius are important considerations for player comfort and feel.

Longer-scale-length guitars have more volume and clarity.

The more a guitar is played, the better it sounds.

# Chapter 11:

## Acoustic Guitar Miking Techniques

Photo by Rich Tozzoli

The techniques used to record acoustic guitars vary widely from engineer to engineer, producer to producer, and guitar player to guitar player. Depending on the type and quantity of microphones, DIs and/or amplifiers in your collection, with a little care, a number of mix-and-match methods can all lead to a great sound. In this chapter, we'll look at ways to record your acoustic guitar, give you some preparation tips, and take a look at the actual recording process.

# Acoustic Guitar Recording 101

Before we get into actual mic placements and recording set-ups, let's take a look at some good practices to follow both before and during the recording.

## RECORDING PREPARATION

It would be nice if all there was to recording was plugging your mic in and playing, but unfortunately, it's not that easy. Before you record your first note of an acoustic guitar, take the following steps.

### Change your Strings

It may seem obvious, but putting on a fresh set of strings may help alleviate potentially problematic issues such as bad intonation and a lackluster tone. Don't be lazy about this step, because unless you're going for a dull sound, a fresh set of strings will make the instrument resonate better, and therefore sound better in the microphones placed around it. Recordings are snapshots of time, and you won't want to listen back after that magic performance and wish you had a clearer, brighter sound because you didn't change your strings. With an electric guitar, you can compensate slightly for dead strings by turning up the treble on the amp—no such luck when recording an acoustic (unless you choose to run it through an amp, of course). Also, fresh strings will hold the guitar's tuning longer, which will in turn make for a smoother recording session. You can even put a little graphite from a pencil in the nut slots to let the strings move a bit easier. Don't forget to keep wiping your strings down during the session, as the dirt and oil from your fingers as well as simple oxidation in the air will shorten their useful life. Remember that the type and thickness of string you use, which will be dictated in part by the type of instrument you play, will also alter the tone of your guitar.

### Tune It Up

Tune your guitar with the most precise tuner that you can get your hands on, and check to see that it's intonated correctly. Do this by tuning each string, then playing its harmonic at the 12th fret and fretting each string at the 12th fret. All three should register "true" on the tuner. If they don't, your intonation is off, so either fix it or be prepared to work around it.

### Listen to the Guitar

Sit quietly with the instrument and play it for a few minutes. Listen closely for buzzes on the neck. They signal positions you should avoid if there are issues that can't be immediately fixed. Get a good feel for how the instrument really sounds now so you can compare it to the recording when you hear it played back.

### Listen to the Room

Listen to how the guitar resonates in the room that you're playing in. A good room will definitely complement the sound of an acoustic guitar. Consider whether the room is worth miking. Do a quick check of the room by loudly clapping your hands and listening for unwanted echoes or reflective "pings." If the room doesn't sound good, it will dictate the type of mic you choose because you'll want to pick up less ambience in the recording. However, if the room does sound good but has too much reverb, your guitar can end up sounding cloudy and less defined. You can sometimes overcome this problem by setting up on a rug instead of the hard floor to keep reflections to a minimum.

A short, bright room sound is best for acoustic guitar recording, especially when the room includes any combination of wood, tile and brick (see Figure 11.1). Carpeting will deaden the sound, depending on the thickness, so use it sparingly. To get a woody room tone in a carpeted space, lay down an area of wood tiles like the kind you find in a hardware store. The sound of the guitar will reflect off the floor, depending on the type of wood and the amount that you laid down. Having the guitarist face a heavy wooden door is another great trick to gain some additional positive reflections, if needed.

*Figure 11.1: Clubhouse Studios – An example of an excellent recording environment*

In mediocre-to-poor-sounding rooms, consider close-miking the guitar with a tight cardioid mic to keep the sound focused only on the projection of the instrument. Avoid using omnidirectional mics in poor-sounding rooms, because the 360-degree pickup pattern will capture unwanted room reflections that will not complement the overall sound.

### Stand Back from the Instrument

If possible, have someone else play the guitar using the same technique (pick or finger-style) as you do, since the sound that you hear from the player's position is different from the sound that the mics pick up. Close your eyes, move around, and to try to listen for that sweet spot where the guitar sounds best as its direct sound combines with the reflections of the room. Is the best sound on the neck, on the body, or both? Do you hear your instrument resonate better from a few feet back, or up close? The only way to know is to listen. The results may surprise you, since different acoustic guitars project in different ways. Remember that the soundhole may not always be the best choice for mic placement. Doing all of this listening will help you make useful suggestions to the engineer (or yourself!).

### Consider the Guitar's Part in the Production

Before you begin, think about the guitar's place in the mix. Is the part you're about to track supposed to fit into a dense mix, a sparse mix, or be recorded solo? Discuss this with the engineer/producer ahead of time, as the arrangement may dictate not only the type of guitar you choose, but also the number of mics you use on it. Do you really need to use stereo mics? The more mics you use, the wider the sonic space you can create in the mix, but this effect might not be what the song calls for.

### Take Off your Clothes

Well, at least take off any offensive items such as watches, rings or other jewelry that might bang against the instrument. Also, certain jackets and/or shirts may have buttons that can cause a problem. And no big belt buckles! Many great takes have had to be redone because of extraneous noise from clothing and jewelry, so remove the problem before it even becomes one.

## CHOOSING A MICROPHONE

The acoustic guitar is a surprisingly dynamic instrument that requires a microphone that is able to capture its transients as well as its wide frequency response. While you can always put up a dynamic mic such as a Shure SM57 (which has been successfully used on countless records), be aware that it (like most dynamic mics) has a limited frequency response and can be slow to catch the instrument's transients. Dynamic mics are tough and rugged, but they may not be right for recording an acoustic guitar, especially when you're relying on a single mic to capture the sound.

### The Condenser Microphone

To capture more of the guitar's details and transients, reach for a good condenser mic, which has enough sensitivity to capture all of the fine details of an acoustic instrument. Many engineers' first choice is a small-diaphragm condenser, such as the classic AKG C451 (see Figure 11.2), Neumann KM-184, Rode NT5, Shure SM-81, DPA 4011 or the Schoeps CMC 5 with an MK4 cardioid capsule. A small diaphragm allows for excellent high-frequency accuracy and a tight pick-up pattern.

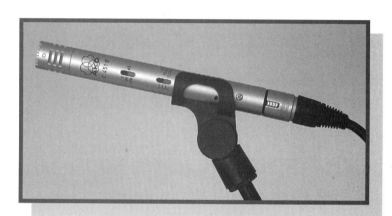

Figure 11.2: An AKG C451 microphone.

You can also choose a large-diaphragm mic, which will have a greater sensitivity due to the larger diaphragm, and a traditionally warm bass response (see Figure 11.3). Well-known acoustic guitar mics in this category include the AKG C414, Neumann U87, U67 and TLM 102, Audio-Technica AT4033 and AT4050, and the Blue Microphones Bluebird and Kiwi.

If your microphone has multiple pickup patterns, experiment with them. For example, the AKG C414 XL II, has nine pickup pattern options, including wide cardioid, cardioid and hypercardioid. Each pattern will have its own subtle characteristic, and the only way to know which one suits your track is to record a little with each and listen back. Some multi-pattern mics also offer omni recording, which can work amazingly well with acoustic guitars.

Figure 11.3: Large-diaphragm microphone placed 12 inches from the soundhole

Omni, or omnidirectional, microphones, have a 360-degree polar pattern. That means that they will record sounds coming from behind the mic as well as they record sounds at the front and sides. This can be very useful when capturing the sound of the room along with your guitar, providing the room sounds good! Many omnidirectional microphones are extremely accurate, offering a very detailed organic recording of the instrument. They also are less prone to proximity effect, so you can place them closer to the soundhole without the additional bass buildup.

To place an omnidirectional mic, start where the guitar's fretboard meets the soundhole, about 6 to 12 inches away from the instrument. As you move further from the instrument, the balance between the direct sound of the guitar and the room sound will begin to favor the room. Omnis work great when placed at a point slightly higher than the spot where the soundhole is pointing, but again, take into consideration the guitar sound in the room and reflections coming off the floor. Use the polar pattern to your advantage, and listen back to a recorded sample in the control room to make sure you don't have too much room sound, since it can't be removed after the fact.

Engineers have had excellent results using omni mics such as the Earthworks QTC40 and M50 (see Figure 11.4), DPA 4006, M-Audio Sputnik, Neumann M150 Tube, Schoeps CMC 5 with MK3 omni capsule, and Blue Microphones' Snowball.

*Figure 11.4:*
*Earthworks QTC40*
*omni mic*

### The Ribbon Microphone

Ribbon mics, with their inherently warm, natural sound and flat frequency response, can effectively capture the full sound of an acoustic guitar. While some of the older, vintage models are rather fragile and can't take high sound pressure levels (SPLs), today's new generation of ribbon mics are built a lot tougher than their predecessors. Aside from their low noise floor and the ability to take high SPLs (upwards of 135 dB!), by design, ribbons have a figure-8 polar pattern. However, the Beyerdynamic M 160 ribbon mic features dual ribbons and has a Hypercardioid polar pattern.

The mic's figure-8 pattern will pick up sound in both the front and the rear of the mic (see Figure 11.5). In fact, the popular Royer R-121 (see Figure 11.6) has a feature in which at distances of three feet or less from the source, the back of the mic has a slightly brighter frequency response than the front. This is very useful if you only have a single mic to work with and want to capture some room ambience, since one mic will record both the direct sound and the room.

Figure 11.6: Royer R-121 ribbon microphone

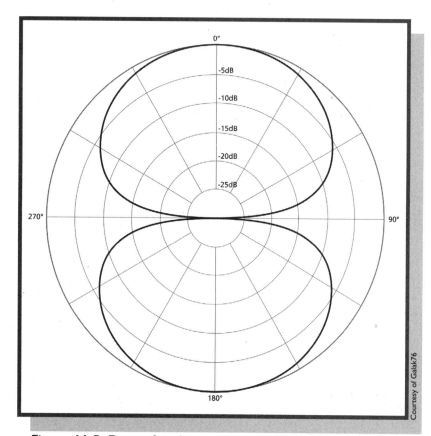

*Courtesy of Galak76*

**Figure 11.5: Figure-8 polar pattern**

Other excellent ribbon mics include the AEA R84, Shure KSM 313, and Audio-Technica AT 4080 and AT 4081. These will all give you that classic warm ribbon sound. Ribbon mics also work especially well in combination with other microphone types.

## UNDERSTANDING RECORDING LEVELS

It's important to discuss the level at which an acoustic guitar should be tracked, since bad levels can ruin an otherwise great performance. Using great mics and paying careful attention to placement means nothing if the recorded track is distorted and unusable. First and foremost, avoid clipping the signal—you can't undo this later. Distortion, unless expressly intentional, certainly won't complement the sound of an otherwise clean guitar.

### Setting Levels

When setting levels, think about the entire signal path. For most sessions, this breaks down to signal going from the guitar into the microphone, into the preamp, then into the recorder (see Figure 11.7). If you have additional outboard gear such as a compressor in the path, take that into account when determining your best gain staging.

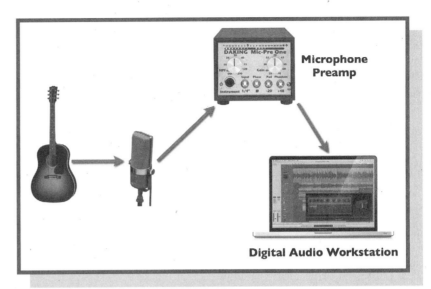

**Figure 11.7: Typical guitar signal path**

When setting basic levels, make sure to play a few chords louder than you will play them when you're recording the actual part. This lets the engineer set the preamp input so it won't clip when you play at a normal level (see Figure 11.8). While it's not always possible to practice real-world playing levels, it's worth taking a few minutes to try to make it happen.

### If You Hear Distortion...

If the signal is clipping, start by making sure that the preamp level isn't too hot, then check any additional outboard gear to determine whether it's clipping. If the signal is still too hot, you may have to back off the input level of the preamp itself, insert an attenuation pad, or move the mic farther away from the guitar. Take the time to set your gain stage correctly. Countless takes have had to be redone

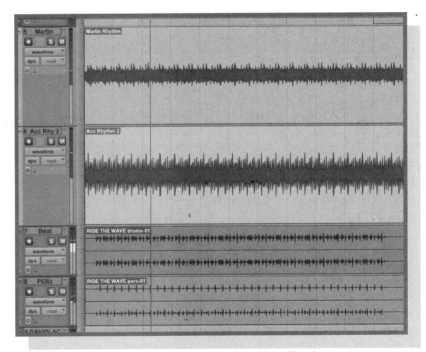

**Figure 11.8: Clean waveform levels in Pro Tools**

because the preamp level was too hot, thereby causing distortion. Leave yourself enough headroom to work with; you can always turn it up later. If everything seems to be operating at the proper level, make sure your mic is working properly and that your cables and connections are all clean.

Also, make sure to inspect the preamp itself. Confirm that the phase button is not switched in (unless you want it to be in). If the preamp is the channel-strip type, make sure you switch effects such as EQ and compression out (more on that shortly). The same applies if you're using a console channel strip. If there's a separate output to the DAW or tape machine, make sure that level is set so it won't distort the loudest signal peaks that the mic captures.

If you're using an internal pickup/DI combination, make sure that the guitar's preamp isn't overloading at the source. Also, if using a DI box, be sure to check its phase as well. Every little detail is important.

**Acoustic Guitar Recording 101**

Change your strings, intonate and tune up.

Listen to the guitar and the room before you record.

Make sure your clothing and jewelry do not add noise.

Remember that condenser mics are good at capturing an acoustic's transients and frequency range.

Pay attention to your signal path before you record.

Check everything in the signal path if you hear distortion.

## Acoustic Guitar Miking Set-Ups

Like with the electric guitar, the acoustic guitar offers a number of miking possibilities and everyone has their favorite. Let's discuss a few widely-used techniques and their variations.

### SINGLE-MIC TECHNIQUES

Using a single microphone is the easiest way to mike an acoustic. If you're using just one mic for recording, consider the wide dynamic range of the acoustic guitar. Here are a few ways to get the most out of a single microphone.

### Single-Mic Technique #1: Where the Neck Meets the Soundhole

To record the true natural sound and acoustic output of the guitar with one mic, place a mic 6 to 12 inches straight out from the point where the guitar's neck meets the soundhole (see Figure 11.9). This technique usually provides a good balance between the ambient room sound and the instrument's highs and lows. If the player tilts the guitar up on his or her knee, make sure to raise the mic accordingly to accommodate the playing position.

**Figure 11.9: Miking an acoustic guitar with a single mic**

To get a brighter sound, move the mic toward the neck, pointing it slightly downward toward the higher strings. For more bass, move the mic down toward the soundhole, and/or point it toward the bottom bass strings. If you're using a directional microphone, moving the mic closer to the soundhole will increase the bass response because of the proximity effect. This technique can be used effectively on acoustic instruments, but be careful not to increase the bass at the expense of the mids and highs. If you move the mic away from the guitar, you'll record more ambient room sound; moving it closer will capture more direct sound.

### Single-Mic Variation #1: Close-Miking the Body

Remember, acoustic instruments need space to resonate and project. The guitar's soundboard is critical to its sound, so consider placing the mic near the body (see Figure 11.10). This technique will typically pick up more bass information than miking the soundhole/neck combination, so make sure that's the sound you're looking for. Remember that you don't have to settle on one style or technique of guitar miking.

Figure 11.10: Miking an acoustic guitar near the body

### Single-Mic Technique #2: Over the Shoulder

Some engineers have achieved excellent results by placing a mic over the player's shoulder or head, facing it down to where the guitar is pointed (see Figure 11.11). Don't be afraid to experiment.

## TWO-MIC TECHNIQUES

Adding a second microphone on an acoustic guitar opens up numerous tonal options. Remember, the sound does not come from the soundhole alone; it's a combination of all the elements of the instrument—its body, neck, strings and overall design.

The two-mic technique provides many positioning options, where each mic can be placed on a different part of the guitar. Several mics can be placed directly next to each other to create a wider sound field. Or, separate them so that one captures the direct sound of the instrument and another records the room ambience, or is placed over the guitarist's shoulder. Although the mics can be grouped onto a single track, recording the mics on individual tracks provides more options during mixing.

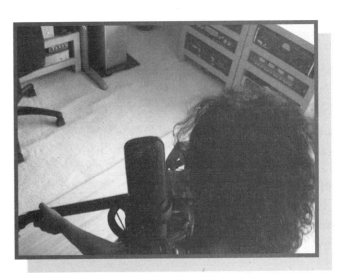

Figure 11.11: Miking an acoustic guitar from over the player's shoulder

### Two-Mic Technique #1: Capturing Multiple Parts of the Guitar

Many excellent guitar recordings have been made by placing one mic at the point where the soundhole and neck meet, and another on the body (see Figure 11.12). For example, place a small-diaphragm condenser such as the AKG C451 on the soundhole/neck to capture the instrument's brightness, and place a ribbon such as the Royer R-121 near the body of the instrument to capture warmth. Or, place the ribbon on the soundhole and the condenser on the body. Don't be

Figure 11.12: Miking the neck and body

afraid to try any mic combination.
Experiment by moving the soundhole mic up the neck, to increase the brightness captured by that mic (see Figure 11.13), or toward the bridge, to darken the tone. When placing a mic on the body, it's best to listen to the instrument first to find the sweet spot, since every guitar has a unique projection. Place both mics at equal distances from the instrument.

*Figure 11.13: Soundhole mic placed farther up the neck to capture a brighter tone.*

It's important to place both mics at equal distances from the guitar to keep them in phase with each other. Any slight time delay between the mics, even if it goes unnoticed during recording, can cause the mics to be slightly out-of-phase with each other, which will cancel out certain frequencies and cause a "washy"-sounding effect. An easy way to check phase is to listen to one of the mic channels switched in and out of phase, either by applying a plug-in (with delay compensation!) that has a phase reversal feature or selecting the phase on your mixing console or microphone preamp. If you notice that one of the mics is out of phase (mostly because the bass response is diminished), either move the mics or adjust the waveforms in your DAW so that they align.

Keeping the adage "there are no rules" in mind, the above information should be taken with open ears. Some very cool guitar sounds can be created by actually recording out of phase, or better yet, by sliding separately recorded DAW tracks by a few milliseconds (see Figure 11.14). This can create a short delay sound, which in certain productions, may actually work sonically to lift the guitar louder in the mix. A few minutes of experimenting should tell you what works and what doesn't.

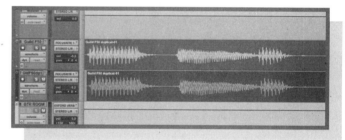

*Figure 11.14: Screenshot of two tracks that are slightly out of phase*

One last thing to think about when you are recording multiple parts of a guitar: If you have one high-quality mic and one that's mediocre, it makes sense to put the good mic in the most important position, which is usually the neck/soundhole. By letting the quality mic do the "heavy lifting" of capturing most of the sound, the other mic can then be placed either on the body or the strings to complete the overall sound.

### Two-Mic Technique #2: Close and Ambient Miking
Another common two-microphone technique involves placing one mic close to the guitar and another back in the room to record the ambience (see Figure 11.15). The first mic, which can be placed either at the traditional fretboard/soundhole position or near the body, will capture the direct sound of the instrument. Place the second mic out in the room, making sure it is at least three feet away from the first mic to maintain proper phase integrity.

This method is quite effective when using either a small-diaphragm condenser or a ribbon mic up close, and a large-diaphragm or omni mic as the distant mic. Make sure to achieve a good recording level on the room mic, because the sound level will decrease as

*Figure 11.15: Close and ambient miking*

you move away from the source. This technique's success depends on the quality of the room and the amount of available room space.

### Two-Mic Variation #1: Shotgun Over the Shoulder

For an alternative placement of the second mic in the room, try positioning it above the player's head or shoulder, facing towards the front of the guitar. This configuration approximates what the guitarist hears at the playing position, and can add a nice sense of depth to an acoustic recording. Try using a shotgun mic. Shotgun microphones are highly directional by design and minimize the recording sensitivity to the left, right and rear, focusing on the sound projecting in front of the guitar.

## THREE-MIC TECHNIQUES

If you have many mics to choose from, try using a three-microphone combination (or more) on acoustic guitar. The technique is especially effective for solo or duet guitar pieces, because it offers a wide array of tonal options for mixing, and can provide an exceptionally wide image in the stereo field.

### Three-Mic Technique #1: Single Guitar Mic, Pair in Room

You can get excellent results when placing a single mic (such as a small-diaphragm condenser) on the soundhole, and a pair of omni or large-diaphragm mics at least three feet away from the guitar and at least three feet apart (see Figure 11.16). This technique creates a virtual "triangle" of sound, and it's especially effective in good, reverberant wooden spaces.

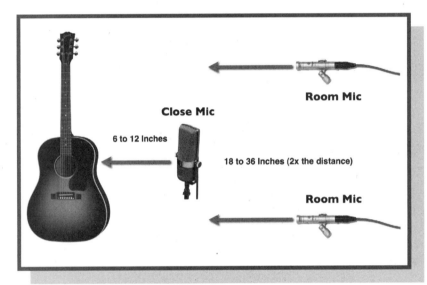

*Figure 11.16: Three-mic technique #1*

### Three-Mic Technique #2: X/Y Pair with Room Mics

Another option is to use an X/Y pair (see section below) and add either a single room mic or a pair of room mics (See Figure 11.17). This method creates an amazing sense of space and depth, as the first pair captures the up-front direct sound of the guitar, while the second mic (or pair) captures the ambience.

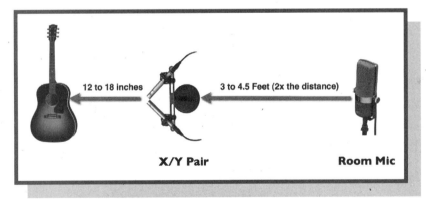

*Figure 11.17: Three-mic technique #2*

## STEREO RECORDING

Recording the acoustic guitar in stereo can create very satisfying ear candy in a mix, providing a lush, deep soundfield. A true stereo recording captures the left and right image of the source, with the information in the middle simply a sum of the left and right signals (called a "phantom center"). There are numerous ways to record in stereo, so let's look at some of them.

### Stereo Mics

A good stereo microphone will accurately reproduce the left/right signal and give a sense of the depth of the space you're recording in. A stereo mic can be used to record multiple instruments at once. For example, it can be placed in front of a pair of guitar players. The accurate localization of each player will be determined by their proximity to the microphone as well as how loud they play.

There are a wide variety of stereo microphone models available; excellent acoustic recordings can be made with models such as the Royer SF-12 stereo coincident dynamic ribbon mic, the Shure VP-88 condenser with 3-way switchable stereo width control, the Audio-Technica AT4050ST stereo condenser, and even the small Audio-Technica AT 8022 (which is also a great videocamera microphone as well; see Figure 11.18).

It's important to remember that when you use a stereo microphone, you no longer have control over the individual placement of two mics. The mic is basically point-and-shoot, since both the left and right capsules are built into the same body. Therefore, you need to make sure your placement on the guitar is correct, and that the mic's distance from the instrument allows for the desired amount of ambience.

*Figure 11.18: Audio-Technica AT 8022 stereo microphone*

Note also that a stereo microphone is different from a stereo pair of microphones. A stereo pair is simply a pair of microphones that are closely matched to each other in terms of frequency response of the capsules. A closely-matched stereo pair is the preferred method for the traditional stereo miking methods below, but a stereo microphone can provide excellent results in the right acoustic environment.

### The X/Y Technique

The X/Y stereo recording technique is an excellent way to reproduce the natural sound of an acoustic guitar. By placing a pair of cardioid microphones at an angle to each other, as close as possible without the tips touching (or just barely touching), you can capture a realistic stereo image of the guitar (see Figure 11.19). The angle of the mics, which is typically set between 90 and 140 degrees, determines the width of the stereo image. The width can also be altered during the mix, depending on how wide you pan each channel.

*Figure 11.19: X/Y mic configuration on an acoustic guitar*

In an X/Y configuration, each microphone captures the sound directly in front of it, so if the pair is positioned near the guitar's soundhole, one mic will capture the neck and one will capture the body, depending how the mics are angled. Remember that the microphone on the left will record the right channel, and the one on the right will record the left channel. This technique produces a very clear, focused, tight image, without a lot of room sound. Be sure to set your preamp controls to capture the same levels, to create the most balanced recording.

Certain microphones, such as the Rode NT4 condenser, are designed to record in an X/Y configuration (see Figure 11.20). Two frequency-matched capsules are mounted in an X/Y configuration on one mic body, meaning that careful set-up of multiple microphones is not necessary.

*Figure 11.20: Rode NT4 X/Y microphone*

Another useful stereo recording tool for acoustic guitars is the Shure A27M stereo microphone adapter (available for around $75; see Figure 11.21), which allows two microphones to share a single stand, and is designed for coincident or closely-spaced mounting at a variety of angles.

*Figure 11.21: Shure A27M stereo microphone adapter, shown with two MXL 603s in ORTF configuration.*

### The Blumlein Pair

A Blumlein pair is a pair of figure-8 microphones in an X/Y configuration, which some say provides the most realistic stereo of the many techniques. This method, named after its creator Alan Blumlein, who patented it in 1931, dictates that the microphones occupy the same space as each other. Since this is physically impossible, a common technique is to stack them on top of each other in an "X" pattern (see Figure 11.22). Be careful to make sure that the middle of the "X" directly faces the sound source and doesn't favor one of the sides, or the image will not translate properly on playback. The figure-8 patterns capture the stereo image in front of, to the sides of, and behind the microphones, with almost no phase cancellations. It's important to record in a really good-sounding room when using this method because the ambient sound will be quite noticeable.

*Figure 11.22: Blumlein pair on acoustic guitar*

### ORTF Recording

The ORTF (Office de Radiodiffusion Télévision Française) technique, originated at Radio France in the 1960s, was designed to recreate the perspective of human ears. Like the X/Y technique, ORTF uses a pair of cardioid microphones (preferably closely matched), that have their capsules positioned at a 110-degree angle from each other, which is about the distance between the ears of a typical human (see Figure 11.23). These measurements are based on research, but you can always experiment to find positions that work best for your needs. Because the cardioid patterns focus on the front source, and not the rear ambience, you can experiment with placing the mics at various distances from the source. This method also provides good mono compatibility.

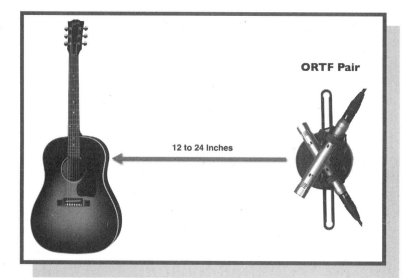

*Figure 11.23: Mics in ORTF configuration*

## OTHER MIKING TECHNIQUES

Today, there are more ways than ever to capture the sound of an acoustic guitar. Here are a few additional possibilities.

### Clip-On Mics

Clip-on microphones, such as the DPA 4099G supercardioid, typically mount to the guitar with a device or clip that positions the microphone near or above the soundhole (see Figure 11.24). Their advantage is that they typically remain in the same position no matter how the player sits.

*Figure 11.24: Guitar miked with a DPA 4099G clip-on*

If you move around a lot while playing, which some players tend to do, a clip-on mic may help capture a more consistent sound. It also can be used effectively when players record themselves, especially if they sit in unusual positions. With larger 12-string and jumbo body guitars that often need to be propped up on a player's knee to accommodate a comfortable playing position, a clip-on mic really comes in handy.

### Combining Mics and Pickups

Does your acoustic have a built-in pickup? Many of today's electroacoustic models feature an internal pickup, transducer or microphone. By plugging the pickup into a DI (direct injection) box, you can capture the sound of the guitar without using any microphones. This technique lets you record without headphones, eliminating the potential for feedback (unless the monitors are incredibly loud, or you have a mic inside the guitar that picks up the speakers in the room).

Some acoustic systems, such as Fishman's popular *Blender* system, combine a mini microphone with an internal pickup (see Figure 11.25). With both the mic and pickup mounted inside the instrument, it offers independent control over the bass, treble, phase and level (trim) of the acoustic output. Fishman's *Ellipse Aura* system features a control panel that's mounted directly on the top of the guitar, providing easy access to tone shaping. These systems can help create a blended and shaped tone to send directly to the mixing board.

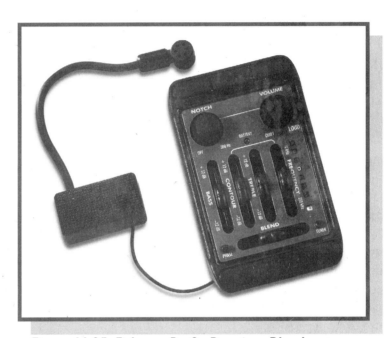

Ultimately, an internal pickup should be combined with a microphone to achieve the best results. Even the best internal systems can't reproduce the full natural spectrum of an acoustic guitar, but combining them with mics will give you more options when it comes time to mix.

*Figure 11.25: Fishman Prefix Premium Blend system*

### Acoustic Preamps/DIs

Some companies make DIs specifically for the acoustic guitar. For example, the popular LR Baggs *Para Acoustic DI* combines a direct box with a preamp and a 5-band equalizer, and includes features such as phase inversion, an effects loop, and a balanced XLR output. The LR Baggs *Venue DI* direct box also includes a tuner and mute and boost footswitches (see Figure 11.26).

Fishman's *Pro EQ Platinum Acoustic Preamp* handles the same duties, and includes a ground lift, 5-band EQ, phase switch and ¼-inch and XLR output capabilities. Taking things a step further, the TC Electronics *G-Natural* multi-effects processor features programmable delays, reverbs, compression, boost and other effects, and also includes a mic input, letting you combine a DI and mic signal in one unit.

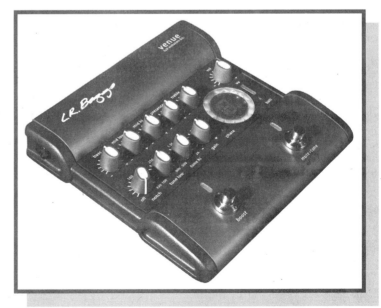

*Figure 11.26: LR Baggs Venue DI direct box*

Any of these pedals and DIs can be used both onstage and in the studio, if your acoustic guitar has an internal pickup with a ¼-inch or XLR output. In the studio, you can run the XLR signal from the pedal's output directly into a recording channel and combine it with a mic for further tonal options.

### *Miking an Acoustic Guitar and an Amp Together*

If your acoustic guitar has a pickup, consider running the signal into an amp instead of into a DI, and miking both the amp and the guitar. This technique will provide two distinct guitar sounds to work with: the instrument's natural, acoustic sound, and its amplified sound. Or, just mike up the amplifier and leave the guitar unmiked for a nontraditional sound.

If you do mike the guitar, try to isolate the amp so that it doesn't bleed into the acoustic mic. This set-up will let you keep the sounds separate in your mix. Each signal can then be treated independently, in terms of effects, EQ, compression and so on.

This technique is especially effective if you run the acoustic into an amplifier that has a nice, deep reverb (see Figure 11.27). It will create a "washy," ambient sound that can't necessarily be duplicated with a plug-in or outboard reverb. Acoustic guitars can also sound good with the addition of an amplifier's vibrato or tremolo effect. Interesting results can also be achieved by letting the amp sound "bleed" into the acoustic mic, creating a natural blend.

*Figure 11.27: Acoustic guitar plugged into a Gibson Falcon amp*

## RECORDING GUITAR WITH VOCALS

Capturing both an acoustic guitar and vocal track at the same time has its challenges. Since you would typically use a vocal mic on the singer and one or more mics on the guitar, and the mics are in close proximity to each other, phase issues can occur.

Some engineers angle the vocal mic (usually a large-diaphragm condenser) up toward the singer's mouth and away from the guitar. The guitar mic or mics (usually small-diaphragm condensers) are angled downward toward the instrument and away from the singer's mouth (see Figure 11.28).

Using a hypercardioid mic with a very tight polar pickup pattern on the guitar may help alleviate vocal bleed if it becomes a problem. However, hypercardioids tend not to record the wide tonal spectrum of an acoustic guitar as well as other mics, so they must be positioned carefully.

*Figure 11.28: Recording a singer and an acoustic guitar at the same time*

For another approach, try figure-8 mics on both the voice and guitar (see Figure 11.29). They must also be carefully positioned so that the 90-degree null point of each mic points towards the sound you want rejected. However, due to the nature of figure-8 patterns, you will also be capturing the sound at the rear of the mic, which may or may not be ambience or room sound that you really want.

Since there is virtually no way to prevent the voice from bleeding into the guitar mic and the guitar from bleeding into the vocal mic, you must take the bleed into consideration when recording and mixing. When mixing, you won't be able to apply independent effects to each "instrument"—for example, if you add EQ to brighten up the vocal, it will also brighten the guitar sound that bleeds onto that track, and so on.

Many guitarists need to sing and play at the same time, so for them, recording each part individually may not be an option. But sometimes, the bleed in each mic can actually enhance the recording, giving it a truer live feeling.

*Figure 11.29: Recording songwriter Chris Pierce's voice and guitar with figure-8 mics*

### Tips for Miking Acoustic Guitar

A mic positioned at the junction of the neck and soundhole usually provides a balanced response.

Move the mic up the neck for a brighter sound.

Move the mic down the body for a mellow sound.

A second mic provides more possibilities to widen and deepen the sound.

Stereo mics or miking techniques are another way to widen the soundfield.

When recording guitars and vocals together, use mic polar patterns to isolate the voice from the guitar.

# Chapter 12:

## Acoustic Guitar Production Techniques

Once you record your acoustic guitar parts, you're done, right? Well, probably not. Even if your project is a solo acoustic guitar recording, certain production techniques can help make the guitar sound better. From making sure the levels are clean to creative use of panning, EQs, reverb and other effects, paying attention to a few small details can help your acoustic tracks shine in a mix.

# Production from a Player's Perspective

Although it's nice to have great gear, fitting a part into a track all comes down to the player. Here are a few typical performance situations that might come up.

### PUSHING THE TRACK

In pop, rock and country recording situations, the acoustic guitar player has the unique ability to drive a rhythm section, and therefore the track, by his rhythm playing. Most of the time it's more important to lay in with the rest of the band (see to Chapter 7 for more on playing with a rhythm section), but sometimes the rhythm of the acoustic guitar sets the groove.

While laying into the track means melding seamlessly into the groove, pushing the track means playing just a little bit on top of the beat to push it forward and create excitement. Often this is the drummer's job, but the acoustic guitar player is equally capable of accomplishing the task. The trick is to play in the "pocket," but on the front end of the beat.

So what exactly is the pocket? The term pocket was born in the middle of the last century, when a strong backbeat (snare drum strikes on beats two and four) became the backbone of popular music. When the backbeat is slightly delayed, creating a laid-back or relaxed feel, the drummer is playing in the pocket.

Today, the phrase "in the pocket" has broadened a bit, suggesting that if two musicians (usually the bass player and the drummer) are feeling the downbeats together and placing beat one (the downbeat) at the exact same time, they are said to be in the pocket. Whether you are playing ahead (in front) of the beat, or behind (on the back) of the beat, or right on top (middle) of the beat, as long as two musicians (i.e. bassist and drummer) feel the downbeat at the same time, they're in the pocket.

When you push the beat, you're slightly on top of the pocket, playing on the front end of the beat, but the whole trick is to be able to identify the front, middle and back of the beat and everything in between. If you play too much on top of the beat, the track will feel uncomfortable.

### VARIETY COUNTS

You may have the greatest-sounding pre-war Martin or a stunning Gibson J-45 around, but if it's the only acoustic guitar that you have for the session, you're probably limiting yourself a great deal. Even more so with electric guitars, you need a variety of acoustics to be sure that you find the right sound for the track. You can change the sound of an electric guitar pretty easily by selecting a different pickup or amp channel, but with an acoustic, what you hear is what you get.

Just like you seek out the diversity of a Strat and a Les Paul, look for that diversity in acoustics too. An ideal combination is one guitar with a rosewood body and another with a mahogany body, which will give you one choice with more low-end and another that's a bit tighter on the bottom. Having a dreadnought or jumbo along with a small-body could work as well. Sometimes even having the exact body types with the same wood can still yield a substantially different sound, depending upon the age and make of the guitar. So before you begin recording, cover your bases and borrow or rent several different acoustics.

## TUNINGS

The standard tuning for an acoustic guitar is E–A–D–G–B–E (low to high), referenced to a standard pitch (A=440 Hz). However, it is easy to change guitar tunings to create a whole new palate of sonic possibilities. These tunings can be placed into several subcategories such as open tunings, lower tunings, higher tunings, dropped tunings and double drop tunings, which work for both acoustics and electrics.

### Open Tunings

Open tunings let the guitarist play a chord without any fretting, and has long been a favorite of the blues greats, especially those specializing in the slide guitar. You've heard *Open G tuning* (D–G–D–G–B–D) on many Rolling Stones hits, including "Start Me Up," "Brown Sugar" and "Honkey Tonk Woman." It was also a favorite tuning of Mississippi Delta bluesmen Son House, Charlie Patton, and Robert Johnson.

*Open A tuning* (E–A–C#–E–A–E) was famously used by the White Stripes on "Seven Nation Army" (although on an electric), and *Open D* (D–A–D–F#–A–D) is favored by '60s folk giant Richie Havens.

Another popular tuning, D–A–D–G–A–D, is sometimes called *D modal* or *Celtic tuning*. You've heard it on Led Zeppelin's "Kashmir" and "Black Mountain Side," and the Doobie Brothers' "Black Water."

### Drop Tunings

Drop tunings lower only the sixth string of the standard tuning, with *Drop D* being one of the most popular tunings. Drop D is tuned as D–A–D–G–B–E and is used by Soundgarden ("Spoonman"), Creed ("Higher"), Radiohead ("Optimistic") and Led Zeppelin ("Moby Dick"). *Drop C* (C–G–C–F–A–D) is a full step down from Drop D.

With double–drop tunings, the first and sixth strings are dropped a full step, so *Double–Drop D* is D–A–D–G–B–D. This tuning was used by Neil Young on his hits "Cinnamon Girl," "When You Dance, I Can Really Love," "The Loner" and Crosby, Stills, Nash and Young's "Ohio." *Double–Drop C* tuning (C–G–C–F–A–C) is a full step down from Double–Drop D.

### Lower Tunings

In lower tunings, all six strings are tuned down. An *E♭ tuning drops* each string down a half-step and has been very popular with some of the greatest guitar players of our time, such as Edward Van Halen, Stevie Ray Vaughan, Jimi Hendrix and Slash.

*D tuning*, in which each string is tuned down a full step to D–G–C–F–A–D, is a favorite of John Fogerty and Dream Theater, and is used on the Nirvana hit "Come As You Are."

In *C tuning*, strings are tuned down two full steps to C–F–B♭–E♭–G–C; this tuning has been used by Queens of the Stone Age and other metal bands. Lower tunings are favored by Swedish death metal bands, but string tension will be quite low on some of these tunings, causing tuning and intonation problems.

## High Tunings

Higher tunings, which are not used often with acoustic guitars, will increase the string tension. *F♯ tuning* is one full step up from standard tuning, with the strings at F♯–B–E–A–C♯–F♯; *G tuning* (also sometimes called *third tuning*) is G–C–F–A♯–D–G. Not all acoustic instruments can handle these tunings, so it might be better to use a *capo* instead.

### Popular Alternate Tunings

| Name | Open String Tuning (Low To High) |
|---|---|
| **Standard** | E–A–D–G–B–E |
| **Open Tuning** | |
| Open G | D–G–D–G–B–D |
| Open A | E–A–C♯–E–A–E |
| Open D | D–A–D–F♯–A–D |
| D Modal (Celtic) | D–A–D–G–A–D |
| **Drop Tuning** | |
| Drop D | D–A–D–G–B–E |
| Drop C | C–G–C–F–A–D |
| Double–Drop D | D–A–D–G–B–D |
| Double–Drop C | C–G–C–F–A–C |
| **Low Tuning** | |
| D Tuning | D–G–C–F–A–D |
| C Tuning | C–F–B♭–E♭–G–C |
| **High Tuning** | |
| F♯ Tuning | F♯–B–E–A–C♯–F♯ |
| G (Third) Tuning | G–C–F–A♯–D–G |

## CAPOS

Another way to change the sound of an acoustic is by using a *capo*, a device that shortens the scale of the guitar and raises the relative pitch of all of the strings when it's placed across the neck of the guitar at different fret positions. Capos are great for transposing songs, developing new chord voicings and simply creating new ideas.

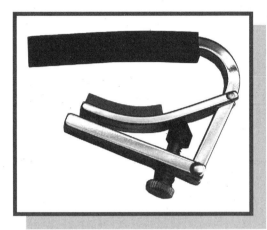

*Figure 12.1: Shubb CN1 capo*

Many manufacturers such as Shubb (see Figure 12.1), Kyser, Planet Waves and Dunlop make guitar capos. Partial capos are also available, which let guitarists clamp selected strings, leaving others unclamped.

Placing a capo on an acoustic guitar creates new options for chord voicing, and the actual timbre of the guitar will change, due to its shortened scale length. In other words, playing an A7 in the first position on a guitar with standard tuning will sound different than playing an A7 on a guitar that has a capo placed across its 5th fret.

In addition to providing new voicings, capos also let guitarists easily transpose songs. As you can see from the capo chart below (see Figure 12.2), the form of a standard G chord played with no capo becomes an A chord when capoed on the 2nd fret. The A chord with no capo becomes a D chord with a 5th-fret capo, and so on.

*Figure 12.2: Capo chart – Indicates the key of the chord shape when a capo is attached to a fret.*

| Capo On Fret | C | G | D | A | E | B | F# |
|---|---|---|---|---|---|---|---|
| 1 | Db | Ab | Eb | Bb | F | C | G |
| 2 | D | A | E | B | F# | Db | Ab |
| 3 | Eb | Bb | F | C | G | D | A |
| 4 | E | B | F# | Db | Ab | Eb | Bb |
| 5 | F | C | G | D | A | E | B |
| 6 | F# | Db | Ab | Eb | Bb | F | C |
| 7 | G | D | A | E | B | F# | Db |
| 8 | Ab | Eb | Bb | F | C | G | D |
| 9 | A | E | B | F# | Db | Ab | Eb |

**Production From A Player's Perspective**

An acoustic rhythm guitar can create excitement in a track by pushing the beat.

Having a variety of acoustic guitars is important during recording.

Alternate tunings can significantly change the sonic qualities of an acoustic guitar.

A capo can significantly change the sonic qualities of the sound of an acoustic guitar.

# Common Acoustic Guitar Production Techniques

Most of the production techniques in Chapter 7 regarding electric guitars apply to acoustic guitars as well. However, acoustic guitar has its own considerations.

## PROCESSING DURING RECORDING

Decisions about adding processing such as EQ or compression during recording an acoustic must be made on an individual track basis. The adage "If it sounds right, it is right" applies here. However, many engineers would rather take the time to position a mic correctly before reaching for an EQ or compressor to keep processing during recording to a bare minimum. Remember that if you record with compression or EQ, this processing can't be removed after the fact.

If you choose to record with compression, be careful to set it so that it doesn't squash the guitar's important transient attacks. Depending on how an acoustic guitar is played, it can project quite a wide range of dynamics, from extremely quiet to harshly aggressive. Base your compression settings on the intensity of the sound at the mic during recording. Sometimes, adding just a touch of compression can help bring out the attack of a pick or fingers striking the strings, especially on softer songs. If you record with compression, try using a ratio of around 3:1 or 4:1, with a medium/fast attack and a relatively fast release. Also, set the threshold so the loudest peaks have no more than 3 to 5 dB of gain reduction. If you feel you don't need any compression, don't use it!

The same rule applies with EQ: If you don't need it, don't use it. That said, engineers will often apply a highpass filter on the preamp, or the mic itself, to reduce low-end rumble. If you feel the need to apply EQ during tracking, try moving the mic first, or try another mic. Remember that EQ can always be added later, during the mix.

## THE PREAMP CHOICE

Although just about any good preamp will get the job done, many engineers tend to have a favorite model for recording acoustic guitars. Here, we're talking about a microphone preamp that connects directly to your recorder, not the kind of DI or preamp that you plug your guitar directly into, such as an L.R. Baggs Para Acoustic DI. To properly capture the lows, mids and highs of an acoustic guitar, many engineers combine a good mic with the most neutral preamp possible, one that does not impart any sonic color of its own onto the guitar.

Since everyone has different ears and opinions, the type of preamp to choose is an open-ended topic. But if you have one that has a transparent sound, try that first. If not, use the highest-quality preamp possible.

## PANNING

Panning the guitar in the stereo soundfield is an important step in your production. Panning is a creative mix technique that has virtually endless possibilities, but the type of track and style production tends to dictate pan positioning. For instance, solo acoustic guitar recordings will probably have different pan positions than guitars in a dense mix filled with instruments.

### Listen First

A great way to get inspired by the production potential of an acoustic guitar track is to listen to some of your favorite recordings. Focus on nothing but how the acoustic guitars sit in the mix, both in terms of pan and level. For example, Led Zeppelin's "Going to California," on *Led Zeppelin IV,* opens with the acoustic guitar panned hard left and right with virtually no reverb or delay on it. A mandolin then appears in the left channel, followed by another acoustic picking the main part in the right channel. This wide panning creates plenty of room for Robert Plant's vocal to be heard loud and clear. The positions remain consistent throughout the entire mix.

To hear an opposite effect, listen to the mono placement of Steve Earle's "Sparkle and Shine," on *Washington Square Serenade.* Sitting almost directly on top of his vocal up the middle, the dry, tight guitar lets the width of the drums be heard, as well as the bass, which is panned slightly to the left of it.

Neil Young's classic "Old Man" starts with his guitar panned on the right side and the piano on the left, with some bass and his vocal up the middle. When the drums enter, they are panned slightly to the left of the center image. When the steel guitar enters, its reverb can heard clearly in stereo, which creates a distant, haunting sound. The relative isolation of the guitar on the right, in its own space among all the other instruments, almost announces: "This is a guitar song."

Listening to the production of other artists' songs can help inspire your own work and provide fresh, creative ideas. It's also a great reference point to help you begin a session.

### Mono Panning

The best way to determine panning for a mono acoustic guitar in a full mix is to simply sweep the panner left to right and listen. Find out where it sounds good, and it doesn't step on other instruments.

If you've recorded with a single microphone or DI, your panning choices are a bit limited because it's a matter of where the guitar fits best with the other instruments in the stereo field (see Figure 12.3). With a mono acoustic, you need to make sure it has its own "space" and can still peek out when needed. Sometimes you can achieve this effect through level-setting, but if you find the right pan position in the mix, you may not need to add as much volume as you think. Adding less level improves the clarity of a mix, since you won't mask the sound of any of the other instruments.

If there's only one electric guitar in the mix, it often makes sense to place the acoustic on the opposite side of it. This is a common mix technique to create a wide blend of guitars. Then again, it's all a matter of what sounds best to the artist, mixer and producer.

*Figure 12.3: Mono panner in Pro Tools*

### Two-Mic Panning

With two microphones, your panning options increase dramatically. Panning a pair of acoustic guitar tracks lets you create a narrow or wide soundfield, depending on what the track calls for. With an X/Y recording, for example, get the widest image by panning one microphone hard-left and one hard-right. As you narrow the pan, the left/right sonic image tightens.

However, the pan position of two different microphones doesn't always have to be split wide and can sound great when they're placed next to one other in the soundfield. Since the two mics each have their own sound, their tonal properties will be different. By placing them close together, you can create different frequency blends based upon how loud each mic is in the mix. You can also process each mic differently in terms of equalization, compression and effects. Of course, you'll have to experiment with what works best for the track, but two mics give you a lot more options.

### Panning Three or More Mics

The creative panning of three or more mics introduces many possibilities. If a single mic is used close to the guitar and a pair of mics is on the room, you can create an extremely wide soundfield. If you pan the close mic near the center and the room mics hard-left and hard-right, the image will fill the entire stereo field. By raising and lowering the level of the room mics, the ambience level can be adjusted.

If an X/Y pair is used on guitar, along with a pair of room mics, you have the choice of a narrow or wide direct soundfield and a narrow or wide ambient field, which gives you the most options to fit the guitar exactly in the right place in the mix.

### Creative Panning of Room Mics

If you record with room microphones, you don't have to pan them hard-left and hard-right, or even in the same position as the close mics. The benefit of capturing the room is that you can create a sense of depth and space that works in your production.

Properly captured in a good room, room mics can be used in place of reverb. For example, panning the room mic(s) to the opposite side as the guitar widens the soundfield of the instrument and deepens the listener's acoustic image. The width and depth of that image can also be changed by raising or lowering the volume of the room mics, as well as widening the panners. Room mics also do well with a bit of compression and input gain on them. If the room mic picks up too much low end, it can be EQed out or even brightened, so don't be afraid to experiment with the processing.

### Reverb Panning

Like room mics, reverb returns can be panned to create space and depth. With a mono guitar, adding a short stereo room setting (less than a second of decay) and panning the returns opposite the guitar will create a sense of ambience and space (see Figure 12.4). The width of the ambience can then be adjusted, depending how wide you pan the reverb returns. If you use a mono reverb, you can pan it alongside the guitar, or opposite it, depending on the amount of space you want.

*Figure 12.4:*
*Panning mono guitar with stereo reverb returns*

## ADDING SPATIAL EFFECTS

As with electric guitars, it's important that acoustic guitars have their own ambient space. But because of the acoustic instrument's organic nature, choosing the perfect effect for the track sometimes requires a bit more care.

### Reverb

Like salt and pepper, reverb is added to taste. It also depends on what the track's style calls for, be it a ballad or piece with a lot of energy. Some engineers choose not not add reverb to acoustic guitars, which keeps the guitar sound more immediate and in-your-face. Adding reverb will create the exact opposite effect, placing the guitar farther back in the sound field. However, every track is different: your track might call for exactly that sense of space and depth on the instrument.

There are countless types of reverb, ranging from plates to halls to emulations of real acoustic spaces with impulse response/convolution processors (see below). Although stereo reverb is most common, mono reverb can be used just as effectively to add width to a mono recorded guitar.

The length of the reverb will usually be dictated by the type of song. For example, longer reverb times, above 2 seconds or so, will add an extended trail to the end of each note. If the song has the space, long reverbs can create quite a lush acoustic guitar sound. Reverb times over 2 seconds tend to work best on slower songs where your ear has time to catch the subtleties. If the song has a faster tempo or a lot of instruments in the mix, a reverb time of 2 seconds or more may get lost, or even worse, cloud up the mix. Try using a shorter reverb time, around 1 second or so. This will create a tighter, drier sound but it won't feel as dry as having no reverb at all.

Many engineers apply several reverbs, with different lengths and characteristics, to their tracks. For example, you could have a short, 1.5-second plate reverb on one channel, and then a longer, 3-second hall on another. Then you can add reverbs to the guitars as needed, and even automate the reverbts to change in each section of the song.

### EQing the Reverb

EQing the reverb can be very effective in making the effect fit better around the instrument and in the mix. During the '60s and '70s, it was very common to EQ the send going to a plate or chamber to limit the bandwidth. You can hear this effect on any of The Beatles' records, or anything that came from the famous Abbey Road Studios since they routinely rolled off the low end at 600 Hz and the high end at 10 kHz. Sometimes rolling the high end off at a point as low as 3 or 4 kHz can give you a sense of space without the track jumping out of the mix.

Although most outboard reverbs and plug-ins have built-in EQ, you'll get a completely different sound if you EQ the send going to the reverb, just like they did in the old days. Try it both ways and see which sound fits better in the track.

### Convolution Reverb

Convolution reverbs, such as the Audio Ease Altiverb (see Figure 12.5), Waves IR-1, Apple Logic Pro Space Designer and McDSP Revolver, use a sonic impulse to sample the characteristics of a real acoustic space, then extrapolate the parameter settings during playback.

*Figure 12.5: Audio Ease Altiverb convolution reverb*

After playing a sine wave sweep or shooting a starter pistol in a space, the room's acoustic response is recorded and put through a process called deconvolution to yield an impulse response. From that, an acoustical representation of the real space is available for use in your music. The process is not limited to acoustic spaces since any hardware processor can also be sampled.

This means that a convolution reverb lets you artificially place your acoustic guitar in any number of fine rooms, studios, chambers, classic effects units and even concert halls. For example, say you're forced to record the guitar dry in a small, carpeted bedroom, and you want to add a little natural ambience to the sound. You can call up an impulse response reverb and place the guitar into a sample of a medium-size recording studio. While the effect may not sound exactly like you recorded the guitar in that particular room, it will provide a nice sense of realism.

### Delay

While you may not think that a nice, natural acoustic guitar sound needs delay, delay can be creatively applied in certain situations. For example, if you record a single acoustic guitar with one mic, you could pan that signal either to the left or right, say at the 9 o' clock or 3 o'clock position (or even a harder pan). By adding a short delay or slap in the 40 to 100ms range with no repeat, then panning it opposite the guitar, the acoustic soundfield will get wider (see Figure 12.6).

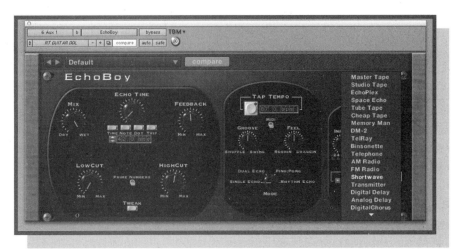

*Figure 12.6: Screenshot of Sound Toys delay set to 42ms*

The level at which you mix the delayed signal will affect how the listener perceives the width of the instrument. By mixing it at a lower level than the guitar itself, say 3 to 6 dB down, it will blend in smoothly.

Another nice technique is to EQ the delay return. This technique can usually be performed on the delay itself (providing it has a filter), or by placing an EQ in the delay's return path to the DAW or console channel. If you remove some of the delay's high frequencies (at around 5 kHz and above), you can darken the signal, which will create a warmer feel. The opposite also applies: If you want to brighten the sound of the instrument, add high end (above 6 kHz) to the reverb. This can be done with an equalizer, but many reverbs have EQ built into their interface. Use them if you've got them!

While you're at it, consider removing low frequencies (in the 200Hz range and below) from the delay, since they usually won't be audible in a mix, and can make the low end muddy.

### Duplicate the Track

With today's DAW's, it's easy to instantly make a copy of a guitar track. By duplicating the track, and then panning the two tracks opposite each other, you have more to work with. Since the tracks are exactly the same, try offsetting the timing of one of them by 20ms or more, simply by sliding the channel's audio waveform (see Figure 12.7).

This will create a very short delay; by turning one channel's volume down lower than the other, you'll create a sense of distance. At this point, you could even apply different effects on the two tracks. Note that the farther in time (milliseconds) that you slide the channels away from each other, the longer the echo or delay time.

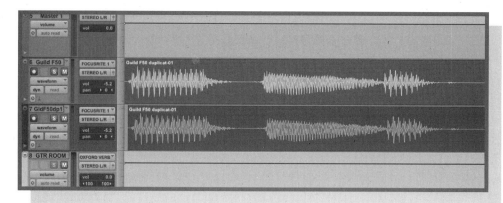

*Figure 12.7: A duplicated track in a DAW*

## USING EQ

Acoustic guitar EQ is usually applied on an as-needed basis, which, of course, is totally subjective. Here, several factors come into consideration, such as the quality of the recording, and the frequency response of the mics that were used. Each song has its own needs, and a dense mix may very well may require different EQ settings than in a sparse ballad to allow the acoustic to be heard.

If the instrument had old, dull strings during the recording, you may need to brighten up the sound in the mix. Usually the boost would start in the 8kHz area, but you may need to go up to the 10 to 14kHz range, which is often referred to as adding "air" or "brilliance."

Another important consideration for EQ use is how bright or dark the guitar sound is. Sometimes an acoustic guitar sound needs to be thinned out in a mix. For example, in a dense mix, a rosewood guitar that's been recorded with a large-diaphragm mic may have too much low end in the context of the song. It may be a good idea to apply a highpass filter to cut boomy frequencies, especially in the 100Hz area and below (see Figure 12.8). If necessary, cut even more low end, around 120 to 140 Hz, which will create room in the mix for additional instruments, such as bass and kick drums.

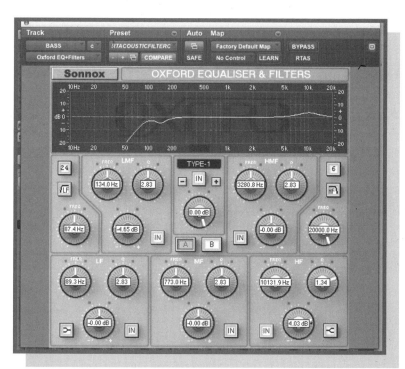

*Figure 12.8: Oxford Acoustic EQ filter screenshot*

If you've used more than one microphone or recorded the mics with a DI, you can equalize independent channels on an individual basis. For example, since some DIs tend to emphasize the midrange, you could pull those frequencies out on the DI channel while leaving them alone on the mic channel.

When EQing an acoustic guitar within the context of a mix, don't be overly concerned about the way it sounds when it is soloed. It may sound terrible by itself, but if it sounds great within the mix, that's all that matters.

| Typical Acoustic Guitar EQ Points | |
|---|---|
| **Frequency** | **Characteristic** |
| 80 Hz | Fullness, but too much will make it muddy. |
| 240 Hz | Body, but too much will make it cloudy. |
| 2 to 5 kHz | Presence, but too much will make it shrill. |
| 10 kHz | Brilliance, but too much will make it sound thin. |

## USING COMPRESSION

Compression can be used during the recording process, but it's often better applied during mixing. Since the production goal of most acoustic tracks is usually to retain the natural attack and character of the guitar, the compressor should be set with a longer attack time to let those transients through. If you need to reduce the transients, applying a faster attack with just a dB or two of gain reduction should do the trick.

If you're trying to get an acoustic guitar to punch through a mix, this is the time for more aggressive compression. However, if the peaks hit the compressor too hard and create unnatural attacks, it's best to either back off the threshold or simply use volume automation (if the compressor is set post-fader). You can push the acoustic guitar's volume up using the compressor's gain function, which helps compensate for signal reduction that occurs when pushed beyond the set threshold.

### Acoustic Guitar Production Techniques

Applying processing during recording can't be undone later.

Creative panning can add space or pop the guitar out of the mix.

Reverb pushes the guitar back in the mix.

A convolution reverb can place the guitar in a realistic-sounding acoustic space.

EQing the reverb can help it blend into the mix better.

Short delays can add width to a mono guitar track.

A guitar that doesn't sound good soloed can sound great in the mix.

Applying compression during mixing can take away the realism of the instrument but can bring it forward in the mix.

# Chapter 13:

## Other Instruments in the Guitar Family

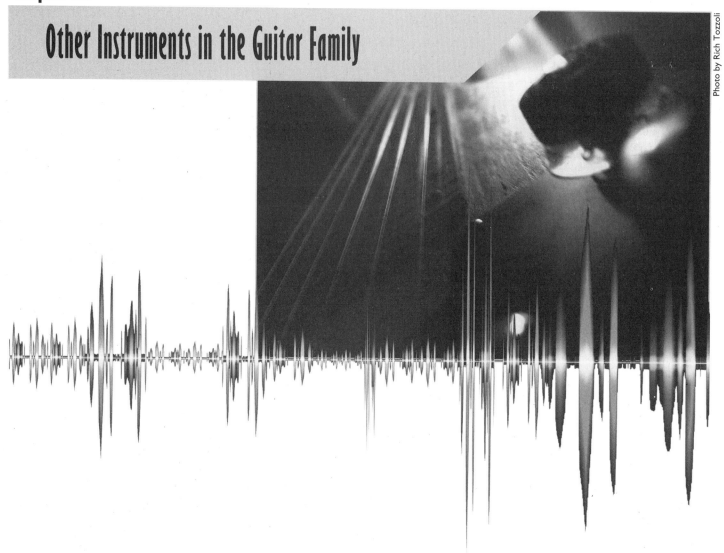

Photo by Rich Tozzoli

Although electric and acoustic six-string guitars are the most common instruments in the guitar family, you'll likely encounter many other styles when recording. The following are some of the most common alternative guitars.

# 12-String Guitars

12-string guitars, both acoustic and electric, feature six courses (pairs of adjacent strings) of two strings each. The treble strings are tuned in unison, while the bass strings are tuned an octave apart. Some players also tune the G string in octaves, whereas some prefer them in unison.

The instrument is believed to have originated in Mexico, and the first American 12-strings were built in the late 1800s. 12-strings came to public attention in the 1920s through blues players such as Blind Willie McTell and Leadbelly (see Figure 13.1), as well as many Mexican-American artists.

The 12-string, with its shimmering, natural chorus effect, became a signature sound on many hit songs of the '60s and '70s, as it was featured on The Beatles' "A Hard Day's Night," The Byrds' "Eight Miles High," Led Zeppelin's "Over The Hills and Far Away" and Pink Floyd's "Wish You Were Here," to name a few. Players such as Glen Campbell, Leo Kottke and Roger McGuinn have became synonymous with the 12-string guitar.

*Figure 13.1: Leadbelly, with a 12-string*

Because of the six extra strings, the tension on the neck of a 12-string guitar is enormous, often forcing the builder to use additional bracing. And because of the constant pull, 12-string guitars (especially acoustics) are notorious for their bridges eventually lifting up.

## TUNING THE 12-STRING

12-strings are commonly tuned to the traditional E–A–D–G–B–E tuning, and sometimes even tuned lower and capoed to reduce neck stress, although this is generally no longer necessary because of today's advanced materials and construction techniques. Like with six-string guitars, many players also use alternate 12-string tunings (such as D–A–D–G–A–D) and various open and dropped tunings.

12-strings are often challenging to tune. Even if you play with your fingers, it's easiest to tune a 12-string with a pick. Here's how you do it:

1. Starting with the low E-string course (in standard tuning), carefully pluck the low-octave string only, and tune with an ordinary electronic tuner.

2. Once the string is in tune, play both strings in the course and tune the higher-octave string to the low one.

3. Repeat the process for all strings, plucking the lower string in each the course (the one closest to you) first.

Famous 12-string electric guitars include the Rickenbacker Model 360/12 (see Figure 13.2), the Gibson EDS1275 Double Neck and the Danelectro 12SDC. Classic acoustic 12-string models include the Guild F512 (see Figure 13.3), Martin D12-28 and Ovation 6756 LX Legend.

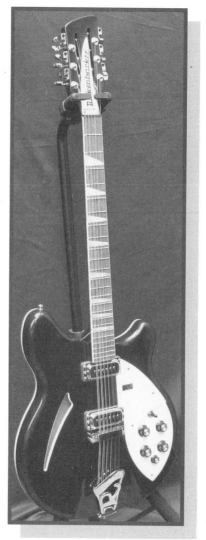

*Figure 13.2: Rickenbacker 360/12 electric 12-string*

*Figure 13.3: Guild F512 12-string*

## HIGH-STRING/NASHVILLE TUNING

To achieve the bright, chimey sound of a 12-string with only six strings, use a high-string guitar, also called Nashville tuning. A guitar strung as a high-string uses the thin strings of a 12-string set: The high E and B are tuned to their traditional pitch, but the G, D, A, and E strings are all tuned up an octave.

If you don't want to use up half of a 12-string set, D'Addario makes an electric set called the High-String/Nashville tuning set under the model name EXL150H (see Figure 13.4), as well as the EJ38H phosphor bronze acoustic set.

A high-string guitar sounds great alone or as an overdub in conjunction with a traditional six-string. Configuring high-string tuning is the perfect use for an older or lesser-used acoustic that may be sitting around your closet or basement. Just dust it off and string it up as a unique-sounding instrument.

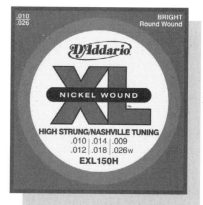

*Figure 13.4: D'Addario EXL150H high-string/ Nashville string set*

# Resonator Guitars

The resonator guitar was invented in the late 1920s by John Dopyera as a way of mechanically amplifying an acoustic guitar. Dopyera's first guitar, called a Tri-Cone, featured three 6-inch aluminum discs that sat on the guitar's top, attached with a t-shaped bar called a spider (see Figure 13.5). When the strings were struck, the discs mechanically vibrated, creating its unique tone.

*Figure 13.5: A National Tri-Cone Resonator Guitar*

The first resonator guitars were manufactured by Dopyera's company, the National String Instrument Corporation. As a result, National eventually became synonymous with guitars of this type. National also created a resonator model that used a single 9.5-inch cone, often referred to as a single-cone guitar (see Figure 13.6). Resonator guitars found popularity with blues and bluegrass players because of their increased volume and unique sound.

*Figure 13.6: 1932 National single-cone resonator guitar*

## DOBRO

Dopyera eventually lost control of National and went out on his own to build a different kind of resonator guitar. He and his brother formed Dobro, which is short for Dopyera brothers. Dobro guitars are also resonators, but use a single, inverted-bowl-shaped metal cone (see Figure 13.7) which is louder than a National Tri-cone and cheaper to produce. When the Dobro is played, the outside of the cone resonates as string vibrations pass through the bridge (spider) and are amplified by the body. Because of its inverted cone, the Dobro has a slightly different type of sound from either of the other National resonator guitars.

*Figure 13.7: Dobro guitar*

## MIKING A RESONATOR

Recording a resonator guitar is a little different than recording a standard steel- or nylon-string instrument. The reason lies in the basic construction of the instrument; the sound of a resonator comes not only from the metal cone and bridge, but also from the body cavity and sound holes on the top. The very nature of this resonator is to provide volume and a bright metallic sound that cuts through other instruments. However, since there are several types, they each have their own distinct sound.

Have the player sit comfortably with the instrument either on his or her lap or upright, depending on the preferred style. Then listen to the sound of the guitar. Where does it sound good? From up close, out a foot or so, near the bridge or on the body? Determining the best-sounding spot will give you an idea of where to place the mic.

A resonator's true sound is often best captured with at least two microphones, but a single mic can still get you that classic sound. When using a single microphone, place it six or more inches away from the cone, pointing in front of or behind the bridge (see Figure 13.8). The amount of brightness you want will determine exactly where the mic faces. For a more open, roomy sound, move the mic back a few inches, where the instrument tends to "breathe" a little better.

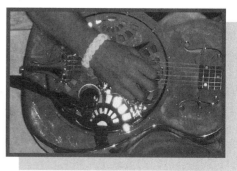

*Figure 13.8: Miking a resonator guitar with a single mic*

If you have a second mic, place it on the instrument's sound hole(s), which will provide a warmer tone. By blending in the bright, metallic-cone/bridge mic with a body mic, you'll get a much fuller tone.

# Lap Steel Guitars

The lap steel (see Figure 13.9), which is typically played on the player's lap or on a stool in front of the seated player, was invented by Joseph Kekuku in 1885 and was hugely popular in the '20s and 30's. The main feature of a lap steel guitar is that the strings are raised at both the nut and bridge ends of the fingerboard, which makes the frets unusable, so the player must use a slide, or tone bar, to play the notes. This also makes it quite difficult to play chords, which is why you will often hear lap steels play single notes or melodies.

The lap steel has several variations. Resonator guitars, since they're sometimes played in the lap, are sometimes referred to as lap steels, as are lap slide, or Hawaiian guitars.

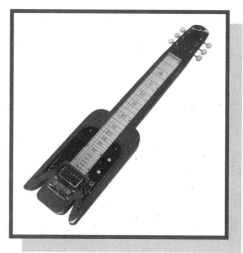

*Figure 13.9: An electric lap steel*

## STEEL GUITAR TUNINGS

Lap steels are not typically tuned to a standard E–A–D–G–B–E guitar tuning. To accommodate chord work, they are often tuned to open tunings such as Open G (D–G–D–G–B–D), Open D (D–A–D–F♯–A–D), E7 (B–D–E–G♯–B–E) or Altered G (G–B–D–G–B–D).

Pedal steel guitars (see Figure 13.10) were developed from lap steels, but use knee levers and foot pedals to change pitch. Many feature dual necks, in which one often has a C6 tuning (C–E–G–A–C–E) and the other an E9 tuning (E–G♯–B–C♯–E–G♯). They also use a standard 10–string Nashville E9 tuning (B–D–E–F♯–G♯–B–E–G♯–D♯–F♯).

*Figure 13.10: Pedal steel guitar*

# Tenor Guitars

Tenor guitars are four-string instruments that were developed so banjo players could easily double on guitar. They're smaller than traditional six-string acoustics, can be either electric or acoustic, and and are usually tuned in fifths (C–G–D–A).

Tenor guitars have been used in recordings by Sting, Ani DiFranco, and Wes Borland from Limp Bizkit. They have been built by companies ranging from Gibson and Fender to National and Guild (see Figure 13.11)

*Figure 13.11: Ovation tenor guitar*

# Baritone Guitars

A baritone guitar combines elements of a bass with a traditional six-string guitar. Baritone electric guitars were first manufactured back in the 1950s by Danelectro (see Figure 13.12), but now are made in varying styles and scale lengths by several companies. They feature larger bodies than six-string guitars and a longer scale length. Baritone guitars are frequently used as doubles for either bass or guitar parts. In fact, this is such a common practice on country records that the baritone guitar has been named a "tic-tac" bass part.

*Figure 13.12: Danelectro baritone guitar*

## BARITONE GUITAR TUNINGS

Baritone guitars use heavy gauge strings in sizes that range from .012 all the way up to .080. For example, D'Addario's XL157 Baritone Guitar Nickel Round Wound XL set features .014, .018, .026, .044, .056 and .068 gauge sizes.

Baritones can be tuned in several different ways. Common tunings include a perfect fifth below standard (A–D–G–C–E–A), or a perfect fourth lower (B–E–A–D–F#–B). Some players also use the fourth-lower tuning and drop the low B to A, so it's tuned as A–E–A–D–F#–B, and others tune it to major third below standard (C–F–B♭–E♭–G–C). Fender's Jaguar Bass VI Custom (see Figure 13.13) features a 28.5-inch scale length and is tuned an octave below standard (E–A–D–G–B–E).

Baritones have been played by the likes of Jack Bruce, Robert Smith, Johnny Cash and Pat Metheny. Popular electric baritone guitars include the Fender Bass VI and Jaguar Baritone HH, and the Danelectro Dan '63. Acoustic bartiones are made by luthiers such as Linda Manzer and Joe Veillette, as well as companies such as Alvarez and Paul Reed Smith.

*Figure 13.13: Fender Jaguar Bass VI Custom*

### Notes on Additional Instruments in the Guitar Family

12-string guitars put enormous strain on the guitar top.

High-string/Nashville tuning gets a 12-string sound with only six strings.

Resonator guitars are noted for their mechanical amplification and distinctive sound.

Baritone guitar frequently doubles the bass or guitar part.

# Part Three:
## The Interviews

## Chuck Ainlay: Recording Engineer

Grammy-nominated engineer/producer Chuck Ainlay's kindness belies his intensity in the studio. That's why artists such as Mark Knopfler, George Strait, Peter Frampton, Eric Clapton and Vince Gill often call on his services. We caught up with him at his Nashville-based BackStage Studios to learn his tips for recording guitar while he was waiting for Lee Ann Womack to listen to the mix he had just finished for her.

### How did you get started in audio?

Like everybody, it's been a long, hard slog, working my way up. I was interested in audio since I was a child. My uncle had a little home studio that he built, and anything technical always fascinated me. After high school, I went to Indiana University for a year to study music. There was a studio in Bloomington that offered a little program to teach you about recording, so after taking the course, I decided that being an engineer was what I wanted to do.

The following year, I ended up going to Belmont University in Nashville, which had a four-year music business degree program that was one of the first of its kind. I did that for about a year and a half, then dropped out to get a studio job.

### What was your first studio job?

My first job was at Future Sound Studio, which was a place that actually had tour buses full of people coming through. We'd do a little skit about recording and show them how it's done, then in the evenings we'd record and edit demos and so on. We had an 8-track Scully and a Langevin tube console that sounded amazing. They also had some decent mics, like a U47 and some AKGs. It was just a starting place for me.

Then I took an assistant job at Quad Studios, and that led to another job at a place called Sound Lab. That was cool, because we also built a remote truck and had a house that we could use to record called the Rock House. With that truck, we got to record Journey, The Police, and all kinds of cool stuff. The Sound Lab was really a rock studio, as we weren't doing a lot of country. Then Jimmy Bowen heard some stuff that I had done at a time when he was looking to do something different with country music. He asked if I'd start mixing for him, and that's what kind of got me into the whole country world.

All that experience mixing led me to work with producer Tony Brown, and do some great records with him. At that point, Mark Knopfler heard about me, and you know how it goes…one thing leads to another.

### So what is your current set-up down in Nashville?

I have a studio within SoundStage Studios called BackStage. We have a small tracking space, but primarily it's a mix room. I have an SSL 9000J and some great speakers (ATC 300s) in the wall and a bunch of outboard gear. Most of it's what I carry with me, but there's a fair bit of stuff that stays here even when I'm working somewhere else. It's a great room because it's in the back of the building, and there are doors that open outside so I can get some daylight in. It has the feel of a home with all the support of a commercial studio.

### What would you consider a great acoustic guitar sound?

It varies so much, depending on what the purpose is. Personally, I like a warm, natural-sounding acoustic that's not all hyped on the top end. I like something that has some meat to it, yet without all the low-frequency thud that kind of just muddies up the tracks. So I look for a really warm, natural tone that's not too exaggerated.

**What's your initial approach to capture that sound?**
The first thing I do, if it was an acoustic that sits in a rhythm track, is to probably do an X/Y stereo miking, with the mics sitting about six to eight inches away from the guitar. They'd sit in front of the soundhole, up the neck a bit, usually with one mic pointing up the neck and one back at the sound hole.

My first choice of mics would probably be a DPA 4011, with some great mic preamps like the Upstate Audio ones that I have. They just sound super on acoustic guitar. I might put a Neve 33609 on there to just lightly compress it, and I'd probably roll out some of the low frequencies around 60 Hz on down, and then put a bit of 10 or 12kHz shelf on the top. Beyond that, it's just what you gotta do for each sound.

**Do you ever use room mics?**
On acoustics, not typically. If I wanted a more roomy sound, I'd either go to something more like a U67 and maybe open it up in omni, with the mic placed a little further away. But no, I probably wouldn't do a room mic.

**What would you say you have learned about electric guitar recording from Mark Knopfler?**
Well first, it's all in the fingers. The microphone and the gear you run it through are of little importance. You're going to get a great sound out of him just putting a [Shure] 57 in front of the amp. It doesn't matter, because he's got this great, beefy tone. He doesn't use a pick so what you hear is all his fingers.

With him, you don't really want to use a compressor. Some of the things you might do to a guitar in a rock record, say, putting a 57 through a Neve with a compressor, you wouldn't do with him because compression limits what he does.

It's really about him, the guitar he chooses, and the amp. You just try and stay out of the way until he settles on whatever that is, and then refine it from there. You might work with some different mics and positioning and so on, but first you have to let him settle into what it is that will draw the emotion out of his playing. But you record everything!

**What would be in that recording chain?**
Normally, we would always have a 57. That's kind of the first thing on any electric guitar. It works, and you know it will work, so that would go into a Neve 1073, and I would record that on one channel. Then I might put a [Neumann] 67 on there as well, backing off from the amp a little bit. I tend to really like 1073s for recording electric guitar, or an API channel might be another possibility.

Depending on what we're doing, we might do some ambient-miking too. It could be a pair of anything, but something like [Neumann] M149s or 67s in the room. Sometimes we even do a Decca Tree of [Neumann] M50s to try something different to get a big room sound. A lot of times though, the room mics just kind of end up muddying everything up. It doesn't always necessarily make it bigger.

**When you're cutting a typical Nashville-style session, how live is it?**
Generally there's a large group of musicians who are going down live on the track. You'll have bass, drums, one or two acoustics, one or two electrics, piano, maybe some B3, fiddle and steel. That can all be going down live with the lead vocal, so you really

can't dedicate a lot of ambient miking to individual instruments. If I want to get a more ambient sound on the electric, I put the amp in the main room with the drum kit and let it bleed into the room mics for the drums. These guys are so good, they just don't make mistakes. It goes down live, and I really like that.

If I know the musician and I know he can nail it, I may just put him out there with the drummer because the more you can track like that does kind of glue everything together. Otherwise, you might end up isolating the amp in a booth and not use any kind of ambient miking. That would typically be like a 57 with a Royer 121 type of thing.

**How do you deal with mixing acoustic and electric on a record with a lot of layers?**
Because there's generally a lot going on in a country record, I like to use a lot of wide panning. Even if there's not a lot going on, I still like to pan wide and use up the whole stereo image. I'm not one of these kinds of guys who just piles everything into the middle, so I'd spread the electric way left and the steel way right, then maybe have the acoustic panned off center, opposite the hi-hat to fill out the center. That helps everything have a space, instead of piling everything on top of each other in the middle.

When you do have a pile of guitars, you might end up having to roll out some bottom end, especially on the acoustics. On their own, it might sound thin, but when you put it all together, you have to clear out that bottom or it all becomes a big wash. You've got to designate frequency areas where each instrument is going to live, with the electrics carrying sort of more of the middle and low mids, and the acoustic carrying more of the highs. That's not to say that's the only frequency spectrum the acoustic fills up, that's just more of its area.

**How about your use of delays and 'verbs?**
It's track-dependent on where you're headed. I like to use no reverb at all if I can get away with it, because that makes everything sound that much more immediate. When you start putting reverbs and delays on, it starts sinking everything back in the mix and you end up having to turn things up louder for it to be heard. Reverbs make everything more grandiose, and if that's what you're going for, it's cool. I take every song on its own. It has to ask something of itself, and it draws something from inside me and I just follow that.

**How about compressing acoustics when mixing?**
Generally, it's a slower-attack kind of thing, not any real steep ratios; something under 4:1. Probably a slower attack and maybe a quicker release, because that holds it up a bit and puts it in your face so you're not messing with the pick attack of the guitar.

With electric, you sometimes want to get that kind of gushed up sound and you might go for it more. If you're going for an Everly Brothers/Tom Petty/Traveling Wilburys-kind of acoustic sound, then you might go for more compression. There's nothing to say you shouldn't compress an acoustic hard.

**Do you mix only on a console?**
For the moment, yes. As long as people can afford to be in a real studio, I'm going to continue to mix this way because I just prefer the way it sounds. But if someone says, "I've only got so much money and I can't afford your studio," I'd mix in the box if the circumstance is right. For now, I'm sticking to my guns. I don't want to sacrifice the quality just to get some work!

*To learn more about Chuck Ainlay, visit www.chuckainlay.com.*

# Paul Antonell: Recording Engineer/Studio Owner

As founder and owner of Clubhouse, a recording studio in beautiful Rhinebeck, New York, Grammy-nominated producer/engineer Paul Antonell knows his gear. That's why artists ranging from Natalie Merchant to Hall & Oates to Earl Slick to Rusted Root call the Clubhouse home. Although the studio features a Neve 8058MKII and racks of vintage compressors, preamps and mics, it's his amp collection that gets guitarists excited. With more than 50 classic amps to choose from, Antonell can get virtually any sound that guitarists are looking for. Sitting in the studio's spacious control room, we asked him a few questions about his approach to guitar recording.

**Tell us how you first got into recording.**
I went on a studio tour when I was 16 and just fell in love with all the analog synths and stuff. I was already doing sound for a few bands at the time and eventually, when I was 18, I ended up becoming a partner at Valley Recorders in Red Hook, New York.

**What kind of tape machines were in there at the time?**
When I first got there, it was Crown tube 4-track machines. There were also Crown 2-tracks, and the console was a Teac Model 10. We eventually upgraded to a 2-inch, 16-track Ampex MM-1100 and an Apsi console, which was quite nice. I ended up working in New York City for years and then eventually moved back upstate in '86 to start the original Clubhouse, which was in Germantown, New York. I had the same gear from the old studio, but ultimately built it up and bought the Neve and a Studer 24-track. So I ran the Clubhouse in Germantown for 12 years until I built this place here in Rhinebeck in 2001.

My goal was to build a residential commercial recording facility where people could actually come to stay and work. It's all-inclusive, with a kitchen and accommodations right across from the studio.

**How did you build up the guitar amp collection?**
It started when I first opened the studio in Germantown. I had to make a decision on what kind of amp to buy, so I bought a Marshall from Mandolin Brothers. As I started doing sessions with bands, I started to see more and more great amps. I would work with all these amps, and I'd be like, "I gotta get one of these!" I'd just talk to people, and they would bring amps over. Some would say, "I have one in my closet, do you want it?" I literally got one from my plumber. We'd go to yard sales, and some people traded a couple for studio time. It took about 10 years to find all the different amps and build the collection.

When it comes to recording, different amps make a huge difference. You really need a lot of different guitar amps for pop projects, not just one. It especially wakes you up when you start working with really good guitar players and realize how they get those sounds. Of course, it's not just the amplifier, it's really the guitar player, and that's where it all starts. The amps are great, though; there's no question about that.

**What's your go-to approach for electric guitar recording?**
Certainly, I begin with the genre of music. There seems to be a few different main categories: the distorted sound, the clean sound, the Marshall sound, the Brit/pop sound like an AC-30, and so on.

What we normally do is set up about three or four amps if the guitarist doesn't have an extensive rig. We'll listen to what they're doing, then try a few in combination. A lot of times these days, for modern rock records we'll use multiple amps and split the signal. Generally speaking though, we'll hone it down to one or two amps that they'll flip between when recording.

**Does your distorted-mic set-up differ from a clean one?**
Yes, it probably does. Generally speaking, when I record rock amps I use three mics: a dynamic, a condenser and a ribbon. I bring them into the console, listen to all three of them, check the phase, and start there.

With a clean guitar I may just use one mic. Usually I'll use an old tube mic for that, depending on the sound we're looking for. There is no right way and there is no wrong way, but there is a way to make it different and have it cut through.

Back to the rock sound, I like a Shure SM57, a Sennheiser 421 or the Neumann KM84 condenser, which has a 10dB pad. You can put it very close to a rock amp and it adds a super-clean top. I'm a huge fan of the AEA R92 ribbon mic on rock guitar amps. They just sound fantastic placed right up on the grill.

**Being that you have such a nice room, do you use it with the amps?**
Not as much as you may think. A lot of people do record the room sounds, but I tend to do more of a tight rock sound where I'll put the amps in the room but still mic them fairly closely. What I've noticed is that sometimes the room takes away from the punch, especially on rhythm rock tracks. But for a solo, it does sound cool.

**How vital is your choice of preamp?**
Vital. I love the Neve console preamps on electric guitars for a simple reason—they have a really classic sound and an enormous amount of headroom and clarity. It's just a great rock and roll guitar sound through the Neve. They make you smile when you use them. I do use other preamps, but for electric guitars, I tend to stick the Neve with a Universal Audio LA-3 limiter.

**Do you EQ and compress to tape?**
Sometimes, maybe for a little midrange, but mostly it's clean. I do love the way guitars sound through the LA-3 so I'll put just a tiny bit to tape.

It's important to note that we send the amp signal at speaker level to the cabinets. A lot of times what we'll do here is have the amp in the control room, and instead of running a quarter-inch cable through the wall, we plug a short guitar cable into the head and send a speaker level signal to the cabinet in there [the tracking room] live. There's much less degradation of signal to send the speaker line out there and keep the guitar cable as short as possible.

**How about acoustic guitar recording?**
Well, for rock I love using a nice Neumann U67, which is a key choice for me. The standard mono sound is great, and I have them double the part, which is very effective.

For alt rock, I really love using a pair of Schoeps CMC5s with the M4 capsules. I also often use a pair of the Telefunken Schoeps 221s, which are cardioid tube condensers. They sound absolutely amazing on acoustic guitar.

### How about the positioning?

Usually, a foot away is my starting distance, but I like using ORTF stereo miking, which I would normally use with the CMC5s. I'll pan them hard left and right. If you want it to sound just like the acoustic sounds in the room, use that technique with good mics like those. It sounds amazing.

I do sometimes use a Blumlein setup as well, which is a stereo configuration with two figure-8 mics. That's set up about a foot and a half away from the guitar. My personal choice for those are Neumann M49s. They sound amazing. It all depends though, as I've also done X/Y technique with a 45-degree angle, and X/Y at a 90-degree angle. My preference is to do the ORTF because I really think it's a better image for me when I'm mixing.

With acoustics I don't use any compression and EQ to tape. With these kinds of mics you don't usually need EQ. I do like the Neve preamps on acoustic as well, but I also use the Chandler TG channel as well as a pair of Telefunken V76s. Each adds its own color, and the older pre's give it kind of a classic sound. Instead of adding EQ the pre's can add that color.

On acoustic I don't use room mics because I'm already miking them about a foot back so I'll naturally get some room reflection in there. I think a lot of people mike acoustics too close because when you have a good room sound you get a fuller tone by keeping them back a bit. You can then turn the pre up a bit, and to me, it's a warmer sound than miking them too close and keeping the pre low in level.

### Do you ever suggest that guitar players change their amps?

Yes, all the time. One of the advantages of having all these amps is the ability to do so. Obviously certain guitar players have certain sounds and that's their thing. But when you're in a situation where something is not working, I will often suggest trying a new amp because not every guitar amp works for every sound.

It's really important to have good amplifiers. I'm lucky to have a lot of these classics, but there are a lot of good ones that I don't have, like the Sommatones, and so forth. There are some great amps out there.

*To learn more about Clubhouse Studios, visit www.theclubhousestudios.com.*

# Dick Boak: Director of Artist Relations and Signature Editions, Martin Guitars

Dick Boak has worked just about every job that you can think of at Martin. After learning to build guitars on his own, Dick started at Martin as a draftsman in 1976, and eventually worked in the wood and production division, the string-making division, built prototypes, created in-house advertising, and even ran the sawmill. We wanted to find out about tonewoods, and Dick knows more about them than almost anyone else on the planet.

***When did you start making guitars?***
I've been working for Martin Guitars for 34 years, but I've been interested in guitars since hearing Elvis sing "You Ain't Nothing but a Hounddog." When The Beatles came out with *Rubber Soul*, I really wanted to learn guitar, so I started to build guitars in my basement out of old oak doors and balsa wood and leather and anything I could find. From the age of 12, I started building instruments. I didn't have any books; I was just doing it.

It wasn't until the Whole Earth catalog came out that I saw the first book about building guitars by Irving Sloan called *Classic Guitar Construction*. That was a wealth of information, but I still didn't have access to materials. I was living in Bethlehem and teaching art at nearby Blair Academy and one day discovered Martin Guitars by driving past it in Nazareth. I took the tour, and being a woodworker all my life, was completely blown away by it. After the tour I asked if they had scraps of wood, and they showed me a full dumpster on the side of the building, so I filled my Mustang up with it all. After that, I went nuts building everything out of Martin's scrap rosewood, ebony and mahogany.

***How'd you get the job at Martin?***
I kept coming back almost every week for the better part of four years. One day I met the foreman, who had gotten to know me from being in the dumpster at the back door. He had saved some wood for me and asked what I was doing with the stuff. I showed him two guitars that I had made from the dumpster scraps, and he paraded them around the shop. C.F. Martin III happened to be walking around the shop at the time, so Harvey [the foreman] showed him the guitars. C.F. said that I should apply for a job. I went around the front of the building and did just that. They had a job opening for a design draftsman, and I had been teaching design drafting for four years and was really quite good at it. They also wanted someone with woodworking experience who knew about guitars, so I handed them the guitars I built and played them a song. They brought someone up from personnel who asked if I could start tomorrow, so I started doing drafting for Martin in 1976.

***How did you get from drafting to the job you have now?***
I went from drafting to prototype building, and from there I worked in production. Through drafting I learned every aspect of the guitar; literally, every dimension of every piece of every model the company made. At home instead of watching TV I would experiment building guitars in my basement. I would try out different tonewoods, sizes and shapes, and eventually I built about a hundred guitars.

Spurred on by Chris Martin's D-45S Gene Autry Limited Edition guitar project in 1994, I initiated a project with Eric Clapton that led to the formation of the artist relations department. The Clapton project earned the company a great deal of money and a lot of publicity, so the company had me stop doing all the other jobs and do just that. Over the past 16 years, I've worked with over 150 artists, like Johnny Cash, Willie Nelson, Sting, Paul Simon, Mark Knopfler, Dion, Tom Petty, John Mayer, Crosby, Stills and Nash, and even Neil Young. I wrote a book about that called *Martin Guitar Masterpieces* that is the nutshell of my experience with artist collaborations. Then with Richard Johnston I co-wrote a two-volume book set called *Martin Guitars: A History*, which is the more technical and historical Martin story.

**Haven't you done a few things outside of Martin as well?**
I helped form an organization called the Association of Stringed Instrument Artisans (ASIA), which is the international group of instrument makers. At the peak of my reign in that organization we had more than 2,500 guitar makers from all around the world. Everybody was in it including Bob Taylor, Bill Collings, Richard Hoover, and all of the other smaller individual guitar makers.

I then wrote and published a magazine called *Guitar Maker*, and we also put on symposiums of guitar makers from all over the world to share information and advance the art of instrument building. So that put me at the center of guitar making and I got to know everybody through that. Those contacts continue to be incredibly valuable to me. Now I'm on the board of directors of NAMM and involved in lots of different segments of the musical instrument field.

**Let's talk about tonewoods.**
The first thing to understand is that a guitar needs to be thought of as a drum. The back and sides of a guitar are the shell of the drum, whereas the soundboard is the skin that stretches across the back and sides.

With respect to tonewoods, Brazilian rosewood has always been considered the optimum material for back and sides because it's hard, dense and resonant, as well as tremendously good at reflecting sound [see Figure 16.1]. Those are important traits as wood for back and side material, but in the process of absorbing the vibrations from the top it flavors the tone with a complexity and balance that's kind of unprecedented. Unfortunately, Brazilian rosewood is extremely rare, regulated, and near extinction at this point so it's probably a moot point to talk about how wonderful it is. It's also probably inappropriate because of the devastation of those trees and the illegal trading of it.

*Figure 16.1: Brazilian rosewood*

**If Brazilian rosewood isn't available, what do you use instead?**
There are many different species of rosewood. East Indian rosewood is the most available [see Figure 16.2]. It's not quite as dense as Brazilian, but it has a nice tonal flavor to it and a nice, rich, warm bass response. Rosewood is always valued for bass response. In a worst-case scenario, it could be criticized for being muddy or thick, but it typically has tremendous and pleasant low end.

*Figure 16.2: East Indian rosewood*

There's also a Honduras rosewood [see Figure 16.3], but the tree is quite small, and you only occasionally find one big enough to make guitars out of. It's the primary material for making marimbas since it just rings when you hit it, and it's easy to get xylophone mallets out of small logs. It would be a great material for guitars if only the tree were a little bigger.

*Figure 16.3: Honduran rosewood*

You also have Amazon rosewood, which is a close relative to Brazilian but not restricted as of yet [see Figure 16.4]. Cambodian rosewood is similar in properties to Amazon rosewood. Madagascar rosewood [see Figure 16.5] has a close visual appearance, and even a lot of the tonal properties of Brazilian rosewood, so we are quite encouraged to have acquired some beautiful sets of that tonewood.

*Figure 16.4: Amazon rosewood*

*Figure 16.5: Madagascar rosewood*

Tulipwood is also a member of the rosewood family, as is Kingwood. The big problem is availability, quality, and sizes large enough to make guitars.

### Is there any other wood besides rosewood that's suitable?
The complete opposite spectrum for back and sides is Mahogany [see Figure 16.6], which is an extremely lightweight material. It's actually not as reflective, but it has an absorptive quality that produces a very light, crystalline and glassine tone. Guitar tone can sometimes be thought of in the same breath as its weight. A light guitar is typically more responsive and vibrant than a heavy one, so mahogany is very underrated as a tonal material since it produces a crisp, clean, bright sound that is really valued in the recording studio. Rosewood guitars might not be as appropriate in the studio because they might be too bottom-heavy, depending on the needs of the track.

*Figure 16.6: Mahogany tonewood*

Between mahogany and rosewood, you have a whole spectrum of different tonewoods that vary in weight and density. Koa from Hawaii [see Figure 16.7] is popular for guitar making since it has a density that falls nicely between mahogany and rosewood.

### It seems like tonewoods are getting tougher to find these days.
Guitar makers are going to have to experiment with other woods a great deal because of the difficulty in acquiring the traditional tonewoods. They will need to experiment with more localized woods like walnut, cherry, ash and maple because they are temperate domestic hardwoods that don't come from the rainforest.

*Figure 16.7: Koa tonewood*

At Martin, we're trying to educate our customers about the viability of those as tonewoods, but it's tough because guitar players tend to be environmentally conscious. As environmentally consciousness as they are, they don't necessarily want to give up the tone.

Cherry is actually an excellent material and so is maple. Maple is a traditional choice for violins and many other instruments [see Figure 16.8], but it's extremely hard and doesn't have the resonance of rosewood. While it's also very projective in tone, it's sometimes considered harsh without the flavor or character of rosewood and mahogany. But with the right combination of soundboard wood maple can result in an absolutely wonderful, projective and powerful guitar sound.

*Figure 16.8: Maple tonewood*

Other woods are ovangkol, also called shedua or African teak [see Figure 16.9], which has an olive coloration and is kind of like walnut in its tone as it's a bit dark sounding. It also is not as dense as rosewood.

*Figure 16.9: Shedua tonewood*

### How do you rate the different woods?
With just about any wood you choose you can look up its density in comparison to the density of water. What they do is weigh a square gallon or meter of water and compare that to a square meter of the selected wood. If you get a number like .9, it means the wood is not as heavy as water and it will float. If a wood is 1.1, it will sink in water.

Ebony is very close to sinking in water and African blackwood sinks in water as does ironwood so those woods are probably too dense to use for a guitar, but any of the woods that fall between mahogany and rosewood are viable as tonewoods. There are a lot of choices.

### Which woods are used for the guitar top?
When you move on to top materials, it's a totally different picture because the real goal of a top is to vibrate. Firstly, all woods need to be cut quartersawn, which means a radius from the center of the tree outward. If you look at the grain rings [the annual rings on the board], they would stand as vertical lines like little I-beams of strength. Each winter growth is what you see as a grain line. The summer or spring growth is the softer wood between the grain lines.

So what you want is the strength on the top to withstand the pull and pressure of the strings, but you also want a vibrating quality, which comes from its lightness. Spruce has the highest strength-to-weight ratio of any of the woods and that's why it was even used for Howard Hughes' Spruce Goose aircraft. It's light but strong, so that's a typical choice for a guitar top.

### What else is used besides spruce?
There are other choices like cedar or redwood for top materials. Mahogany and koa wood have also been used, but none of them are as light as spruce so they produce different tones.

Note that there are many different kinds of spruce. There is Sitka spruce, which grows from the Oregon coast up to the panhandle/Sitka region of Alaska [see

Figure 16.10]. There is Engelmann spruce from the Rocky Mountains ranging from New Mexico all the way up to the Canadian border. There is Adirondack red spruce [see Figure 16.11], which grows from Upstate New York all the way down into Tennessee. There is Carpathian spruce from the Carpathian mountains near the Ukraine. The wood Stradivarius used in his violins is high-elevation Italian alpine spruce. There are many other spruces in uncharted areas like Siberia.

Figure 16.10: Sitka spruce

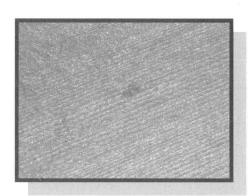

Figure 16.11: Adirondack spruce

Different spruces have different tonal characters. This is subtle to an untrained ear, but people who play guitar can really hear those differences in the wood.

### Can you describe those differences?
When you tap a piece of spruce, you either get a low boom, a high-pitched sound, or everything in between, depending on what kind of spruce it is. They are all viable, but they tend to show their character more on bigger guitars. Smaller guitars have more treble response and bigger guitars have more boom and warmth.

Adirondack spruce is highly prized and was used on Martin guitars prior to WWII. The problem was that President Roosevelt decided to make the entire Adirondack forest into a state park, which pretty much shut down all the logging and forced Martin to seek their spruce on the West Coast from Oregon up to Alaska. So for many years, there was no Adirondack spruce in the marketplace.

Adirondack spruce typically has a wide grain. The wood between the annual ring's grain lines is soft and light, which probably contributes to its good tone. Sitka spruce typically has a tighter grain and is usually old-growth wood. It's very strong and stiff as well as being quite available, so that has been the logical choice for most guitar tops.

Engelmann spruce is rarer but has a very light weight and produces a very open, old sound, but because it's not as stiff, it perhaps has less longevity. The same is true of cedar.

Carpathian and Italian alpine, which are spruces from Europe, are traditional spruces that have great complexity of tone. They come at a premium price, like the rare Adirondack spruce, but they make extraordinary guitars that are somewhere between Sitka and Adirondack in their tonality.

### What's usually used for the neck?
The other woods on a guitar contribute less, but every little piece of an instrument contributes to the tone. Mahogany and cedar are the typical woods used for necks, with cedar being a little lighter in weight. Mahogany is extremely stable and very easy to carve.

Ebony is often used for the fingerboard and bridge. It's very dense and durable for the amount of wear that a fingerboard gets. Rosewood is also a good material for fingerboards and bridges.

The only other real parts are the lining, which is the point of transition between the vibrations of the top into the sides and back. I feel Spanish cedar is the best material because of its lightness in weight.

All of that energy is being transformed through the lining into the sides and back. Much of the guitar's tone comes from the absorption of the top's vibration into the sides and back, combined with that reflection of the tone out the soundhole.

### How important is the soundhole to the tone of the guitar?
Actually the soundhole is only there to be able to get a clamp into the inside of the guitar and access the internal braces for repair and to glue a bridge on. The soundhole benefits only the extremely low registers of the bass response, probably below 70 to 80 Hz, so it is possible to make guitars without a soundhole.

### What else determines a guitar's tone?
Scale length, for one. A shorter scale length can be strung to a higher pitch, so mandolins, which have very short scale length, have an incredibly powerful sound because the strings can be tuned to a much higher pitch. That gives them tremendous volume.

Longer-scale instruments are tuned to a lower pitch, but can be strung tightly to really produce vibrations in the top. Short-scale guitars of the same size have the bendability and expressiveness that long-scale instruments don't have. For Martin guitars, the long scale length is 25.4 inches, and the short scale is 24.9 inches.

### How about the size of the guitar?
The size of a guitar is also of primary consideration when it comes to tone. Many companies make one size of guitar, but Martin makes many sizes, some from antiquity— starting at size 5, 4, 3, 3.5, 2.5, 2, 1, 0, 00 (which is slightly bigger than 0), size 000, size 0000, which we call M size, and size D. We also have Jumbo and Grand Jumbo, as well as the Performing Artist Series.

The main thing here is that small guitars produce crisper, cleaner treble response, and larger guitars produce a thicker, more resonant bass response. In between the span of small and large guitars, there are extremely small guitars like Requintos, up to big mariachi basses. The search is on by all guitarists to find the sweet spot where treble and bass balance out and where sweetness wins out over muddiness and tinniness. That sweet spot is really somewhere between a 00 and a dreadnought. Dreadnoughts have a great tone and they are certainly the most popular guitar size in the world, but the small-bodied guitars have really had a resurgence in popularity and are recognized to be quite amazing.

Long-scale orchestra models are great instruments for fingerstyle playing. They are extremely responsive and versatile for rhythm playing as well as individual notes. You can't always do that on a 12-fret instrument. Big, thick guitars like the more bass-heavy dreadnoughts are not always great for finger style, but are excellent for rhythm and vocal accompaniment.

The M-size guitars are close to the 000s, which are great for recording. Martin did a project working with George Martin trying to optimize a guitar for the recording studio. It focused on the M-size guitar with mahogany back and sides for crisp and clear tone with an Italian alpine spruce top. We were trying to utilize George Martin's vast experience in addressing the difficulty of recording acoustic guitars.

### Can you tell us about the guitar aging process?

There are three basic steps in the aging process of a guitar. It begins when it comes fresh off the line, assuming that real lacquer is used. The lacquer has plasticizer, which softens the finish to enable it to be polished. During the early stages of the guitar, perhaps three to six months, the plasticizers are expelled from the fuming of the lacquer, with the result being a hardening and slight shrinking of the lacquer. This really has an impact on the guitar's gradual transition to maturity and opening up the sound.

In the course of three to five years, the finish will further shrink, expelling more of the solvents in the lacquer until the finish probably achieves about half of its original thickness. It also gets used to vibrating in sync with the top, back and sides. The playing of a guitar gets the lacquer and the wood vibrating as one unit, so there is no question that a guitar that is played or excited or vibrated in some way benefits the instrument. Most players would recognize that a guitar that's been played for an hour or two starts to "wake up." Guitars should sound good immediately after being made though, so that all they can do is become better over time.

Fresh wood has a lot of moisture inside the cells, and a plank of well-aged wood will start to develop a dry, pithy or powdery texture. That's what I liken to the expelling of moisture from the cell. Old guitars have a very dry, lightweight feel. We have been weighing guitars a lot lately here at Martin to see how much a new guitar weighs in relation to an older guitar. It's amazing—built with the same specifications, they seem to lose a significant amount of weight. I certainly attribute lightness in a guitar to wonderful tone. Ironically, a heavier rosewood guitar can benefit in resonance from the extra weight. I often compare this phenomenon to strumming a zither or autoharp on a dining room table. The vibrations are transferred to the table and the tone is enhanced, so it seems to work both ways.

We try to ensure that all Martin guitars start out with great tone, but there is little question that a well-made guitar with well-chosen tonewoods and a thinly lacquered finish does indeed improve with age.

*For more about Dick, visit his website at dickboak.com.*

# Jim D'Addario: CEO and Chairman, D'Addario & Company

As CEO and chairman of D'Addario & Company, Inc., the world's largest maker of musical instrument strings, Jim D'Addario is truly the definition of a hands-on executive. A longtime guitar player and musician himself, he's constantly seeking to improve the quality and design of his family's products, which feature a heritage dating back to the late 1600s in Italy. In this informative interview, his knowledge of the past and passion for the future of the string business clearly shine through.

**Tell us a little bit about the history of your company.**
My grandfather came here in 1905 from a little town in Italy called Salle. They were shepherds there, and whatever was in the soil and grass that the sheep grazed on made for very good-sounding and strong music strings, since the gut strings were made from the intestines of the sheep. The little town of Salle, Italy became pretty famous for making fine-quality gut strings.

There are actually many string making families from Salle, some of which are still in business today; the Mari family (LaBella), the Galli family in Naples and the D'Orazio family all still make strings today.

When I traced the family tree about 12 years ago, I hired a genealogist to research the church and town records in Salle. We traced our family tree all the way back to 1680.

So Salle had a heritage of string making. In winter they would make strings from the sheep's intestines because the strings were kind of a byproduct and a trade that they learned as a secondary way of getting more value from the sheep they raised. Unfortunately they were not very proud of their string-making craft 150 years ago because to clean the intestines and prepare them for string making was a difficult, dirty job.

Essentially that was the trade my grandfather came here with when he was 14. He came here with his dad, however his father couldn't adjust to the New World and left his son Carmine here with some relatives in Astoria, Queens, which had an area there where all the Sallese people gathered. It was pretty traditional for any group of immigrants to stick together with their townspeople when they came to America. The Mari, or LaBella, factory was actually just a stone's throw away from my grandfather's factory when it was in Long Island City.

Originally called C. D'Addario & Son, the company eventually evolved into Darco Music Strings. It began in the basement of my grandfather's home in Jackson Heights, Queens, but it was eventually moved into a factory loft on Astoria Boulevard when my grandfather retired. From 1959 to 1969, Darco grew to be a significant string manufacturer. I started working there in 1969 when C. F. Martin & Company bought Darco. For five years, my brother, my father and I all worked there in various capacities, and it was a great period of learning. Unfortunately, we really didn't enjoy being part of a larger organization and we decided to branch off on our own again in 1973.

**So they hadn't used the family name before that?**
No. Prior to that time my family never used the name D'Addario on their strings. String making was kind of a blue-collar trade so they weren't as proud of it like we are today. We have very little archived history from this period, because although it was truly an art, they never took many pictures from that era and they never put their family name on the product.

We had a very strong work ethic in our family and nothing was ever taken for granted. My father squeaked by earning a modest living. He never really made a great deal of money and we lived in a middle-class area in West Hempstead, Long Island. He didn't understand how to market his own brand of strings.

But timing is everything in life, and while finishing my last two years of college, I was lucky enough to work as the Martin Guitar sales rep in the New York metro area, which was a crash course in music marketing. I learned so much during that period, and because of that knowledge I was able to capitalize on opportunities when they would later come our way.

In '73 and '74, when we were starting over, we were making a lot of private-label strings, which was essentially 90 percent of our business at the time. We had many accounts, but our biggest account was Guild, which then was a very popular brand of strings. I convinced my dad and my brother that we should take the profits that we were making selling strings to private label customers and advertise our own D'Addario brand of strings. At that time, nobody placed full-page ads for strings in magazines, and marketing was always an afterthought for the market leaders. At most, you would see a sixth-page ad, and even the string specialists didn't really advertise aggressively.

When we started the D'Addario brand, we took our chances. There were only a few media outlets, like *Guitar Player* and *Pick'in* magazine, and we decided to go full throttle by taking out full-page ads in every issue. By taking a full-page ad in *Guitar Player* to introduce the D'Addario brand, we instantly received recognition in export markets like Australia, England, France, Germany, and so on. People thought we were a lot bigger than we really were!

### So that strategy really worked?

Yes, it turned out to be a brilliant strategy that we stuck to for quite a while. We kept reinvesting our profits into marketing the D'Addario brand, and we got better and better at the ads. Today it's not as simple since you can't just take out a full-page ad and get into the string business, or any other business for that matter. And the Internet has certainly changed things as well.

At the time though, we not only changed the paradigm for how you market a string, but also for how you design and build a string as well. We spent a lot of time tinkering, doing research and development, and testing new materials. We introduced nickel-plated steel, phosphor bronze, and the half-wound concept, which took off like crazy in the '70s. So we did some innovative things that set us apart from every other string company.

We advertised that a lot and drove the message home from a technical point of view. The ads included illustrations of hex cores or cross-sections of half-round string windings and lots of scientific information. We helped people understand what our innovations in string-making meant. We tried to communicate that there was something technically superior about the way we were making our product. I think that we've maintained that reputation. In fact, over time, a lot of people have mimicked it. We built a great foundation in the late '70s and early '80s, and have been able to continue build off of that.

### What do you think makes a great guitar string?

Certainly that's a matter of opinion. It comes down to the tone you are looking for. However there are some common denominators that are key ingredients for making a great string. The most important things are consistency in diameter, shape, and the mass of the string from one end of the vibrating length to the other. If there are fluctuations as you're winding or making the string and the mass of the string varies at any point along its length, the intonation is going to be horrible and the harmonics will not be true.

As we developed the expertise to design and build our own machinery in the '70s, we developed ways of controlling the variables that are involved with the manufacturing process. One of the most important variables is the tension that you put on the wire as you wrap it around the core. I would say it's one of the most critical variables in string making. Because we use soft-temper wires, we can actually elongate the wire significantly during the process and end up with a completely different-diameter finished string. Tension is a critical aspect of making a string!

**What are some of the innovations you came up with in string manufacturing?**
Twenty years ago we developed a closed-loop system where we actually measure the tension on the wire just before it goes on the string. Utilizing a load cell and a digital control that adjusts the tension, we always maintain perfect tension specifications. You can't do that when you wind a string by hand, and you can't do that with a mechanical tension device. It has to be closed-loop and digital. It's really very similar to an autopilot in a plane. Our machines are constantly making minute corrections to hit the tension target.

The other breakthrough innovation we developed was a way of tracking the angle that the wire was being fed onto the core, which is also extremely critical. Many competitors are still using machinery with mechanical drives that feed the wire, but back in 1979 we developed a system that tracks the wire feed angle and makes adjustments on the fly to ensure the windings are perfectly spaced. It is one of the reasons why our strings are so consistent. We designed this in 1979, so you can imagine how expensive the electronics for that were back then.

If you control the basics, core tension, wrap tension and feed angle, then it's a question of designing the string properly. Here's where we create your choices for string tone. A flat-wound string is very mellow sounding, a half-round string is a little brighter, and a round-wound string is even brighter. A nickel-plated steel round-wound string is bright; a stainless steel string is a little brighter, etc., etc.

It's like going to a restaurant and looking at the menu. What flavor would you like? You want the chef to do a great job at cooking all the things on the menu, but you want to be able to select the flavor that you're looking for. Picking and designing the materials that should go into the strings is like picking what you like off the menu. Personally, I like very bright-sounding strings. I like uncoated phosphor bronze strings on acoustic, but because I have so many guitars and can't change strings often enough, I use coated EXP strings. I actually like our 80-20 coated strings better than coated phosphor bronze. I don't know why, but I do. Over the past ten years, we've gotten the coating process on our EXPs down to be so thin that I can't even hear the difference between a coated and a uncoated string anymore.

EXP is a micro coating on the wrap wire that's only 2/10,000ths of an inch in thickness. What it does is seal it from the environment so it doesn't corrode and doesn't get affected by your body chemistry. Those are the key elements that break a string down and make it lose its tone prematurely.

**So there's no tonal difference?**

I can't hear it anymore. In the beginning, there was a difference because we didn't have the technology that we have now. We've actually invested in our own wire-drawing and coating factory. The technology is very sophisticated, with laser micrometers at the front end and back end of the line to monitor and control the thickness of the coating precisely to within plus or minus .0002 inch. The less coating you put on, the better the string sounds, but if the coating is too thin, the string will corrode prematurely. Over two years of R&D went into developing this process, and we've landed on a spec that we can now control and repeat.

Adding a plastic coating to a string can add acoustic damping if you're not careful. As coated strings have developed, the technology has improved so that the amount of acoustic damping on our coated strings is virtually nonexistent.

We have a very sophisticated acoustic lab where we can measure the acoustic damping on our strings. We can compare an uncoated to a coated string, or various coated strings to each other, and look at quantitative data that tells us what kind of acoustical damping exists.

Ten years ago, coated strings might exhibit damping of ten percent or more on the upper overtones; now, the damping is unmeasurable. Today most people who try our coated strings find they are as good as their uncoated counterparts, however they last three or four times longer.

**Is that an average?**

It really depends on where you live and how much you play. Also, it's about your body chemistry and how hard you play. Our coatings are extremely durable because we're using a urethane that's extremely tough with excellent adhesion.

**What's next for the guitar string?**

Wow, it's hard to keep innovating, but that is our culture. We keep exploring new technologies. In the violin string and bowed strings areas there is still plenty room for innovation.

For bowed strings, we actually want to add damping. It's the opposite challenge of a guitar string. A violin string sound is sustained using a bow. With the guitar, when you pluck the string you want it to sustain as long as possible on its own. Those are two completely different design challenges.

While innovation in guitar strings might be more challenging, we're always pushing the envelope. At our steel wire mill in Massachusetts, we're making big advancements in the material itself. We've been testing new, microstructure raw material from the tire core industry that is 20 percent stronger than the standard high-carbon steel used in music strings. We have also developed a new tin-plating process that puts four times as much tin coating on the steel as the standard techniques. We're striving to perfect material that will make a much more durable plain steel string and core wire.

We're always trying to improve the materials and the processes we use to assemble those materials into music strings. It's a culture of continuous improvement at D'Addario and all our affiliate companies.

*To learn more about D'Addario, visit www.daddario.com.*

# Al Di Meola: Guitar Player Extraordinaire

Al Di Meola has long been one of the most influential guitarists in the world, first as a member of fusion's first supergroup Return to Forever in 1976, and later as an artist in his own right with his group Tour de Force and his current World Sinfonia band. But Di Meola's technique goes beyond the electric guitar, as he's also successfully delved into the intricacies of the nylon-string guitar with his recordings and tours with John McLaughlin and Paco de Lucia. Di Meola was kind enough to share some of his insights on guitar tone.

**What did you play the first time around with Return to Forever?**
The Les Paul was the first axe of choice when I started with Chick Corea. It was the appeal of the long sustain of the notes, which were more attractive to me, coming from a 335. The way the bridge was set up was really comfortable for my right hand to rest on, especially the way that I pick and mute. It's obviously very different than it would be if I had played a Strat. However, I still love the sound of a Strat; it was just never comfortable enough for me, so I always gravitated toward the Les Paul.

I had a fortunate situation in which I met Paul Reed Smith backstage at a Return to Forever show on a co-bill with Santana. He was just a kid at the time, as I was, and he was showing his guitars. So I went for it, and within a year, I bought three or four of them. In fact, I had one of the first ones ever made.

The PRS has a wonderful sound that's different than a Les Paul. I just view the 'Paul as a thicker, meatier sound than the newer versions of the PRS. I feel these guitars have a more fluid, focused and concentrated sound. However, both are great. My '59 Les Paul has a sweet, fat sound, and the PRS's that I've played and owned are also sweet. They're just different kinds of sweetness.

**When you're in the studio, do you think PRS or Les Paul, or just electric?**
Right now, I'm really enjoying the PRS with a tremolo on it. It's unusual for me, but it's kind of cool at times to throw it in. Also, I have my own PRS model so I'm gravitating more toward that than a big, wide kick-ass Les Paul sound. Onstage, I'm only using the PRS now.

**How about amplifying your guitars, both in the studio and live?**
When I started, it was Marshall 50-watts, which was the way to go then. I don't remember if it was by choice or by chance, but I found out soon after that the 50s were maybe not enough wattage, so I went to the 100-watts and noticed the sound wasn't as good. When I asked around to people who knew about the amps better than I did thought the 50s were better-sounding. So I accumulated a few of those and stuck with that.

Then, when I went out on my own after Return to Forever, 50-watts weren't enough, live, but I liked the sound of them, so I coupled them with some of the early versions of the Mesa Boogie. I had a small wall of sound that was so loud, I have permanent ear damage as a result.

**How do you handle the volume now?**

I've been primarily involved with acoustic groups, but I throw some electric tunes in the mix. I keep it on the shallow side of sound, not so big and loud. I've gone back to using a Mesa Boogie Mark III or IV. They are small and compact, and the sound is awesome. I don't need more, since I'm not amassing the sound with heavy keyboards and such. I don't have to punch through extremely loud drums and percussion. We now have our dynamics worked out so well in rehearsal that there isn't that need for overkill.

**You've begun recording with a Dumble. How come?**

Wow, yeah, that thing is the king. For years, I always had a love/hate relationship with electric guitar and electric music because I could hear the difference between the human ear and the microphone. It's a big dilemma for me.

The human ear in a room hears the [amp] sound as smooth, loud and big. Then, when you put a mic up to it, it hears it in a different sense. So during playback, you're going to hear what the mic hears. A lot of times it was so different from what I thought it sounded like, and usually not better—in fact, sometimes, much worse.

What I heard was more of an uneven kind of sound, almost described as having hard raspy edges. It didn't represent what I'd heard, and it wasn't pleasurable, either. For me, what I heard in my head was a sound that was smooth. I've come close to it with certain amps, and I've tried so many different ones it's not funny.

But I'd heard for a long time about this amp that was ridiculously expensive, called the Dumble. Finally I met someone who had one, and he happened to be working with us on the new record. Funny enough, when he bought it over he mentioned this one had belonged to John Mayer, and I happen to run into [Mayer] on tour in Tokyo, and we sat down and talked for a while. I told him I used the Dumble, and he said, "Yeah, that was my amp!"

Anyway, when recording in the studio, I immediately heard in my headphones this smooth sustain and gorgeous tone for the first time ever. And headphones are usually the place where everything sounds the worst.

It immediately clicked for me, that this is the reason why the amp is so expensive. A tiny little amp can be 50K, but there are no hard edges. All of a sudden, the electric guitar sounds beautiful to me, instead of harsh and ugly. That's the difference.

**Your favorite reverb is a Lexicon 200. Why is that?**

Yes, but they are not road friendly because they break all the time. In the beginning, when I did have them on the road and they didn't break so much, it was the most gorgeous reverb to me. I feel they still haven't made one that comes close to it. The ones we use now don't stand up to that, so I just use what I have. What I liked is that it wasn't so clean. It didn't have a lot of high end, which I liked too. All of these reverbs with the upgraded technology don't sound as warm to my ears.

Another dilemma for me is not having the predelay set properly. It's hard for engineers to get it where you hit the note and you hear that note with reverb. My dilemma, which I still can't seem to get somehow, is that you hit the note and it's bone dry, then the reverb follows. That doesn't work live because the trail is happening within the music of the other musicians, and all you really hear is a dry note. It's a weird phenomenon, but it's part of what I go through.

**How about your steel-string guitars?**

Onstage I still play the Ovation if I do play steel-string. In the studio, it's mostly an old Martin. That guitar has sustain for a week and a half. It's an old '48 Martin, and there's something about the wood, the age and the sustain on each note that is not to be believed. It also has that amazing clarity.

**Which mics do you choose for your acoustic sounds in the studio?**
I prefer Schoeps because they have the full tonal range with clarity. Doing all the A/Bs that I've done over the years with all different mics, those are the ones that seem to sound the best to me. They first came to my attention after discussing the tonal quality of ECM records with the late great engineer David Baker. When I started working with him, he brought those to the studio, and it was pretty clear right off that they were the mics of choice. Sure, there are other damn good ones out there, but I bought the Schoeps. They work on nylon, steel, piano and cymbals. I don't use them live, but they are great in the studio.

**Let's talk about your nylon-string guitars.**
The Conde Hermanos is the one. I just got a new model that has a bit more rosewood integrated into the construction of the body. The one I've used for the last 25 years is that bright orange one. That's actually a cyprus guitar, so it has more highs, but when you don't have the added rosewood, you lose some of the bottom. I've been really into using the new one because it's fuller and richer sounding. I had it custom-made, and it's a cutaway model.

They sound great, they project really well, and they punch. I look for the rhythmic articulation of an instrument, so those two just have great attack. The construction of the instruments is A-1. They are amazing instruments that withstand a lot of stress and tension, and I travel all over the world with them. I never have any problems like the necks bending, or dilemmas with tuning.

This is a family that's been making guitars forever. I always liked Paco's sound, even before I was playing with him. When I first hooked up with him, I ended up getting a Conde in Madrid, and that was the beginning of my association with it.

I have to say, though, it took a lot of years for me as a player to rise to the ranks of where I could feel comfortable playing that kind of instrument. It's like swinging four bats. It's certainly much harder to play than the Ovation. You can fly on an electric guitar, but an acoustic will be a level or two more challenging. It could be the gauge of strings, the wider neck or just how it's laid out.

When going to a nylon guitar, it's even double or triple that effort. So it took a while to get to that comfort level where I can graduate as a student from steel to nylon and play with that kind of technique. It's not so easy. Still, I can fly better on my steel, but I love the richness of the nylon.

**When working in the studio, you're also very conscious of the panning of your guitar parts.**
Well, when working with three guitarists, back with John and Paco, if you have them all mixed in the center and wide, it would be a mess. It's just logical to separate them so you can pick out who's who. This is especially true when you're trading licks, because it's more exciting to hear everyone in their own space. When you're mixing a record like that with a group, it's also important to keep that space open.

This goes back to the days of listening to The Beatles. I always loved when Ringo was on one side and the bass was on the same side! The only thing coming out of the other side was John or something. Damn, was that hip! It's still hip, but nobody mixes like that. You have to go back sometimes and listen and see what they were doing. Then do your own thing with it.

*To learn more about Al Di Meola, visit www.aldimeola.com.*

# Rob DiStefano: Veteran Guitar Tech

Since 1963, Rob DiStefano has been building, assembling, modding and repairing all manner of electric and acoustic guitars, electric basses, mandolins, banjos, ukuleles and any other instrument that uses frets and strings. He now runs Fret Tech, a shop that provides just about any service on a stringed instrument you can think of. A good recording instrument is one that is well maintained, and Rob was kind enough to give us some tips on the best way to do so.

**What's the biggest problem with guitars that come into your shop?**
Playability is number one, for sure. Some players don't have instruments that are playable enough to meet their needs, so they just don't perform well on them.

**Do you take a person's style into consideration when tuning up his or her instruments?**
Absolutely. You'd be crazy not to, because there are pick players, finger players and hybrid players, and the way they attack their instrument is super-important for me to see. My biggest nightmare is a 14 year-old kid who brings in an Ibanez RG with a Floyd or Kahler [vibrato system], and wants to have it set up so the action is so low he could breathe on the string and it would play itself. And that's while using 9s and it's dropped down to C! Sorry, can't do it.

**What is the biggest issue you come across when the instrument itself lacks tone?**
Well, of course it depends on the instrument and whether it's acoustic or electric, but first and foremost, it starts with the player. Pick your favorite player and give them a $99 Fender junker or a $5,000 custom shop model, and they pretty much will sound like themselves. To structure the tone, it's a combination of their brain and their fingers. Second is going to be the pickup. Third will be the amalgam of the guitar, not just the strings or the body or the wood. There's an in-toto thing about an instrument: It just either comes together, or it doesn't. Its not the cryogenic bridge or the custom electronics, it's the whole of the instrument itself, once you get beyond the pickups.

Of course, if you're a player who needs a lot of effects, then a lot of what we just talked about goes out the window because your inherent tone and ability to play makes it into something completely different. Then there's the amplifier, with all of the ramifications of speakers and tubes, which you can go on and on about.

**What about acoustic instruments?**
What you see is what you get. It's either built right or its not. I'm afraid that's just the way it goes. With an acoustic, you pay for tone. See, with an electric guitar, you can kind of modify it, because there's a good amount of versatility there to where you can tweak it. There's not much tweaking that can be done with an acoustic.

Let's think about it. What can you tweak? The truss rod...but really, its not there for tone. It's there to give you a little bit of relief for the bass strings so they don't bang against the frets. You can tweak the saddle up and down, maybe the lateral length there a bit, too. You can tweak the nut for relief, and maybe even use a little bit better material. But look, it's in the wood. You're paying for good wood and for somebody to put it together correctly.

**For players at home, what's one thing they can do to take better care of their instrument before they have to come to you?**
Humidify. All instruments need to be humidified. It's a huge problem, and it's always seasonal. People come in and want to know why the frets are cutting their fingers. The answer is typically because they haven't humidified, particularly over the winter when things get dried out because of the dry heat.

So you really need to be cognizant of humidity. You're looking for around 50 percent or so, and you don't want it to go down below 35 or 40 percent. It's better to be wet than to be dry; dry means the wood is going to shrink. Typically, when the wood shrinks, there's a point where it's not coming back. If it's wet, you can kind of get over that.

But note that this is true for all instruments. People say, "I have a Les Paul; why do I have to humidify? There's nothing acoustic about it." Yes, it is an acoustic instrument! It's got wood in it. Wood is organic. It reacts to temperature and humidity, so you need to take care of all your guitars that way. With acoustics, you really have to be on the ball for them. You have to use your humidifiers and keep the guitars in their case with humidification.

If you do have the guitar open in a room, make sure the room is humidified. Also, don't think that just because it's the summer and the air is humid that the instruments won't need care in that respect. Chances are, you're going to have those guitars in a room where there is air conditioning. What does A/C do? It sucks water out of the air. What is that going to do? It's going to dry your instrument out. What does that mean? It means you're going to be knocking on my door for an appointment.

*To learn more about Fret Tech, visit www.frettech.com.*

# John Holbrook: Recording Engineer/Producer

Multi-Grammy Award-winning engineer/producer John Holbrook has recorded a lot of artists during his career, but working with guitarists ranging from B.B. King to Todd Rundgren to Ernie Isley (of the Isley Brothers) to Brian Setzer has given him perspective on how to get great guitar sounds. He sat down with us on a lazy country afternoon to talk about some tales of the tone.

**Tell us about your background in music.**
At some point as a kid I started playing guitar, but I was also really interested in electronics. I got a Philips tape recorder that actually had an add-on ability to bounce tracks. That was my first recorder, and I had it at the same time as I was learning guitar. Eventually, when I got thrown out of university, I thought it would be cool to work in a recording studio, so I found the address of a bunch of them in London and wrote some letters.

Fortunately, I got hired at a studio called I.B.C, which was actually one of the early independent studios in London. It got me a start, and my gig was disc mastering. They had a stereo room and a guy who only wanted to do mono, so they wanted to train someone else to cut the stereo discs—we're talking about those round black plastic things with wobbly lines cut in them! Soon, I started doing things on the weekend in the studio. It's funny, I remember how many Neumann tube U-67s were on the floor there; it was amazing! It was quite a big room, and they used to do a lot of orchestral dates. They would just put 67s on everything. The 67 was a great mic, and I remember my roommate worked on *Tommy* with The Who, and said they had 67s on everything for that record too.

So I started recording with friends, where we would do a full album over a weekend, and that type of thing. I also ended up working for EMS, which was a synthesizer company in London. Then a friend of mine actually talked me into coming over to Woodstock, New York. He said the scene was happening, with Todd Rundgren and Albert Grossman and so on. I made it over here and just barely survived somehow, as I didn't know as much as I should have! They sent me out on the road doing live mixing for the Bearsville acts such as Paul Butterfield and Todd Rundgren and Utopia for a few years back in the '70s. That was my *Spinal Tap* introduction to America!

I eventually started to do more engineering at the Bearsville studios, which was really great back then. I really learned on the job, and did both outside clients and inside Bearsville clients like Jessie Winchester, Paul Butterfield, and The Band. I also worked on three or four albums with the Isley Brothers.

**How about Ernie Isley's guitar sound?**
There were plenty of pedals. It was basically his fuzz box—I think it was a Big Muff—a wah-wah pedal and the Mutron Phaser—the one with the big, colored buttons. He also had a Roger Mayer Octavia pedal, and we did some stuff with a Leslie guitar too. The amp didn't really matter, because it was all about him and those pedals.

So much of it is in the player that if you've got a guy who's got the touch, he's going to have a sound. You can give that same guitar and rig to someone else and it won't sound like him. It almost has less to do with the microphones than it has to do with the guy who's playing. Same with drums, but that's a different story.

**What is a great guitar sound to you?**

One that works in the track! On its own, it could be a wanky guitar sound, but it just might be the perfect thing to set off the track, so there are no rules. My default approach, until I really know what's going on, is to try and get a full spectrum of sound where the guitar has a pretty wide range. You have the high end with the harmonics, then the edge of the midrange, and then down on to the bottom. I just try to capture what's coming out of the amp. If the amp sounds like crap, it doesn't matter; I could put a $5,000 mic on it and it would still sound bad, because so much of the tone is in the player and the rig.

**What would be a classic mic setup?**

Well, it's varied over the years, but we know that a 57 is a good thing, but I also fancy a nice tube 67 if I can get my hands on one. Most of the time I'll have a 57 right on the grill cloth after I've found the sweet spot, but then I'll take a 67 and put it a little further away so you're getting the whole picture of the amp. As for a preferred preamp, I'd certainly take a Neve if I could.

**How about working with Brian Setzer?**

Well, on the first day I came in, his roadie had set him up with two Fender Bassman amps, which is what he would set up onstage with. But live, he only used one, and the other one was a spare. For some reason—this was at The Village in Los Angeles—he had them both on and it was loud! So that was part of the sound. The other thing is that he overdrives the input with the Roland Space Echo. The Roland is hitting it a little harder than the guitar normally would, so he's overdriving the front end a little bit.

So I put a 57 and a 67 on each of the cabinets, with the 57 on the grill cloth and the 67 backed off a bit. Depending on how edgy it would sound, I would go off-axis a little with the 57. It's a question of tuning it to get a sweet blend of the frequencies. So the first session on the *Dirty Boogie* album, we used four mics on his guitar.

But something sounded out of phase. Not 100 percent out of phase, but something was bugging me that I couldn't quite figure out. I was checking the phase buttons on the four mics, and no matter what I did, it sounded out of whack. The problem was that Brian was raring to go, and we had a good sound, so we just started recording. As we're playing it back, I'm thinking to myself, "Something is not right," but everyone else thought it sounded great, so we stuck with it, and that whole first album was recorded that way.

I subsequently found out one of the speakers in one of the cabinets was wired out of phase unintentionally. When we got to the second project, I went through that with his guitar tech, but it actually created a cool sound. When you listen back to it, it created this interesting stereo field that works because it's not 100 percent in-phase. So if you want to create this sort of unique guitar sound, you take two cabinets and reverse the polarity of one of the speakers!

**Do you generally compress at the mix stage, or does it depend on the track?**

It completely depends on the track. A lot of times, I don't feel that guitars need a lot of compression anyway, because the distorted tones already have inherent amp compression. There's really not a whole lot of point in compressing that, although maybe it might make some difference on the attack of the sound. When you're talking about a clean setting, you can compress it though. It all depends, because there are no rules.

**Do you ever give the guitarists feedback that their sound may be too distorted?**
Yes, sure, especially if it seems like they want it [the feedback about the sound].
Working with Brian [Setzer], he always wanted to know how it was sounding. Also,
he would check if there was too much delay and stuff like that. He would ask, but
some people don't want to. I think generally, people are willing to adjust if you feel it
strongly enough.

I think it's a good idea if the guitarist has the patience to run a little piece of the track
and then let them come hear it. If they're out in the room, they're hearing it in a
different way, so roll a half a minute or so and have them come in and see if it sounds
right to them.

**Do you have a preferred acoustic recording method?**
I go back and forth with large- and small-diaphragm mics. I do tend to go with a small
one, and usually the default position is over the 12th fret, pointing back toward the
sound hole. I know other people do that, but I kind of arrived at that position on my
own by just experimenting. I also like a single 67 on an acoustic. I'm not necessarily a big
"mic everything in stereo" guy, so I do find sometimes that one guitar needs just one
mic. To me, if you can get it in the sweet spot, it's all good!

*To learn more about John Holbrook, visit www.johnholbrook.biz.*

# Hernan Romero: Flamenco Guitarist

Born in Buenos Aires, Argentina, Flamenco guitar virtuoso Hernan Romero infuses his music with elements of flamenco/gypsy, Middle Eastern, classical and jazz to produce a style that is uniquely his. A frequent collaborator with Al Di Meola, he has played with a variety of artists ranging from Stevie Nicks to John McLaughlin. Hernan was kind enough to give us his views on what he looks for in a flamenco guitar.

### Tell us a bit about your background.

My mom, Estela Raval, is a Grammy Award-winning singer, and my dad is also a great musician. I actually started playing guitar on my own when I was around 9 years old. When I was 11, my mom sent me to study with Roberto Lara, who was one of Andrés Segovia's disciples and a really great teacher. So I spent around four years with him, and then went to Andalucía, Spain to do additional studies. Then I moved to the United States and went to college for music there. I played around New York for many years and started doing sessions, eventually hooking up with artists ranging from Stevie Nicks to Al Di Meola. I've done many records with Al, but also I tour nationally and internationally as a solo artist with my band.

### What do you personally look for in a flamenco guitar?

First, it needs to be very responsive, with a lot of both high and low end. Low end is especially important to me because I play very percussively on my instruments. With flamenco, you can play very delicately, but overall, it's more dynamic.

### To you, what's the difference between a classical and a flamenco guitar?

With a traditional classical guitar, you can only do certain things. With a flamenco, you can be both delicate and aggressive. To me, it's simply a more versatile guitar. Flamenco guitars project more, and although the scale is typically the same, it's louder, depending on the wood. I tend to also like the action a bit higher on my flamenco guitars versus classical, but that's obviously up to the player. With flamenco, you need to have a lot of space to do your *golpe*, which is the percussive striking. Classical guitars do not respond well to that.

### What kind of strings do you use?

I use different ones, but primarily D'Addario EJ44Cs, the Extra Hard Tension ones. Extra hard tension is important, because you can get hard tension, but after I play them once, the volume of the strings dies. I play very hard, and these EJ strings will last a week to two during a tour. You can actually bring them to life again if you de-stretch and stretch them again. I know people like Paco [de Lucia] will use his strings for like two months, but I like them when they're fresh. I've also occasionally combined sets, using the lows of the D'Addario and the highs of a Savarez set. The strings make a huge difference tonally, especially for flamenco, because I need volume.

### What about your nail care? Is it critical for your sound?

Oh yes. I settled on nail glue with an acrylic powder. It actually uses your own nail, but it's reinforced with a layer of glue and a little powder, then another layer and so on to make my nail a little thicker. I keep them pretty short because for the best tone, I play with the flesh of the finger and the nail. It's the most versatile sound for me. I keep my thumbnail pretty long because I use it like a pick. The nail is also for the percussive attack on my guitar—the *golpe*.

**How do you translate your studio sound to the stage?**

Well, I really do not like the sound of internal pickups, especially on nylon guitars. I've tried all the different models and blender systems with mics in the guitar and so on, but I really like microphones onstage with no DIs. I will bring the Earthworks SR 30s with me and place them right in front of the guitar. I also found it works great for my voice, so I use a pair. There are also some great stage mics from AKG and Sennheiser, but I'm very happy with the Earthworks, so I travel with them wherever I play.

**So how do you travel with a flamenco guitar?**

I have a pressurized hard-shell case with a humidifier, and it always goes in the cabin with me. No exceptions, unless I'm in a very small plane where I watch them walk it in. 99% of the time I carry my guitar, which can be a pain in the neck, but I wouldn't have it any other way.

**How do you care for the guitar on the road?**

It's not easy. My last tour, which was through Russia and Poland, had a lot of flights and it was quite cold. The top of my guitar actually developed a huge crack on that tour in Siberia, because temperatures mess with guitars. When you go out of the hotel there, even just to walk for a minute, the case protects it, but only a certain amount. The ideal thing is to have two guitars. I like to have my Hermanos Conde on stage all the time, and I had another one with me in the dressing room while warming up. If you warm up with the same guitar you go onstage with, it will go out of tune because it's always colder or hotter. So I'd tune the main guitar and leave it on the stage, because when I came out to play, it was settled and ready to go.

**Is your studio guitar also your live guitar?**

Yes, I play my Conde both in the studio and on tour. I also use a Ravasa from Spain, and Carmen Guitars built me a signature model on my last tour as well—a flamenco model. But in the studio, I will use all my guitars, either my Carmen or Conde flamenco guitar or sometimes my Ramirez, which is a classical model. It's whatever the song calls for.

*To learn more about Hernan Romero, visit www.hernanromero.com.*

# Chip Verspyck: Amplifier Tech

Chip Verspyck is surrounded by recording gear all day, but instead of tweaking knobs to get the perfect mix, he's fixing it all so you can keep working. As owner and chief technician of Tech it Out in New York State's Hudson Valley, Verspyck has worked in countless studios and repaired literally hundreds of guitar amps. We talked to him while he was encircled by a collection of vintage Fender amps, all of which were in his shop for a tune-up.

*Credit: Fender black face collection in foreground courtesy of Jeffrey Resnick. Background amps courtesy of Clubhouse.*

### How did you get started fixing gear?
I started out as an assistant recording engineer and hung out with techs in the shop. I ended up helping the techs out in the studio a lot, and eventually ended up doing full-time maintenance at Bearsville Studios in Woodstock, N.Y. At the same time, I was also going to night school for electrical engineering. I worked at Bearsville from 1997 until 2002. Even while I was at Bearsville, I was freelancing around the area full-time. I was working my ass off and learning a lot.

When Bearsville was on the brink of closing down, I left and went out on my own. I moved my shop to Clubhouse Studios in Rhinebeck and run my business, Tech it Out, out of there.

### So between all those studios, you've seen a lot of amps.
Oh, yeah. As far as tube guitar amps go, I learned it all out of necessity, being in a recording studio. I play sax and trumpet, but I'm not a guitar player. Maybe that's a good thing, because I take an objective approach, and don't get hung up on tweaking for the perfect tone. I get it by taking an amp back to the way it was designed, but if a client wants a custom tone, I can work with them on achieving that. Guitar amps are refreshingly simple compared to a lot of high-end pieces of recording gear. Vintage Fender amps and the like are so easy to work on.

### Why is that?
Because everything is point-to-point wired, and it's so easy to get access to the components. Point-to-point wiring is where everything in the amp is hand-wired, versus having a printed circuit board—that's where everything is on copper traces along a board, and the majority of new guitar amps you buy today, even the reissue Fenders and Vox's, are made that way.

Now, there's nothing wrong with that if the layout is done right, but are they hard to fix? Sometimes yes, because in order to replace a pot, or get inside and troubleshoot, it's all sandwiched in. You have to take the whole thing apart because it's all built as the cart before the horse, which makes it difficult to safely troubleshoot while it's still powered. You're dealing with very high voltages—around 400 volts DC—and that is really quite lethal. With any of the old Fender, Ampeg, Marshall, classic Vox's or any '60s amps, everything is very open and laid out in a way that you can easily get to it all.

### So what makes those amps so great from a design point of view?

Well, it's the simplicity. Most pro studio equipment and hi-fi is clinical and has to have a flat frequency response, low distortion and super-wide bandwidth. But in a tube guitar amp, there's usually no negative feedback in the preamp, and the gain stages are so basic. Feedback, in this sense, is when you have a closed-loop circuit that's controlling the distortion and frequency response. The preamp is running open-loop and single-ended Class A—hence, you get that open sound. You get more second-harmonic distortion, which is the good distortion that we all like, so its very musical, even when playing clean. There's not a lot going on in there to constrict the sound, which is what allows the amp to have its signature tone or harmonic coloration.

### What's the most common problem you see when an amp comes in for repair?

Broken connections are super common. They're called cold solder joints; when the solder develops a crack from vibration if the amp has been on the road or just moved around. The connections get loose and funk also builds up in tube sockets and pots, which causes noise.

Tubes go bad too. They're like light bulbs in that they have a certain life span, then they start to wear out, short out or get noisy. Capacitors, or caps, also go bad as well. They have an average lifespan of about 20 years. Most of the amps I see are way older than that, so the caps just go. Symptoms of a bad cap results in hum, mushy tone, ghost notes, crackling and lack of power and gain. It just makes the amp not perform the way it should.

### What's a symptom of bad tubes?

Noise, low gain, poor headroom or just a complete failure. Also, some tubes go microphonic, which is when the amp has this "ring" to it.

### Do you have an opinion on new tubes versus new old-stock (NOS) tubes?

Actually, I try not to get into all the mojo of that stuff. You can get so caught up in it that it can distract you from what's really important. If somebody wants to take the time to tube roll and listen to the subtle nuances, that's great. You can certainly go crazy with it.

I do agree that the NOS tubes like Mullards, Telefunkens, RCA black plates and so on were made to a better standard than today's tubes are. There's really only a few tube manufacturing plants left in the world. There's JJ, Sovtek (which is owned by New Sensor), the EI plant in Yugoslavia (I don't know what's up them these days), and the Chinese tubes. With any of those, you can get a lot of duds in a batch. The new manufacturing is not held to the same standards as the old ones were.

With the NOS, a lot of them are called JAN tubes, which stands for Joint Army-Navy. They were made for military equipment and tested to a military standard, so they were built to withstand hot and cold temperatures, excessive vibrations and so on. If you have a tube with that JAN stamp, usually from Phillips, GE and so on, you've got a good bet that tube will be pretty robust.

### So what's the best thing somebody could do to maintain their tube amp by themselves?

Keep it out of humidity and don't put it in your damp basement. Be gentle when transporting it! Tubes are in sockets and they can jostle loose. There's really not too much the user can do without opening it up, but tubes on most amps are generally replaceable by the user. Every now and then you should tighten all the accessible screws and nuts that hold it all together because the hardware connections all inevitably loosen over time from the vibration of the speaker. If anything is loose, the cabinet will have an annoying buzz on certain notes and sound like you have a blown speaker.

You can also troubleshoot an amp by swapping tubes. If you're on the road, keep a spare set of every tube in your amp. If you've got a problem, you can swap them out one by one. If there's not something wrong with the circuit, you may be able to get the amp up and running.

Sometimes just pulling a tube out and pushing it back in can clean off enough of the funky oxidization that builds up on the pins or socket. You can also take your finger and lightly tap the glass, with the gain set low, of course. If you hear a high-pitched noise or ringing, it's microphonic, which means it's susceptible to vibration. There's something mechanical in the tube that's gone bad. You can hear it because the gain in the tube is amplifying that problem.

*Find out more about Tech it Out at studiomaintenance.com.*

## Jim Weider: Telecaster Slinger

There are Strat guys, there are Les Paul guys and then there are Tele guys. Jim Weider, with his vintage '52 over his shoulder, is undeniably one of the latter. He's hit the road for 15 years with The Band, played or recorded with Los Lobos, Bob Dylan, Paul Butterfield and Mavis Staples, and toured the world with his own group, Project Percolator. Below, JW digs into a conversation about all things Tele.

*Photo by Mike Thut*

**Tell us how you first got into the guitar.**
Well, my father had an acoustic guitar when I was a kid. Back then in the early '60s, you could get a pickup and stick it on an acoustic guitar. My uncle actually built my first amp out of this radio and put an input jack on it, so I had the acoustic guitar plugged into that, trying to play Scotty Moore stuff. Eventually, when I got an electric guitar, everybody got like a Japanese copy, and mine was a two-pickup Kent, although I really wanted the one with the three pickups!

I had a little Silvertone amp that had three inputs, and we put one vocalist and two guitar players into it. You didn't have a bass back then. You had one guy playing rhythm, one playing lead, and a guy with a mic. We were playing rock and roll, or whatever we could play. You know, Ventures, Stones, Beatles stuff, although that was always harder than the Stones. We'd hit "For Your Love" from The Yardbirds, or whatever was happening at the time.

I'd always wanted a Telecaster. Back then, the Telecaster was one of the most popular guitars because you actually saw guys on TV playing Teles, like James Burton on The Ricky Nelson Show and Steve Cropper with the Hullaballoo band. Even Jeff Beck with the early Yardbirds had him on the album cover playing a Tele.

It was also a little cheaper than a Strat or a Paul. I got mine for $130 at Manny's. That was the cool guitar back then before the Strat became popular, which kind of happened with Hendrix. Still, there were enough guys playing a Telecaster that I just loved it, but when I heard Roy Buchanan doing feedback with one, well that was it.

**Teles are guitars you have to fight. Have you ever gone to other guitars?**
No, I've always been a Tele guy. You're right that you have to work hard on a Tele. I've had other guitars, like an old [Les Paul] Junior in the '60s, but quickly got rid of it to go back to the Tele. I went all the way out to L.A. in search of a '50s Tele, and that's where I found my '52.

Hearing Buchanan play that blonde black-guard Tele, I felt that the flat-pole pickup was more like the lap steel pickup they used in the '50s. They had more girth, and it wasn't so twangy. Everybody thinks of the Tele as being a real twangy country guitar, but there are different styles. With the old '50s ones, you could do blues and rock because they just had this presence and sustain from the back pickup.

**What made those pickups different?**
Well, those pickups had more windings, so they were a bit more powerful. The magnets were flat-poled, and I think they used different magnets than the later '60s ones. It was basically a lap steel guitar put on a plank of wood that had the fixed brass bridge, which just had some sustain to it.

**So your style was literally built around a Telecaster?**
Yes, it makes you play a certain way. You have to work a little harder and play a little harder. Sometimes you don't use your pick and use your fingers and change your tone

just by the way you touch the strings, unless you're playing like Albert Lee, who's got a really light, fast and articulate right hand. That's a different style of flat-picking Telecaster playing, but if you're playing blues and digging in like Roy [Buchanan] and Albert Collins, you play really hard.

The early cats who played Teles played them hard, although there were guys like Jimmy Bryant, who did have a light touch and influenced Albert Lee. They could do that really fast country/jazz-swing stuff. In my case, I was more of a rock, blues and country player, mixed all together.

### Did you take lessons?
I mostly taught myself by using the old nickel-on-the-record-player-to-slow-it-down trick. I just learned as much as I could and along the way I was lucky enough to meet Lenny Breau, and got three or four lessons from him, but mostly I just taught myself.

### What year did you start in The Band?
In 1985; I toured with them for 15 years, until the end of 1999. I also do a lot of session work, and I've worked with people ranging from Mavis Staples to Los Lobos to Scotty Moore, to just so many people. Besides my solo group, PRoJECT PERCoLAToR, I'm also currently playing with the Levon Helm Band.

### How about amps?
I've always used Fenders. The way I would set up my Tele to get the best sound out of the amp is to raise the rear bridge pickup as close as I could to the strings without the strings hitting the magnets. I also did the same with the rhythm pickup. I'd put it up as far as I could get it. Of course, you're always experimenting with getting better rhythm pickups in there.

For years, I used an old Vibrolux and would just crank it up. Guys like Buchanan would get two of them, put them on 10 and operate his guitar with the volume and tone controls. Eventually, I went to a Deluxe Reverb for years, even when I was out touring with The Band.

I would soup up a Deluxe because they will break up sooner than a Vibrolux. I'd change out the speakers and put a 50-watt Vintage 30 in there, as well as a pair of 6L6s [power tubes—the Deluxe comes with 6V6s]. Cesar Diaz modified it and put in an old Bassman output transformer, so it was really mismatched, but it had a definite sound. That thing could really kick ass.

But any normal old Deluxe with a Tele and a good speaker in it could get that break up at a lower volume. Sometimes I would also use Naylor 50-watt speakers, but now I'm just using old Celestions. I also like playing through a 4x12 if I can.

### What's your current rig?
Right now, it's the Two Rock Type 3, which is kind of a Dumble-esque style amp with a real nice black-face sound and a great, natural-sounding distortion. It has two 6L6s and a couple of Mullard dual-rectifier tubes. That goes into one old greenback G12M Celestion and one old 1265 Celestion in a 2X12 Hermida cab. When playing with the Levon Helm Band, I use two old vintage brown-and-gold-back Jensen 12s in a Hermida closed-back cab that's ported. I change it up to get the more rootsy, Fender-sounding thing. In my band, where I'll use more gain, I use the Celestion loaded cabinets. It's working really good.

### How about your strings?

10-48. They're standard except for the 0.48 on the bass and 0.16 on the G string.

### How often do you change them?

Usually every week before the gigs. If I have four gigs in a row, I'll change at least the top strings, otherwise impending doom awaits!

### Do you use any pedals?

I use a King Of Tone by Analog Man, which I really like. It's kind of like a Tube Screamer in that it boosts without loosing your bottom. I helped design it to make it sound kind of like a Fender Deluxe. We modified it until we got it sounding like my Deluxe breaking up. We kept changing the chips until we found the right ones. I use that in places when I want a more compressed sound, but I also use the built-in natural amp distortion live.

### Talk about recording your Tele.

I've got a Manley stereo mic pre, and I use a [Shure] 57 off-center, and usually one other really good mic, on another cabinet at the same time only a little bit back. I've had good luck with that combination.

The hardest part is actually taking the time to find the guitar tone for the track. I'll spend more time on that than actually performing. When recording, I like to not use any distortion boxes and prefer to just use certain amps. I'll set up a few of them maybe with a few different cabinets, then I'll just experiment until I find the right tone for the track. I then go back and listen to see if the amp works. If it does, then I can check out moving the mics. I have to say, that's the luxury of recording at home. In the studio, you usually have an engineer that can move the mics around, but at home you can take your time.

### So your road and studio rigs are different.

Yes, I have more amps at home to record with. Sometimes you might want a Marshall, a tweed [Fender], or a little amp like a Supro or Gibson. There is just nothing like getting the sound out of the amp cranked; that inspires you. Then I crank it as loud as I can stand it through my monitor speakers, and play in the room with the track playing really loud so it's like playing live.

### So really, what is it about a Tele?

The Tele just stands out in a track. It really cuts. It can sound sweet to nasty just by switching from the rhythm pickup to the middle [both pickups] to the back and working the tone controls. It also makes you an individual player because you learn how to do double bends with two or three strings, which you can of course do on any guitar, but they seem to cut better with a Tele. Learn how to really make that back pickup functional by turning the tone control down a bit and using your volume swells. Teles just stand out with that.

### Have you grown as a player?

Yes, and you grow by playing fewer notes in the wrong places! I practice, and I try to move my hands every day to keep them in some kind of shape. I like to play to tracks online, which has been a blast. I'll just turn that up and turn up my amp and just jam. I'd rather do that then play a bunch of scales. That really warms you up.

### So how do you keep your Teles in shape?

In the early '70s I started putting the really big Gibson-style frets on it, which I learned from Roy Buchanan, and that makes them play a lot easier. The finish is worn off the back of mine from use, but on a couple of new Teles like the Fender Roadworn series, it comes with the finish off. If it doesn't, I'll just sand the finish off myself. The Roadworns are actually nice guitars.

I also wear both the volume and tone pots out, so I change them every couple of years or so when they really start getting scratchy. RS guitar works makes really nice straight-shaft brass pots for the Telecaster that are high end, and that's what I use. I'm always changing my tuning pegs because they wear out. I also have the three bent brass bridge pieces that intonate a little bit better. A bunch of manufacturers make them. On my old Tele, the neck and body and back pickup are vintage, and I modify everything else. Those things have made playing the Tele much easier for me.

To learn more about Jim Weider, visit www.jimweider.com.

## Glossary

**active**—an electronic device or circuit that requires AC or DC power to operate.

**ambience**—the sonic character of an environment.

**attack**—the first part of a sound. On a compressor/limiter, a control that affects how that device will respond to the attack of a sound.

**attenuation**—a decrease in level.

**attenuation pad** (sometimes called a pad)—a small passive circuit that decreases the input level by a set amount. The pad can be either inline or available as a selection on most preamps. The amount of attenuation is usually in 10 or 20dB increments.

**balanced cable**—uses two conductors to eliminate electronic interference.

**bandwidth**—frequency range. A human being can hear from 20 Hz to 20 kHz so the bandwidth of the human ear is 20 Hz to 20k Hz.

**Bias**—sets the operating point of an amplifier's power tubes, and has a huge influence on both the way the amp sounds and the longevity of the tubes.

**Blumlein**—a stereo miking technique using two figure-8 microphones.

**bottom**—bass frequencies, the lower end of the audio spectrum.

**bottom-end**—see bottom.

**bout**—the outward curve in the side of a guitar.

**boutique gear**—high-quality, hand-built musical or audio gear with a limited production run.

**bleed**—acoustic spill from a sound source other than the one intended for pickup.

**bpm**—beats per minute. Used as a measure of tempo.

**break-up**—distort.

**cardioid**—a pickup pattern of a microphone that's heart shaped.

**Class A**—the tubes are conducting all of the time. This class has the least distortion of all the classes, but offers the least power, and runs very hot.

**Class B**—the tubes only conduct 50 percent of the time. This design is very efficient and produces more power and less heat but produces a lot more unusable distortion.

**Class AB**—is found in virtually all guitar amps because it has the best of both Class A and Class B. It's efficient, offers more power than Class A, and can be configured to have a variable amount of distortion. Class AB amps always use a pair of power tubes; the more closely-matched, the better.

**Class D**—used in solid-state amps with output transistors that operate as switches, turning on and off at a very high rate. This increases the efficiency, making the amp more portable and capable of being battery-powered.

**Class H**—used in solid-state amps where voltage rises as power demand goes up. Like Class D, Class H is very efficient and allows for a very high-power yet lightweight design.

**clean**—a signal with no distortion.

**clipping**—the point where input electronics overload because the incoming audio level is too high.

**close-miking**—placing a mic close to an instrument or speaker in order to minimize room reflections or other sound sources.

**compander**—used in early wireless systems as a way to reduce noise, the circuit compressions on transmission and expands when it receives.

**condenser microphone**—a microphone that uses two electrically charged plates (creating an electronic component known as a capacitor) as its basis of operation.

**convolution reverb**—a processor that uses a sonic impulse to sample the characteristics of a real acoustic space, then extrapolates and recreates parameters.

**DAW**—Digital Audio Workstation. The computer software and hardware system for recording and editing audio.

**Decca Tree**—A stereo miking technique used primarily for orchestral recording, which uses a spaced pair with a center mic connected to a custom stand suspended over the conductor.

**DI (Direct Injection)**—an impedance-matching device that lets the guitar record direct, eliminating the need for a microphone.

**Dobro**—a resonator guitar that features a single, inverted-bowl-shaped metal cone.

**double**—to play or sing a track a second time. The inconsistencies between both tracks make the part sound bigger.

**direct**—to "go direct" means to bypass a microphone and connect the guitar, bass, or keyboard directly into a recording device.

**direct box**—see DI

**dynamic microphone**—a microphone that converts acoustic energy into electrical energy by the motion of a diaphragm through a magnetic field.

**envelope**—the attack and release of a sound.

**excursion**—a speaker's travel back and forth from its resting point.

**f-hole**—the soundhole on an arch top guitar that has the shape of an italicized "f."

**feel**—the groove of a song and the emotion felt when playing it or listening to it.

**flip the phase**—selecting the phase switch on a console, preamp or DAW channel to switch a channel in and out of phase in order to find the setting with the greatest bass response.

**footballs**—whole notes. Long sustaining distorted guitar chords.

**figure-8**—a microphone with a polar pattern that picks up sound equally at its front and rear.

**gain staging**—setting the gain of each amplification stage so that one does not overload the next in line.

**Headroom**—the difference between the normal operating level and the onset of distortion.

**high end**—the high-frequency response of a device; the high range of a frequency bandwidth.

**highpass filter**—an electronic device that allows frequencies above a set threshold to pass through while attenuating the low frequencies. Used to eliminate low-frequency artifacts such as hum and rumble.

**humbucking**—a guitar pickup that uses two coils in reversed polarity to eliminate outside noise and interference ("buck the hum"). Humbucking pickups have much higher gain than single-coil pickups.

**hypercardioid**—a microphone with a pickup pattern that is much more directional than a normal cardioid pickup pattern.

**impedance**—an electronic circuit's resistance to alternating current.

**input pad**—an electronic circuit that attenuates the signal, usually between 10 and 20dB.

**iso booth**—isolation booth. A soundproofed room that eliminates leakage in or out.

**impulse response**—the acoustic response of a physical space in response to a short-duration audio signal.

**intonation**—the pitch accuracy of a guitar across the fingerboard.

**latency**—a measure of the time (in milliseconds) that it takes for a signal to pass through an system during the recording process. This delay is generated by the time it takes for your computer to receive, understand, process and send the signal back to your outputs.

**leakage**—sound from another source "bleeding" into a mic pointed at an instrument.

**lining**—a piece of wood used to attach an acoustic guitar's top and back to its sides.

**lowpass filter**—a circuit or device that allows only low frequencies to pass.

**luthier**—someone who makes or repairs stringed instruments.

**microphonic**—when a tube or pickup acts like a microphone and captures the surrounding mechanical vibrations.

**mono**—a recording using only a single channel that offers limited spatial sensory information.

**modulation**—modifying a signal with a second signal. A chorus effect uses a very low-frequency signal to modulate the audio signal.

**null point**—the point on the microphone pickup pattern where the pickup sensitivity is at its lowest.

**nut**—the piece of bone, stainless steel, plastic or other material positioned where the fretboard meets the headstock that guides the strings from the tuning pegs to the fretboard.

**off-axis**—a sound source away from the primary pickup point of a microphone.

**omnidirectional**—a microphone that picks up sound equally from any direction.

**ORTF**—a stereo miking technique developed by the Office of French Radio and Television Broadcasting using two cardioid mics angled 110 degrees apart and spaced seven inches (17 cm) apart horizontally.

**out of phase**—see phase cancellation.

**overdrive**—when a device is driven beyond its maximum operating level and begins to distort. A device that intentionally drives the next device or stage to distortion.

**pan**—placing a sound in the stereo field.

**peak**—a short, temporary rise in signal strength.

**passive**—circuitry that operates without any additional AC or DC power.

**phantom center**—the image seems to come from exactly in the center of two speakers.

**phase cancellation**—when two like waveforms are off time alignment, parts of their frequency components cancel each other out, producing an undesirable audio effect.

**plug-in**—an add-on utility that adds functionality to a computer application. EQ, modulation and reverb are examples of DAW plug-ins.

**polar pattern**—the pickup pattern of a microphone.

**power chords**—long sustaining distorted guitar chords.

**proximity effect**—the inherent low-frequency boost that occurs when directional microphone gets closer to the signal source.

**preamplifier**—an electronic device or circuit that boosts a low signal (usually from a microphone or guitar) to a level that can be more easily transmitted or manipulated.

**presence**—accentuated upper mid-range frequencies (from 5 to 10 kHz).

**point-to-point**—amplifier wiring that is hand-wired and soldered from connection to connection.

**punchy**—sound quality description that infers good reproduction of dynamics, with a strong impact. Sometimes means an emphasis in the 200Hz and 5kHz areas.

**ratio**—on a compressor/limiter a parameter that determines how much compression or limiting will occur when the signal exceeds threshold.

**release**—the last part of a sound. On a compressor/limiter, a control that affects how long that device will take to return to normal after the signal falls below a set threshold.

**returns**—inputs on a recording console or DAW, especially those dedicated for effects devices such as reverbs and delays. The return inputs are usually not as sophisticated as channel inputs.

**ribbon microphone**—a microphone that uses a thin aluminum ribbon as the main pickup element.

**roll off**—to attenuate either end of the frequency spectrum.

**roller nut**—a rolling wheel that replaces a standard nut and reduces string friction.

**rout**—to cut a cavity or edge in a piece of wood.

**scale length**—the distance between the bridge saddles and the nut.

**single coil**—a guitar pickup style based around one coil; found primarily on Fender guitars.

**slack-key**—a Hawaiian style of music in which the strings of a guitar are tuned to a chord.

**soundfield**—the left-right area of a stereo recording.

**spaced pair**—a stereo miking technique in which the microphones are placed several feet apart.

**standing waves**—in certain acoustic environments, room wall reflections reinforce some frequencies the signal and cancel out others.

**sweet spot**—the best listening position, usually providing the truest stereo soundscape.

**sympathetic vibration**—vibrations in a part of an instrument, caused by vibrations in another part, or by vibrations in other instruments.

**surround**—the edges of a speaker cone that connect it to the speaker basket.

**threshold**—the signal level at which an effect begins to work. On a compressor/limiter for instance, the threshold control adjusts the point at which compression turns on.

**top end**—see high end.

**tonewoods**—woods that are generally recognized to have pleasing and consistent acoustic qualities; used in guitar construction.

**transient**—a very short-duration waveform with a very steep rise and fall in volume, i.e. the attack of a guitar note.

**tremolo**—a cyclic variation in volume.

**tube**—(see vacuum tube).

**unbalanced cable**—a cable with a single conductor that is susceptible to electronic interference. A typical guitar cable is unbalanced.

**under load**—operating in standard conditions.

**Unidirectional**—a mic that has a pickup pattern in a single direction.

**unity gain**—a gain of 1, which means that the circuit or device neither adds or subtracts gain.

**vacuum tube**—an electron tube used as the primary amplification device in most amplifiers and vintage audio gear. Tube gear runs hot, is heavy, and some components may have a short life, but most have a desirable sound.

**vibrato**—a cyclic variation in frequency.

**voice coil**—a coil of wire attached to the apex of a speaker cone; the center of a loudspeaker.

**XLR**—a connector for balanced wiring usually used in microphones and high-end audio gear.

**X/Y**—a stereo miking technique where the microphone capsules are mounted as closely as possible while crossing at 90 degrees.

# Bibliography

## Bobby Owsinski

**The Mixing Engineer's Handbook, 2nd Edition** (ISBN #1598632515; Thomson Course Technology) The premier book on audio mixing techniques provides all the information necessary to take your mixing skills to the next level, along with advice from the world's best mixing engineers.

**The Recording Engineer's Handbook, 2nd Edition** (159863867X; Course Technology PTR) Reveals the recording techniques used by some of the world's most renowned recording engineers. You'll find everything you need to know to lay down great tracks in any recording situation, in any musical genre, and in any studio.

**The Audio Mastering Handbook, 2nd Edition** (ISBN #1598634496; Course Technology PTR) Everything you've always wanted to know about mastering, from doing it yourself to using a major facility, with insights from the world's top mastering engineers.

**The Drum Recording Handbook** with DVD (with Dennis Moody) (ISBN #1423443438; Hal Leonard) Uncover the secrets to make amazing drum recordings in your recording studio, even with the most inexpensive gear. It's all in the technique, and this book and DVD will show you how.

**How To Make Your Band Sound Great** with DVD (ISBN #1423441907; Hal Leonard) This band improvement book and DVD shows your band how to play to its fullest potential. It doesn't matter what kind of music you play, what your skill level is, or if you play covers or your own music—this book will make you tight, it will make you more dynamic, it will improve your show and it will improve your recordings.

**The Studio Musician's Handbook** with DVD (with Paul ILL) (ISBN #1423463412; Hal Leonard) Everything you ever wanted to know about the world of the studio musician, including how you become one, who hires you and how much you get paid, what kind of skills you need and what kind of gear you must have, proper session etiquette to make a session run smoothly, and how to apply these skills in every type of recording session, whether it's in your home studio or at Abbey Road.

**Music 3.0 A Survival Guide To Making Music in the Internet Age** (ISBN #1423474015; Hal Leonard) The paradigm has shifted and everything you knew about the music business has completely changed. Who are the new players? Why are traditional record labels, television and radio no longer factors in an artist's success? How do you market and distribute your music in the new music world, and how do you make money? This book answers these questions and more in its comprehensive look at the new music business.

**The Music Producer's Handbook** (ISBN 978-1423474005; Hal Leonard) Reveals inside information and secrets to becoming a music producer and producing just about any kind of project in any genre of music. Topics covered include the producer's responsibilities and all of the elements of a typical production, including budgeting, contracts, selecting the studio and engineer, hiring session musicians and even getting paid! The book covers the true mechanics of production, from analyzing and fixing the format of a song, to troubleshooting a song when it just doesn't sound right, to getting the best performance and sound out of the band and vocalist.

*The Musician's Video Handbook* (ISBN 978-1423484448; Hal Leonard) Learn how the average musician can easily make videos for promotion or final product. The book will demonstrate the tricks and tips used by the pros to make videos look professional, even with inexpensive gear and a shoestring budget.

*Mixing and Mastering with T-RackS: The Official Guide* (ISBN 978-1435457591; Course Technology PTR) T-RackS is a popular stand-alone audio mastering application that includes a suite of powerful dynamics and EQ processor modules. T-RackS is an extremely powerful tool for improving the quality of your recordings, but all of that power won't do you much good if it's misused. Learn to harness the potential of T-RackS, and learn the tips and tricks of using T-RackS processor modules to help bring your mixes to life and then master them so that they compete with any major-label release.

*The Touring Musician's Handbook* (ISBN 978-1423492368; Hal Leonard) For a musician, touring is the brass ring. It's the thing that everyone dreams about from the first time they pick up an instrument. But what do you do when you finally get that chance? How do you audition? What kind of chops do you need? What equipment should you bring? How do you prepare for life on the road? Regardless of whether you're a side player, solo performer or member of a band, you'll learn the answers to all of these questions in *The Touring Musician's Handbook*. As a bonus, individual touring musician guides for guitar, bass, drums, vocals, keys, horns and strings, as well as interviews with famous and influential touring players are also included.

# Rich Tozzoli

**Pro Tools Surround Sound Mixing** (ISBN 978-0879308322 Backbeat Books) This essential guide takes readers through all the steps they need to record, mix and produce music with Pro Tools. It covers preproduction, recording, setup, mixing and delivery of surround music. Various formats such as DVD-Video, DVD-Audio, and SACD—and how to use Pro Tools to deliver mixes for all three formats—are discussed. The book also covers encoding mixes for Dolby Digital and DTS, mixing to picture and the strengths of the Pro Tools platform. A bonus DVD includes Dolby Digital 5.1 mixes of more than a dozen examples of multichannel productions, along with written explanations.

# Index

## About the Authors

### Bobby Owsinski

A long-time music industry veteran, Bobby Owsinski started his career as a guitarist, keyboardist, songwriter, and arranger, but eventually became an in-demand producer/ engineer. He has worked with a variety of recording artists, on commercials, and on television and motion pictures as well. One of the first to delve into surround-sound music mixing, Bobby has worked on over a hundred surround projects and DVD productions for a variety of superstar acts.

Combining his music and recording experience with an easy-to-understand writing style, Bobby has become one of the best selling authors in the music recording industry. His books are staples in audio recording, music, and music business programs at colleges around the world. Bobby is a frequent moderator, panelist, and program director for a variety of industry conferences, and he has served as the longtime producer of the annual Surround Music Awards. He is also one of the executive producers for the "Guitar Universe" and "Desert Island Music" television programs.

For more info, please visit Bobby's blogs and Website:

http://bobbyowsinski.blogspot.com/
http://music3point0.blogspot.com
http://bobbyowsinski.com

### Rich Tozzoli

Rich Tozzoli is a Grammy-nominated engineer/mixer/producer who has worked with artists ranging from Al DiMeola and Ace Frehley to Hall & Oates and David Bowie. A lifelong guitarist and 5.1 surround sound specialist, Rich also composes music for the likes of Fox NFL, Discovery Channel, HBO, and A&E.